LIVING TRUSTS

and Other Ways to Avoid Probate

Third Edition

Karen Ann Rolcik

Attorney at Law

SPHINX® PUBLISHING

AN IMPRINT OF SOURCEBOOKS, INC.®
NAPERVILLE, ILLINOIS
www.SphinxLegal.com

Third Edition, 2002

Published by: **Sphinx® Publishing, An Imprint of Sourcebooks, Inc.®**

<u>Naperville Office</u>
P.O. Box 4410
Naperville, Illinois 60567-4410
630-961-3900
Fax: 630-961-2168
www.sourcebooks.com
www.sphinxlegal.com

This publication is designed to provide accurate and authoritative information in regard to the subject matter covered. It is sold with the understanding that the publisher is not engaged in rendering legal, accounting, or other professional service. If legal advice or other expert assistance is required, the services of a competent professional person should be sought.

*From a Declaration of Principles Jointly Adopted by a Committee of the
American Bar Association and a Committee of Publishers and Associations*

This product is not a substitute for legal advice.

Disclaimer required by Texas statutes.

Library of Congress Cataloging-in-Publication Data
Rolcik, Karen Ann.
    Living trusts and other ways to avoid probate / Karen Ann Rolcik.-- 3rd ed.
        p. cm.-- (Legal survival guides)
    Rev. ed. of: Living trusts and simple ways to avoid probate. 2nd ed. 1998.
    Includes index.
    ISBN 1-57248-165-X (alk. paper)
     1. Living trusts--United States--Popular works. 2. Probate law and practice--United
States--Popular works. 3. Estate planning--United States--Popular works. I. Rolcik,
Karen Ann. Living trusts and simple ways to avoid probate. II. Title. III. Series.

KF734.Z9 R65 2002
346.7305'2--dc21
                                                                        2002017385

Printed and bound in the United States of America.

VHG Paperback — 10 9 8 7 6 5 4 3 2

CONTENTS

Using Self-Help Law Books

Before using a self-help law book, you should realize the advantages and disadvantages of doing your own legal work and understand the challenges and diligence that this requires.

THE GROWING TREND Rest assured that you won't be the first or only person handling your own legal matter. For example, in some states, more than seventy-five percent of divorces and other cases have at least one party representing him or herself. Because of the high cost of legal services, this is a major trend and many courts are struggling to make it easier for people to represent themselves. However, some courts are not happy with people who do not use attorneys and refuse to help them in any way. For some, the attitude is, "Go to the law library and figure it out for yourself."

We at Sphinx write and publish self-help law books to give people an alternative to the often complicated and confusing legal books found in most law libraries. We have made the explanations of the law as simple and easy to understand as possible. Of course, unlike an attorney advising an individual client, we cannot cover every conceivable possibility.

COST/VALUE ANALYSIS Whenever you shop for a product or service, you are faced with various levels of quality and price. In deciding what product or service to buy, you make a cost/value analysis on the basis of your willingness to pay and the quality you desire.

When buying a car, you decide whether you want transportation, comfort, status, or sex appeal. Accordingly, you decide among such choices as a Neon, a Lincoln, a Rolls Royce, or a Porsche. Before making a decision, you usually weigh the merits of each option against the cost.

When you get a headache, you can take a pain reliever (such as aspirin) or visit a medical specialist for a neurological examination. Given this choice, most people, of course, take a pain reliever, since it costs only pennies; whereas a medical examination costs hundreds of dollars and takes a lot of time. This is usually a logical choice because it is rare to need anything more than a pain reliever for a headache. But in some cases, a headache may indicate a brain tumor and failing to see a specialist right away can result in complications. Should everyone with a headache go to a specialist? Of course not, but people treating their own illnesses must realize that they are betting on the basis of their cost/value analysis of the situation. They are taking the most logical option.

The same cost/value analysis must be made when deciding to do one's own legal work. Many legal situations are very straight forward, requiring a simple form and no complicated analysis. Anyone with a little intelligence and a book of instructions can handle the matter without outside help.

But there is always the chance that complications are involved that only an attorney would notice. To simplify the law into a book like this, several legal cases often must be condensed into a single sentence or paragraph. Otherwise, the book would be several hundred pages long and too complicated for most people. However, this simplification necessarily leaves out many details and nuances that would apply to special or unusual situations. Also, there are many ways to interpret most legal questions. Your case may come before a judge who disagrees with the analysis of our authors.

Therefore, in deciding to use a self-help law book and to do your own legal work, you must realize that you are making a cost/value analysis. You have decided that the money you will save in doing it yourself outweighs the chance that your case will not turn out to your satisfaction. Most people handling their own simple legal matters never have a problem, but occasionally people find that it ended up costing them more to have an attorney straighten out the situation than it would have if they had hired an attorney in the beginning. Keep this in mind if you decide to handle your own case, and be sure to consult an attorney if you feel you might need further guidance.

LOCAL RULES   The next thing to remember is that a book which covers the law for the entire nation, or even for an entire state, cannot possibly include every procedural difference of every county court. Whenever possible, we provide the exact form needed; however, in some areas, each county, or even each judge, may require unique forms and procedures. In our *state* books, our forms usually cover the majority of counties in the state, or provide examples of the type of form that will be required. In our *national* books, our forms are sometimes even more general in nature but are designed to give a good idea of the type of form that will be needed in most locations. Nonetheless, keep in mind that your *state*, county, or judge may have a requirement, or use a form, that is not included in this book.

You should not necessarily expect to be able to get all of the information and resources you need solely from within the pages of this book. This book will serve as your guide, giving you specific information whenever possible and helping you to find out what else you will need to know. This is just like if you decided to build your own backyard deck. You might purchase a book on how to build decks. However, such a book would not include the building codes and permit requirements of every city, town, county, and township in the nation; nor would it include the lumber, nails, saws, hammers, and other materials and tools you would need to actually build the deck. You would use the book as your guide, and then do some work and research involving such matters as whether you need a permit of some kind, what type and grade of wood are available in your area, whether to use hand tools or power tools, and how to use those tools.

Before using the forms in a book like this, you should check with your court clerk to see if there are any local rules of which you should be aware, or local forms you will need to use. Often, such forms will require the same information as the forms in the book but are merely laid out differently, use slightly different language, or use different color paper so the clerks can easily find them. They will sometimes require additional information.

CHANGES IN THE LAW

Besides being subject to state and local rules and practices, the law is subject to change at any time. The courts and the legislatures of all fifty states are constantly revising the laws. It is possible that while you are reading this book, some aspect of the law is being changed or that a court is interpreting a law in a different way. You should always check the most recent statutes, rules and regulations to see what, if any changes have been made.

In most cases, the change will be of minimal significance. A form will be redesigned, additional information will be required, or a waiting period will be extended. As a result, you might need to revise a form, file an extra form, or wait out a longer time period; these types of changes will not usually affect the outcome of your case. On the other hand, sometimes a major part of the law is changed, the entire law in a particular area is rewritten, or a case that was the basis of a central legal point is overruled. In such instances, your entire ability to pursue your case may be impaired.

Again, you should weigh the value of your case against the cost of an attorney and make a decision as to what you believe is in your best interest.

INTRODUCTION

During the past twenty years, "how to avoid probate" has become the subject of countless speeches, books and seminars. The cost and time delays of probate and the court system have caused many people (including attorneys) to look for alternatives to the probate process.

Today there are a variety of probate alternatives available. Among these are life insurance contracts, pay on death accounts, joint tenancies, retirement accounts and various types of trusts. For many people, these methods may be used to completely avoid probate without any complications. These probate alternatives are discussed in greater detail in Chapter 2.

The most popular probate alternative is the *living trust*. The living trust is a very effective method to avoid the probate process not only after a person's death, but also during a person's life, in the event the person becomes incapacitated. The living trust is explained more fully in Chapters 3 through 6.

The purpose of this book is to acquaint you with the various probate alternatives and to show you which ones will work best for your estate. A special emphasis is placed on the living trust because it has always been popular. However, you may learn from this book that simpler methods are available. If you do need a living trust, several basic forms are included to help you create your own.

You should keep in mind that each of the probate alternatives discussed can be used in conjunction with one or more of the others. For example, you can use the beneficiary designation in your Individual Retirement Account (IRA) to transfer any assets remaining in your IRA at your death directly to your beneficiaries without making them pass through the probate process. The living trust can be used to transfer your other assets to your beneficiaries without making them pass through the probate process.

As the value of your estate increases, the issues that must be considered change. Under the current federal estate tax (death tax) law, there is no tax payable to the Internal Revenue Service on the first $1 million of property owned by the decedent (including life insurance and retirement accounts) at the date of his or her death. This amount is called the *unified credit.* (see Chapter 3.) This amount will increase in steps until 2010, when it will cease to exist.

If the value of your estate or the combined value of your estate and your spouse's estate exceeds the unified credit and you wish to avoid estate taxes, then you should consult a professional with experience in estate tax planning, generally a CPA or tax/estate planning attorney. Such a professional can give you advise concerning the proper way to structure your estate in order to take full advantage of the tax laws and reduce or eliminate estate taxes at your death.

The forms included in this book are not intended for use by individuals or couples with estates over the unified credit who wish to avoid estate taxes. Additionally, if you own assets of an unusual character, such as royalty interests, partnership interests or interests in trusts or annuities, or if there are complicated beneficiary distributions or conditions you wish to include in your living trust, you should consult an experienced professional. In many communities, living trusts are available for reasonable prices. No book of this type can cover every contingency in every case, but knowledge of the basics will help you to make the right decisions regarding your property.

NEEDING AN ATTORNEY

One of the first questions you will want to consider, and most likely the reason you are reading this book is: How much will an attorney cost? When billing on an hourly basis, estate planning attorneys will charge anywhere from $75 to $300 per hour. Many attorneys, however, have set fees for living trusts and these may range from $400 to $2000 plus.

There are some advantages to hiring a lawyer. First, an attorney will be familiar with all of the state laws regarding trusts and this will save you the time of finding out if your state has peculiar rules governing trusts. Second, an attorney will be familiar with the most recent federal and state tax rules.

The primary advantage to creating your own living trust is that you can save money and be certain that your living trust is completed when you are ready. Many lawyers have heavy workloads that can often result in matters being delayed for various periods of time. If you are creating your own living trust, you can do it at your own pace. Furthermore, selecting an attorney is not easy. As the next section shows, it is hard to know whether you are selecting an attorney with whom you will be happy.

Middle ground between having an attorney handle the procedure and handling it on your own is to find an attorney who will be willing to accept an hourly fee to answer your questions and give you help as you need it. This way you can save some legal costs but still get professional assistance.

SELECTING AN ATTORNEY

A common, and frequently the best, way to find an attorney is to ask friends or acquaintances to recommend an attorney to you. You can also contact a lawyer referral service. This is a service that is usually operated by a local bar association. It is designed to match a client with a lawyer who actively handles cases in the area of law that the client needs. Lawyer referral services are usually listed in the yellow pages under "Attorneys."

You may also simply look under "Attorneys" in the yellow pages. Many lawyers list their areas of practice in their ads and some yellow pages list attorneys under various subheadings such as estate planning, wills, probate, personal injury, taxes, etc.

However you find an attorney, you should have a clear understanding with the attorney regarding the amount of the fee, how the fee will be calculated, and exactly what will be done for the fee. For instance, does the attorney charge a set fee, and if so, what does that set fee include? Is there anything you will need that is not included in the fee, such as transferring your property to the trust? If the attorney charges on an hourly basis, find out how much the hourly rate is and how many hours the attorney estimates will be required to complete the matter. The fee understanding should be reached *before* you actually hire the lawyer.

THE PROBATE PROCESS 1

Probate is the legal process by which property in an estate is transferred to the heirs and beneficiaries of a deceased person (the *decedent*). *Heirs* are persons who are entitled to receive a decedent's property if the decedent died without a will. *Beneficiaries* are persons who are named in a decedent's will to receive property.

BEGINNING THE PROCESS

The probate process begins by presenting to the judge the will of the decedent or, if there is no will, by presenting to the judge a list of the decedent's property and a list of the people to whom it is proposed that the property be given.

Generally, although each state will differ in the specific steps involved in the probate of a will, the following is a fairly representative outline of the probate process:

- A *petition* or *application* is filed with the probate court either asking that a will be admitted to probate or stating that a person has died without leaving a will.

- If there is a will, an order is signed admitting it to probate, and some type of document is issued by the court, giving the personal representative power to act for the estate. This may be called *Letters of Administration*, *Letters Testamentary*, *Letters of Authority*, or something similar. This may be done with or without a hearing, depending on the state and county.

- The executor must meet the qualifications of the state statutes setting forth who the state believes is competent to serve as executor.

- Unless the court grants special permission, the executor must post a surety bond.

- Notice of death is published or sent to the heirs and beneficiaries.

- A notice is sent to creditors to permit them time to file claims against the estate.

- The executor must collect all of the assets.

- Assets may be appraised to obtain a current value.

- An inventory must be prepared and filed with the court.

- The executor must pay the debts of the decedent and the expenses of the estate administration, including accountant and appraiser fees, probate costs, and the like.

- If necessary, assets are sold to raise cash to pay debts and expenses.

- A final income tax return for the decedent must be filed. If there is more than $600 income during administration of the estate, the estate must file an income tax return and, if the estate is over $1,000,000, it must file an estate tax return. In some states, both the state income and estate tax returns must be filed.

- An accounting of the estate assets and the expenses of the estate must be filed and approved by the probate court.

- On petition, the probate court will close the administration of the estate.

- Executor and attorney's fees are paid.

- Assets are distributed to heirs or beneficiaries.

WHEN PROBATE IS NECESSARY

Probate may be necessary whether or not a decedent had a will. A will does not eliminate the need for probate. The will is the primary document used in the probate process. Probate is required if the decedent owned property in his or her individual name at the time of his or her death.

If a decedent died without having signed a will, then the decedent died *intestate* and his or her property will pass to his or her *heirs at law*. The probate code of each state lists the heirs of a decedent, the order in which they will inherit from the decedent, and the amount of that inheritance. In effect, the state has written a will for the decedent and dictates who will receive the property without regard to the wishes of the decedent or the true needs of the decedent's family's situation.

If no living relative of the decedent can be located, all of the decedent's property *escheats* to the state. That is, the state is the beneficiary of the decedent's entire estate.

If a decedent died with a signed will, then the decedent died *testate* and his or her property passes to the individuals named in his or her will, the beneficiaries. If a person challenges the validity of the decedent's will, which is often called *contesting the will*, the probate court will get involved in determining whether the beneficiaries named in the decedent's will are legally entitled to receive the property.

PROPERTY THAT IS SUBJECT TO PROBATE

Not all property owned by a decedent at the time of his or her death has to go through the probate process. Only *probate property* (also called *probatable assets*) is subject to the probate process. Probate property includes property owned in the individual name of the decedent alone or in the individual name of the decedent and another person without survivorship rights. Common examples of probate property include:

- bank accounts, securities, and other assets in the decedent's name alone;

- tangible personal property (e.g., jewelry, stamp collections, furniture, car); and,

- real estate.

If a husband and wife owned property jointly as *tenants by the entireties*, or if two people owned property as *joint tenants with rights of survivorship*, the property passes automatically to the surviving owner and does not go through the probate process. A certified copy of the decedent's death certificate generally is all that is required to show that the entire property interest in such accounts is held by the survivor.

Chapter 2 explains how to set up ownership of your property so that it is non-probate property and passes automatically upon your death.

THE ROLE OF YOUR WILL IN THE PROBATE PROCESS

A will allows you to decide who gets your property after your death. You can give specific gifts of personal items to certain persons and decide which of your friends or relatives deserve a greater share of your estate. You can also leave gifts to churches, schools, and charities.

A will allows you to decide who will be the executor of your estate. Some states call the person who represents your estate and handles the probate process the *personal representative*. This is the same as an *executor*, who gathers together all of your assets and distributes them to the beneficiaries. With a will, you can provide that your executor does not have to post a surety bond with the court in order to serve, a provision that can save the estate money. The executor can also be granted broad powers, in addition to the powers given to executors by law, to handle estate matters.

A will allows you to choose a guardian for your minor children. This way, you can avoid custody fights among relatives and make sure that the person who is most apt and most familiar with you and your children raises your children. You may also appoint separate guardians over your children and over their money. For example, you may appoint your sister as guardian over your children and your father as guardian over their money. Thus, a second person could keep an eye on how your children's money is being spent.

DISADVANTAGES OF PROBATE

There are many disadvantages to the probate process. Each item discussed below is a good reason for trying to reduce your estate's exposure to probate. When all of the items are looked at together, the importance of reducing exposure to probate is unquestioned.

ECONOMIC COSTS OF PROBATE

The costs of probate can be very significant. The size of your estate can be reduced, and you can lose large amounts of property that you worked a lifetime to save. The costs of probate include filing fees, appraisers' fees, executor's fees, and attorney's fees. Each state has its own method by which probate attorneys can determine their fees for probate matters. Probate attorneys' fees may be calculated on an hourly basis, on a specific percentage of the value of the probate assets, or a combination of the two. Under any method, attorney fees for probate can be very significant.

TIME COSTS OF PROBATE

The probate process is very time consuming and can cause long delays in transferring assets to your beneficiaries. Generally, the minimum period required to complete the probate process is four months. It is not unusual for the typical probate to take as many as eighteen months. Many probates can take as long as two or even five years.

During this time, money is tied up and possibly household expenses (other than the bare necessities) and college tuitions can be interrupted until the probate is completed. It may be possible to get some of the assets released prior to the completion of the probate by asking special permission from the probate court. However, this may cost additional money for attorney fees and will generally require a showing of need. This all becomes part of the public record and can at times be embarrassing for the surviving family members.

LACK OF
PRIVACY

Once your will is admitted to probate it becomes a matter of public record. Anyone in the world can go to the courthouse and look at your will. Although some states seal the inventory of the estate, generally the identity of your beneficiaries and the inventory of your assets, including their value, are available for inspection by anyone who asks. It is not uncommon for financial advisors, insurance agents, estate liquidators, etc., to look up estate values in the courthouse and contact the family offering services and assistance to the family.

LACK OF
CONTROL

A will can be subject to challenge by disgruntled heirs. Such controversy can undermine the power of the executor over the distribution of your assets and the implementation of your wishes until the will contest is resolved by the probate court.

ADVANTAGES OF PROBATE

Despite the problems of probate described above, there are several reasons why, in some cases, probate should not be avoided *entirely*. While many people will not view these reasons as "advantages" to probate, there are benefits that can be gained from probate.

GUARDIANS FOR
MINOR
CHILDREN

First, generally only a will can name guardians to take care of your minor children. The probate court will almost always honor a designation of guardian in a will. Only in those rare circumstances that the court finds evidence that the person named in the will is not suitable to take care of and raise your children, will the court appoint someone else who it believes is better qualified. If you have minor children, you should have a will that names a guardian, and the will will need to be admitted to probate. However, you do not have to have any of your assets go through probate.

LIMITING CREDITOR CLAIMS

Second, after the will is admitted to probate, the executor will be required to give notice to any creditor you may have at the time of your death. Often this notice is published in a newspaper. As soon as the notice is given, the clock starts ticking and the creditors only have a limited period of time during which to contact the executor and formally file a claim for payment against the estate.

If the creditor does not file the claim within the prescribed time period, its claim is cut off in the future. This time period is called the *statute of limitations*—a statute that limits the amount of time the creditor has to file its claim. If you have only limited, known debts, this may not be a problem. However, if there are any potential claims against your estate, such as from a business venture, heirs you left out of your will, or unpaid taxes, you may wish to have a probate filed at your death to cut off those claims. Even if only $100 is subject to probate, your will can invoke the protections of the probate system, such as starting the statute of limitations.

TRANSFER OF ALL ASSETS

Finally, if probate alternatives are used, including the living trust, there may be some assets that do not get transferred to the trust or that are not covered by a beneficiary designation. Such assets may include last minute inheritances, lawsuit awards, etc. Your will makes certain that such property goes to the beneficiaries you designate—not to people that the state designates if you die intestate (without a will).

It is not necessary to write a will that names the beneficiaries of the probate assets. Instead, a *pourover will* can be used. A pourover will picks up the assets outside of the living trust, through the probate process, and "pours" them over into your living trust to be administered and distributed according to the terms of the trust. (see form 2, p.137 and form 3, p.139.) Once again, this ensures the privacy of the distribution of your assets. Because each state has different rules regarding the appointment of executors, guardians, and the like, it is important to consult an attorney or a self-help law book that specifically deals with the requirement for wills in your state.

For these reasons, not everyone would be advised to avoid probate completely. Instead, you should take advantage of every alternative available to minimize the contact your estate will have with the probate process, but have a will that can be probated in the above situations. The laws authorize these alternatives and you should take advantage of them to the greatest extent possible.

PROBATE ALTERNATIVES 2

There are several ways to keep your assets from going through the probate process after your death. These probate alternatives include various forms of joint tenancy, contractual dispositions of property, lifetime gifts, and the use of trusts. These alternatives are not mutually exclusive. You can use more than one at a time. In fact, it is often advisable to use several probate alternatives. It is very important, however, that you coordinate the use of the probate alternatives to make certain they do not conflict and that your wishes are carried out.

For example, you may wish to make provisions in your living trust to ensure financial security not only for your spouse and children, but also for your parents. However, if your life insurance and retirement plan beneficiary designations or joint bank accounts name your spouse as the sole beneficiary, your parents, and perhaps your children, will not receive the financial benefits of those assets. In such a case, it would be important to change those beneficiary designations to name your living trust as the primary beneficiary. The property will then be subject to the terms of the living trust and your intentions will not be thwarted. Funding your living trust will be discussed in detail in Chapter 6.

There are many benefits of these probate alternatives. First, of course, is the ability to bypass the probate process and its costs and delays. Second, these alternatives are very flexible. For example, bank accounts can be opened and closed easily and generally without cost to the account owner. Thus, if you want to change the joint tenant on an account, you can simply go to the bank and change the account name and signature card. Third, these probate alternatives are generally very inexpensive to establish. Finally, the time and effort to implement these alternatives is relatively minimal compared to the time and expense of probate.

JOINT TENANCY

Joint tenancy is the easiest and most inexpensive way to avoid probate. A joint tenancy is created by the instrument giving title to the asset. Common examples of this type of instrument are deeds, stock certificates, and bank or brokerage accounts. Generally, three types of joint tenancy can be created, but only two avoid probate.

JOINT TENANTS WITH RIGHTS OF SURVIVORSHIP

The most popular form of joint tenancy is "joint tenants with rights of survivorship" (JTWROS). This form of joint tenancy can exist between any two or more individuals—it is not limited to husband and wife. Common JTWROS assets are real estate, bank or brokerage accounts, stocks, bonds, etc. The most common uses of JTWROS are with regard to bank accounts and real estate.

During a lifetime, each joint tenant has full rights of ownership with respect to only that portion of the property that he or she contributed to, but has full access to all of the property. He or she can withdraw all of the funds, even though he or she may have only contributed a minimal amount to the account. The financial institution is not required to determine whether he or she is withdrawing more than his or her contribution.

At death, a joint tenant's share automatically passes to the surviving tenant and is not subject to the probate process. However, when the surviving tenant later dies, the property is included in his or her probate estate and must go through the probate process prior to being distributed to the beneficiaries. Typically, a JTWROS designation is made by using the word "or". For example, "Thomas or Roberta as joint tenants with rights of survivorship."

Example: Angie puts $10,000 into a bank account and names her son, Dave, as joint tenant with rights of survivorship. When Angie became sick and could not handle her financial affairs, Dave could pay her bills because he was one of the "owners" of the account. There was no need to go through the lengthy process of having David appointed guardian for Angie to handle her financial affairs. On Angie's death, the bank account passes to Dave automatically without going through the probate process. However, at Dave's later death, the assets will pass through the probate process unless he has added another joint tenant to the account.

You must be aware that a JTWROS account is risky. While it provides convenience during a lifetime by giving another person access to the funds, that same convenience can cause problems. If you put your real estate into joint ownership with someone, you cannot sell it or mortgage it without that person's signature. If you put your bank account in joint ownership with someone, they can take some or all of the money in the account without your consent or knowledge. Other problems that may arise with joint ownership of property include the following:

- if they are married, their spouse may claim a portion of the property in a divorce;

- if they get sued, the person getting a judgment may try to take the property to satisfy the judgment; and,

- if they file for bankruptcy, the bankruptcy trustee may try to bring the property into the bankruptcy proceedings.

Example 1: Alex puts his bank accounts into joint ownership with his daughter, Mary. Mary falls in love with Doug, who is in trouble with the law. Doug convinces Mary to "borrow" $30,000 from the account for a "business deal" that then goes sour. Later, she "borrows" $25,000 more to pay Doug's bail bond. Alex does not find out until it is too late and his money is gone.

Example 2: Jane puts her bank account into joint ownership with her son, Joe, who is married to Lisa. Two years later, Lisa files for divorce and claims the bank account as part of her marital property. Now Jane has to hire a lawyer to fight Lisa's claim.

If JTWROS is used (or an estate by the entireties, discussed below), it overrides a will and a living trust. Therefore, if you use tenancy by the entireties or JTWROS, it is very important to make certain that the ownership of the account is consistent with your overall intentions. If you want all of your estate to go to your sister and make her the sole beneficiary of your will or living trust, do not put your assets into a joint account with your brother. They will automatically go to him without even going into your estate.

Example: Bill's will leaves all of his property to his wife, Mary. Bill dies owning a house jointly with his sister, Ann, and a bank account jointly with his son, Don. Upon Bill's death Ann gets the house, Don gets the bank account, and his wife, Mary, gets nothing.

Personal property and joint tenancy. While the issue of who owns personal property does not come up often, if the property is valuable you should take the necessary steps to be sure that it is titled as you wish. Property that is represented by a physical title, such as shares of stock, bank accounts, and real estate, is easy to set up in joint tenancy, but personal property, such as furniture, coins or silverware is trickier. To make it clear what type of ownership such property is in, you need some sort of document for your records. This can be the receipt you received from the store, or a bill of sale. For property you already own, you can transfer it to a third party, such as your sister, and have her transfer it back to you and your spouse, or your children clearly stating that is it owned in joint tenancy.

```
John Smith and Mary Smith, husband and wife, as joint
tenants with full rights of survivorship.
```

Forms 12 and 13 are PERSONAL PROPERTY ASSIGNMENT forms and can be used to convert personal property you already own into JTWROS property as described above. Form 12 (part A) transfers the property from you to another person (called a *strawman*), and form 13 (part B) transfers the property from the strawman to you and the other joint tenant.

The strawman can be anyone over the age of 18 (except the intended joint tenant), but you should be sure the person you use as the strawman does not have any judgments against your proposed joint tenant. Technical aspects of the law in many states require the use of the strawman and the two-part form.

To complete form 12, (part A) (see form 12, p.189.):

☞ Fill in the date where indicated at the top left of the form.

☞ In the main paragraph, type in your name on the line for the "assignor." If you already hold the property with someone else, both names should go on this line.

> **Example**: If you and your spouse currently own the property, and you want to add your daughter's name, then both you and your spouse's names should be typed in.

☞ In the main paragraph, type in the strawman's name on the line for the "assignee."

☞ In the space after the main paragraph, type in a description of the property being transferred. Be as specific as possible in describing the property, including such things as the make, model, serial number, etc., if such information is available.

☞ You (and any other assignors), and the assignee (strawman) need to sign where indicated at the bottom of the form.

To complete form 13, (part B) (see form 13, p.191.):

☞ Fill in the date where indicated at the top left of the form.

☞ In the main paragraph, type in the strawman's name on the line for the "assignor."

☞ In the main paragraph, type in your name, and the name (or names) of the person (or persons) you want to be joint owners with you.

☞ In the space after the main paragraph, type in the same description of the property as you did in form 12 (part A).

☞ Type in the names of the new joint owners in the paragraph after the space for the property description, then check the second box for "as joint tenants with full rights of survivorship." However, if you and your spouse are to hold the property as joint tenants (because your state does not permit tenancy by the entireties), check the third box for "Husband and Wife, as joint tenants with full rights of survivorship."

☞ The assignor (strawman), and you and the other assignee (or assignees) need to sign where indicated at the bottom of the form.

Example: John owns an antique roll-top desk in his own name (or with no written evidence as to ownership). He wants his daughter, Sally, to inherit it upon his death, without having to go through probate. John can convey the desk first to Mike (using form 12), who will then reconvey it to John and Sally as JTWROS (using form 13). When John dies, it automatically goes to Sally, without the need for probate.

NOTE: *In Alaska, only a husband and wife may hold real estate in joint tenancy; in Pennsylvania, it is not clear whether real estate can be held in joint tenancy; and in Tennessee, no property may be held in joint tenancy except by a husband and wife. In Texas, property may be held by a husband and wife in joint tenancy if there is a written agreement signed by them that clearly describes the property and uses language such as: "husband and wife, as joint tenants with full rights of survivorship."*

TENANCY BY THE ENTIRETIES

A second type of joint tenancy is *tenants by the entireties*. This form of joint tenancy is similar to JTWROS but can only exist between a husband and wife and is not recognized in all states. Tenancy by the entireties for real estate is recognized in the following states:

Alaska	Michigan	Oregon
Arkansas	Mississippi	Pennsylvania
Delaware	Missouri	Rhode Island
District of Columbia	New Jersey	Tennessee
Florida	New York	Utah
Hawaii	North Carolina	Vermont
Indiana	Ohio	Virginia
Maryland	Oklahoma	Wyoming
Massachusetts		

If tenancy by the entireties is not available in your state, you should review the previous section on joint tenancy.

Tenancy by the entireties historically served as a form of protection for the interests of spouses in real estate acquired during a marriage. It prevents a husband from selling or otherwise transferring real estate without his wife's knowledge or permission. Each spouse owns an equal share of the asset. Tenancy by the entireties can be dissolved by divorce, death, or sale of the asset. At the death of a spouse, his share passes automatically to the surviving spouse and is not subject to the probate process.

Example: Mike and Joan are married. During their marriage they purchase a home as tenants by the entireties. While they are alive, both have the right to use the property. Neither can sell or give away his interest in the property without the other's permission. When Mike dies, his interest automatically passes to Joan. His will does not control the property and therefore, the property is not subject to probate.

Personal property and tenancy by the entireties. Tenancy by the entireties for personal property is recognized in the following states:

Alaska	Massachusetts	Rhode Island
Arkansas	Mississippi	Tennessee

Delaware	Missouri	Utah
District of Columbia	Ohio	Vermont
Florida	Oklahoma	Virginia
Hawaii	Oregon	Wyoming
Maryland	Pennsylvania	

When personal property is purchased, a receipt or bill of sale (as described in the previous section on joint property) should be used. You must make sure that your receipt or bill of sale lists you and your spouse as follows:

```
John Smith and Mary Smith, husband and wife,
in an estate by the entireties.
```

Once again, you can create a tenancy by the entireties for personal property that you already own in the same manner as described in the previous section. Forms 12 and 13 can be used to accomplish this. You can complete the forms by following the instructions in the previous section on joint property, with the following exceptions:

1. In form 12, the assignees can only be you and your spouse.

2. In form 13, you will check the box for "as husband and wife, in an estate by the entireties."

Example: Bob and Lauri are married. Bob owned personal property before they got married and now wants to make it property that he and Lauri own as tenants by the entireties. Bob can transfer the property to Jake, who will then transfer it to Bob and Lauri as tenants by the entireties.

Two words of caution with regard to forms 12 and 13 and the creation of JTWROS and tenancies by the entireties for personal property. First, there is no guarantee that forms 12 and 13 will be effective in your state. However, there is no disadvantage to using this form. It is always better to have documents, even if they are not for official submission, to support your position and evidence of your intention to create a joint tenancy.

Second, such transfers may be considered a gift, which may have tax consequences if the value of the property is great enough. Therefore, you may want to consult your tax adviser before making a transfer. For more information, see the section on "Outright Gifts" later in this chapter.

TENANCY IN COMMON

The third form of joint tenancy is *tenancy in common*. A tenancy in common requires no less than two people to own the asset. Each person owns an equal share of the property and while alive, each person can use the property. At the death of an owner, his or her share passes pursuant to his or her will, or (if he or she has no will) to his or her heirs at law. Tenants in common does not avoid the probate process.

Example: John and Mary are not married but own a house as tenants in common. While they are alive, both are entitled to use the property. John can sell or give away his interest in the property without Mary's permission. Consequently, Mary can become a tenant in common with a complete stranger. When John dies, his half ownership interest in the house passes to the beneficiaries named in his will. Those beneficiaries now are tenants in common with Mary. Mary still owns her share.

COMMUNITY PROPERTY

Only eight states recognize this method of asset ownership: Arizona, California, Idaho, Louisiana, Nevada, New Mexico, Texas and Washington. However, Wisconsin's system is nearly identical to community property. This is a special type of ownership that exists only between a husband and wife. Special state laws govern and protect the rights of a spouse in property acquired during the marriage.

Generally, similar to a tenancy by the entireties, a spouse owns only one-half of the property and cannot sell, transfer, or encumber the property without the other spouse's permission. Community property status attaches to most property acquired during the marriage. If you live in a community property state, you can still pass property to a person other than your spouse at your death, but you can only give one-half of it away.

TRANSFERS OF PROPERTY BY CONTRACT

Some types of property avoid the probate process through the *contract* that establishes the ownership and ownership rights of the property. The contract sets forth the rules governing how the property may be used during your lifetime and how it will be disposed of at your death. You name the beneficiary of the property, the person who will receive it at your death, and the other party must comply with the terms of the contract and distribute the property to that person after your death. Because the property is subject to a private contract, it is not subject to the probate process.

Two common examples of this are, *annuities* and *stock option contracts*.

PAY ON DEATH BANK ACCOUNTS

Financial institutions will allow you to set up your account so that upon your death it will go to the person or persons you name as beneficiary. This is not a joint account; the beneficiary cannot get the money until you die. You retain complete control of the account during your life. Such an account may be called a POD (pay on death) account, a TOD (transfer on death) account, or an I/T/F (in trust for) account. Lawyers call them "Totten Trusts" after the party who first went to court to settle the issue that they are legal.

With a pay on death account you can change the beneficiary any time you want and the person who will receive the money upon your death does not need to know about it until your death.

Example: Michael opened a bank account in his name "I/T/F Judy." When Michael dies, the account automatically passes to Judy without going through probate. During his life, Michael has complete control over the account and can name someone other than Judy as beneficiary simply by changing the title of the account. Judy cannot withdraw any funds during Michael's life.

PAY ON DEATH SECURITIES REGISTRATION

The drawback of pay on death accounts is that they could only be used for cash in a bank account. Anyone with stocks or bonds has to set up a living trust to keep them out of probate. But beginning in 1990, various states began passing a law allowing securities (stock, bonds, and mutual fund shares) to be registered in pay on death form. This change in the law makes avoiding probate easier for many more people.

Unfortunately, as of 1997, only twenty-seven states have passed this new law. But in a few years it will probably be accepted throughout the country.

The states that allow transfer on death as of publication of this book are listed in the following table, along with the reference to the relevant state statute. If your state is not listed you should call your broker or mutual fund agent to see if the law in your state has changed recently.

State	Statute
Alabama	Code 1975, Sections 8-6-140 to 8-6-151
Alaska	A.S. Sections 13.06.050; 13.33.301 to 13.33.310
Arizona	A.R.S. Sections 14-1201; 14-6301 to 14-6311
Arkansas	A.C.A. Sections 28-14-101 to 28-14-112
Colorado	C.R.S.A. Sections 15-10-201; 15-15-301 to 15-15-311
Delaware	12 D.C.A. Sections 801 to 812
Florida	F.S. Sections 711.50 to 711.512
Idaho	I.C. Sections 15-6-301 to 15-6-312
Illinois	S.H.A. 815 ILCS 10/0.01 to 10/12
Indiana	West's A.I.C. 32-4-1.6-1 to 32-4-1.6-15
Iowa	I.C.A. Sections 633.800 to 633.811
Kansas	K.S.A. Sections 17-49a 01 to 17-49a 12
Maryland	Maryland Code, Estates & Trusts, Sections 16-101 to 16-112
Michigan	M.C.L.A. Sections 451.471 to 451.481
Minnesota	M.S.A. Sections 542.1-201; 524.6-301 to 524.6-311
Mississippi	Code 1972, Sections 91-21-1 to 91-21-25
Montana	M.C.A. Sections 72-1-103; 72-6-301 to 72-6-311
Nebraska	R.S.N. Sections 30-2209; 30-2734 to 30-2746
Nevada	N.R.S. 111.480 to 111.650
New Hampshire	RSA 563-C:1 to 563-C12
New Jersey	N.J.S.A. Section 3B:30-1 to 3B:30-12

New Mexico	N.M.S.A. Sections 45-1-201; 45-6-301 to 45-6-311
North Dakota	N.D.C.C. Sections 30.1-01-06; 30.1-31-21 to 30.1-31-30
Ohio	O.R.C. Sections 1709.01 to 1709.11
Oklahoma	71 O.S.A. Sections 901 to 913
Oregon	O.R.S. Sections 59.535 to 59.585
Pennsylvania	20 Pa.C.S.A. Sections 6401 to 6413
South Dakota	S.D.C.L. Sections 29A-6-301 to 29A-6-311
Utah	U.C.A. Sections 75-6-301 to 75-6-313
Virginia	C.V. Sections 64-1-206 to 64.1-206.8
Washington	R.C.W.A. Sections 21.35.005 to 21.35.901
West Virginia	W.V.C. Sections 36-10-1 to 36-10-12
Wisconsin	W.S.A. Sections 705.21 to 705.30
Wyoming	W.S.A. Sections 2-16-101 to 2-16-112

TRANSFER ON DEATH AUTOMOBILE REGISTRATION

At present only two states, California and Missouri, allow transfer on death automobile registration. However, in the next few years other states may pass similar laws. Check with your motor vehicle registration department to see if this type of registration is allowed in your state.

LAND TRUSTS

Although real estate cannot be registered in transfer on death form, and joint ownership may cause problems, land trusts are becoming popular in many states to accomplish the same thing.

A land trust is an arrangement where you put title to your property in the name of a trustee, but you have all the rights and responsibilities for the property as if it were in your name. This type of trust is typically called an *Illinois-type* land trust, or a title-holding trust. Under such a trust, the only thing the trustee does is hold title.

The trustee can be a bank, your attorney, a relative or even yourself.

Some people set up a separate trust for each property they own. The terms of the trust provide that, upon your death, a named beneficiary becomes the owner of the trust and can immediately take charge of the property. Land trusts offer many benefits other than probate avoidance, such as keeping your name off the public records and keeping the purchase and sales price secret.

Currently, only the following states allow land trusts:

Arizona	Hawaii	North Dakota
Arkansas	Illinois	Ohio
Florida	Indiana	Virginia

However, the American Bar Association is working on a law that can be passed in all states, so they may become more available soon. Land trusts may be created in many other states if they are carefully worded. You should consult an attorney with experience in land trusts if you wish to use such a trust.

LIFE INSURANCE

Another popular probate alternative is a life insurance policy. A life insurance policy is a contract between the owner of the policy and the life insurance company. Generally, the person who purchases the policy, the "owner," is also the person whose life is insured. When the policy is purchased, the life insurance company asks the owner to designate the beneficiary of the life insurance policy. The beneficiary is the person who will receive the money that the policy pays when the owner dies. The owner names a beneficiary and this beneficiary designation becomes part of the life insurance contract.

As long as the owner pays the premiums on the policy, the life insurance company agrees to pay the proceeds of the policy to the beneficiary when the owner dies. Typically, when the owner dies, the life insurance company will require proof of death in the form of a death certificate and that a claim form be completed. The life insurance company then will automatically pay the policy proceeds directly to the beneficiary. This happens completely outside of the probate process.

The cash is available to the beneficiary quickly, which often will help a surviving spouse make mortgage payments, pay utility bills, and pay college tuition bills. Only if the owner has designated his or her estate, or the executor of his or her estate (in his or her capacity as executor), as beneficiary of the policy, will the policy proceeds be subject to the probate process.

Example: Mark buys a life insurance policy from Life Company and designates Rebecca as beneficiary of the policy proceeds upon his death. As long as Mark continues to pay the premiums, Life Company will be required to pay the proceeds to Rebecca when Mark dies. Since the life insurance policy provides that the proceeds are to be paid directly to Rebecca, they are not subject to the probate process. However, if Mark had named his estate as beneficiary, upon his death Life Company would pay the proceeds to his estate and the proceeds would be subject to the delays and costs of probate.

Often a parent or grandparent will name a minor child as beneficiary of a life insurance policy. Typically, the insurance companies will require that a legal guardianship be established for the minor before it pays the proceeds of the policy. Such a guardianship requires filing documents with the probate court, which costs money and takes time. Under a guardianship for a minor, the guardian will be required to hold the policy proceeds for the minor and distribute them to the minor when he or she reaches age eighteen or twenty-one, depending on the state. A living trust can provide that such life insurance proceeds be held for the child's benefit until beyond the age of eighteen or twenty-one.

Although the proceeds of a life insurance policy do not pass through probate, the value of the proceeds is included in the estate in determining if it is over $1,000,000 for estate tax purposes. One way to avoid this is if the life insurance policy is owned by a person other than the decedent. For example, if you wish to purchase a life insurance policy on yourself, you could instead give the money to your son and have him purchase the policy on you. That way he or she owns the policy and it is not part of your estate.

Of course, if the money you gave your son is substantial, you may have to pay a gift tax on it. However, this can be risky. As the owner of the policy, your son can change the beneficiary of the policy. Thus, if you intended that the policy be paid to all of your children equally, your son can change this, without your knowledge, to pay all of the policy proceeds to him.

As you can see, this area of law gets complicated and if you wish to use all the loopholes you should consult an expert in estate planning.

RETIREMENT PLANS

Individual Retirement Accounts (IRAs), company pension plans, profit-sharing plans, and 401(k) plans are very popular. Each of these retirement plans are funded with assets such as cash, stocks, bonds, mutual funds, etc. These retirement plans are essentially a specialized form of savings account subject to very strict tax rules. When a person retires or reaches a certain age (often sixty-two or sixty-five), he or she can begin to withdraw funds from the retirement plan.

If the owner dies before receiving all of the funds in his or her retirement plan, a beneficiary designated by the owner will receive the funds remaining in the retirement plan. Just like the life insurance contract, the owner of the retirement plan will complete a beneficiary designation that will direct the employer, brokerage firm, or bank (if the retirement plan is an IRA bank account) to pay the funds to a specific individual (or individuals) upon the death of the owner.

The employer, brokerage firm, or bank is required to honor the contract and make the payment after the death of the owner.

Example: Kevin worked for USA Company and made contributions to a 401(k) retirement plan sponsored by the Company. He named Glenda beneficiary. Kevin retires and begins to receive payments each year from the plan. Kevin dies, and $50,000 remains in the plan. USA Company must pay the $50,000 directly to Glenda without going through the probate process.

There are many very specialized tax rules governing who may be named beneficiary of a retirement plan. Some tax options are only available to a surviving spouse. If you are considering naming someone other than your spouse (including your living trust) as beneficiary of your retirement plans, you should consult a professional with experience in this specialized tax area.

In addition to the transfers of property by joint tenancy or contract, there are two other commonly used methods to transfer property without going through the probate process—outright gifts and trusts.

OUTRIGHT GIFTS

Property can be transferred to your beneficiaries by means of an outright gift during your lifetime. Under the current federal gift tax law, an individual can give up to $10,000 a year, or a husband and wife can together give up to $20,000 a year, to any number of people, free of gift tax. (This $10,000 or $20,000 amount is often called the *annual exclusion gift*. The Taxpayers Relief Act of 1997 provides that it be indexed for inflation, so it will likely rise slightly over the years.) The person receiving the property must receive it with "no strings attached." The property becomes theirs and is subject to their complete control. The person receiving the property does not have to pay income tax on the property he or she receives.

Federal law also permits you to transfer up to $1,000,000, either during your lifetime or at your death, free of federal estate or gift tax. Thus, in addition to the annual exclusion gift you can make gifts of up to this amount during your lifetime with no gift tax. However, if you give away more than this amount during your lifetime, then at your death every dollar that your beneficiaries receive is taxed and the rate starts at thirty-seven percent.

If you give any gifts in excess of the annual exclusion gift during a year, you are required to file a federal gift tax return even if no tax is due because you are using up your unified credit. This gift tax return is due on April 15 of the year following the year in which you make the gifts. A copy of the **U.S. GIFT AND GENERATION-SKIPPING TAX RETURN (IRS FORM 709)** is included in Appendix C. (see form 18, p.211.)

TRUSTS

For hundreds of years, trusts have been the most popular way to avoid probate, especially for large estates. Today, with pay on death accounts and the other devices described earlier, trusts may not be necessary for as many estates, but they can still provide advantages for many situations.

A trust is a legal entity that comes into existence when an individual signs a legal document that contains certain provisions. A trust can be an *inter vivos* trust (meaning it is created during one's life) or a *testamentary* trust (meaning it does not start until one's death). It can be *revocable* (meaning it can be changed at any time) or *irrevocable* (meaning it cannot ordinarily be changed).

The person who creates a trust and transfers property to it is generally called the *grantor*. A grantor is sometimes called a *settlor, maker, donor,* or *trustor*. The person who presently benefits from the trust is the *beneficiary* and the person who will benefit from the trust after the beneficiary dies is the *remainder beneficiary*.

Beneficiaries and remainder beneficiaries can be corporations, nonprofit institutions, or charities. Beneficiaries may be given different rights in the trust property. Some beneficiaries may be *income beneficiaries*, and therefore entitled to receive only the income from the trust property. This may be interest from a savings account or bond, dividends from stock, rental income from real estate, etc. Other beneficiaries may be *principal beneficiaries*, and therefore entitled to receive the actual trust assets—for example, the money in the savings account, the bond, stock, or rental real estate. Sometimes the beneficiary may receive both income and principal.

The person in charge of managing the trust, who oftentimes is the same person who created the trust, is called a *trustee*. In most states, any person or entity (bank, trust company, and some brokerage firms) who is capable of taking legal title to property can be appointed trustee. Trustees have a legal duty (often called a fiduciary duty) to protect the assets of the trust and make certain that the purposes of the trust as stated in the trust document are carried out. The grantor spells out the powers of the trustee in the trust document. Each state also has specific laws that govern the conduct of trustees to ensure that the trust assets are protected, the purposes of the trust are honored, and the beneficiaries of the trust are protected.

Each trust should also designate a *successor* or *alternate* trustee. This person or entity will take over the management of the trust if the original trustee dies or becomes unable to continue management of the trust. If a successor trustee is not named, the court has authority to name a successor trustee if one is needed.

Example 1: Bob and Helen transfer property to a trust and name Ross as trustee. The trust document states that the income from the trust will be paid to Bob and Helen until their deaths and then it shall be paid to Chrissy.

Example 2: Joe transfers property to a trust and names Jane as trustee. Joe's trust document states that the income from the trust will be paid to Robert until he reaches age thirty, at which time the trust principal will be distributed to Gail.

Example 3: Dan transfers property to a trust and names Dorothy as trustee. The trust provides that Dan's three grandchildren will be beneficiaries of the income and principal of the trust until they complete college. At that time the trust will end and the trust property will be divided equally among Dan's children.

Often grantors name alternate beneficiaries to receive the trust property in case the original beneficiary cannot receive the trust property.

Testamentary trusts are created under the terms of a person's will and take effect only when the person dies. Such trusts, by their very nature, do not avoid probate. The trusts are subject to the supervision of the court and the trustee must periodically file reports with the court to account for the income earned by the trust, the taxes and expenses paid by the trust, and the distributions of income and principal made to the beneficiaries. These reports can be costly to prepare.

Inter vivos trusts (most commonly known as living trusts) take effect during a person's lifetime. Such trusts are created under the terms of a special document separate from the person's will. Property is transferred to the trust and managed by the trustee. Most grantors of living trusts name themselves as trustee during their lifetime. This permits them to continue to manage their assets just as they had before the assets were transferred into the living trust. The grantor/trustee typically names him or herself as income and principal beneficiary during lifetime, and designates the individuals who will receive the income and principal after he or she dies.

IRREVOCABLE TRUSTS

Living trusts can be revocable or irrevocable. A revocable living trust can be changed or terminated by the grantor during his or her life. At the death of the grantor, the trust becomes irrevocable. An irrevocable trust cannot be changed or terminated. A grantor who wants to retain complete control over the property that he or she transferred to the trust and change the trust during his or her lifetime should make certain to include a provision in the trust document that states the trust is revocable.

Why would someone set up a trust that they could not change or revoke? Because such a trust can avoid taxes and in some cases can be safe from creditors' claims.

Example 1: Nancy is involved in an automobile accident and the insurance company for the person who caused the accident offers her a million dollars. She accepts the award on the condition that it be set up in an irrevocable trust for herself and her daughter. Years later, Nancy is found guilty of malpractice. The victim of her malpractice cannot touch her trust because it is irrevocable.

Example 2: Ben owns a valuable piece of property that he bought many years ago. He knows that on his death it will add a million dollars to his estate and that 55% of the value will have to be paid in estate taxes. Ben sets up a charitable remainder trust and donates the property to the trust. With careful planning and the use of life insurance, the property will go to the American Heart Association upon Ben's death and his children will receive a million dollars tax-free.

While irrevocable trusts can offer some excellent benefits, they must be set up carefully to be effective. If you feel your estate would benefit from such a trust, you should consult an expert in the field.

THE LIVING TRUST 3

In the previous chapter you were introduced to the basic elements of a trust and to the distinction between living trusts and testamentary trusts. Living trusts have become very popular as a probate avoidance alternative. In fact, living trusts are perhaps the most efficient and effective method to avoid probate and pass assets quickly to beneficiaries without incurring substantial probate and attorney fees.

All states recognize living trusts as legal substitutes for wills. The living trust is a legal entity that can own, hold, and distribute assets to trust beneficiaries. A living trust is created by a legal document and is funded when legal title to assets is transferred to the trustee. It is a revocable trust that can be changed or amended by the grantor during his or her life. The living trust is called that because it comes into existence while the grantor is living, and—when assets are transferred to the trust to be distributed as the trust document directs—the trust "comes to life." After the grantor's death the trust becomes irrevocable: it cannot be changed or cancelled.

ADVANTAGES OF A LIVING TRUST

Living trusts offer several advantages that wills do not.

AVOIDANCE OF PROBATE

Assets placed in a living trust prior to your death do not go through the probate process. This can save your estate several thousand dollars in probate costs (including the cost of an executor's bond), attorney fees, and appraiser fees. Because the assets in a living trust are not subject to the delays of the probate process, they can be distributed quickly and efficiently to the beneficiaries. Generally, the trustee will only require proof of your death and will then begin to manage the trust assets and distribute them according to the terms of the trust document.

FLEXIBILITY

Because the living trust is revocable, it can be changed or cancelled at any time and for any reason. If your family circumstances change, for instance, if you divorce or if you or a family member becomes ill, or if a beneficiary dies, a living trust can easily be amended. Also, if you move from state to state, the trust will be valid in all states. Wills, by contrast, can be changed or cancelled, but generally the process is more time consuming and expensive because the strict state laws governing the creation and amendment of wills impose many burdens on the person making the will.

PRIVACY

A living trust is totally confidential. It is not subject to disclosure to the probate court as is a will. Wills become public documents and can be read by anyone who takes the time and has the interest to do so. Also, when a will is probated, the court will require that a listing or inventory of the probate assets be filed. These inventories may also be public documents that reveal the assets that comprise the estate.

This is not the case with a living trust. Neither the assets in the trust at the time of death, nor the terms of the trust and the identities of the beneficiaries are required to be disclosed to the public. The only persons who need to be aware of the trust's existence, its assets and its terms are you, the trustee and the beneficiaries.

There are some states that require a trust to be registered with the court where the trustee lives or administers the trust. The trustee must file certain information with the court including the name of the grantor, the name of the trustee, the date on which the trust was created, and some form of written acceptance of the trusts by the trustee. This acceptance is often evidenced by the trustee's signature on the trust document.

Failure of the trustee to register the trusts generally does not result in legal consequences or penalties. This registration requirement impacts and undercuts the privacy advantage of the living trust. As of the date this book was written, the following states have laws governing the registration of living trusts:

Alaska	Maine
Colorado	Michigan
Florida	Missouri
Hawaii	Nebraska
Idaho	North Dakota

CONTROL

While you are alive, you continue to manage and control the assets in the trust just as you did prior to establishing the trust. You continue to direct how the assets will be invested and how the assets will be used during your lifetime. Of course, if you choose to designate someone other than yourself to handle the investment of the assets, you may either name that person as trustee or hire that person to give you investment advice.

In a living trust you will personally select the successor trustee who will control your assets. The living trust will contain your specific instructions regarding how the assets are to be invested and distributed. Property passing through the probate process is subject to the many complex state laws imposing rules on executors that often limit the investments and distributions executors can make.

ORDERLINESS

A living trust will help you to keep your financial affairs in order and the records in a central location. This saves your family a great deal of time after your death attempting to locate and identify your assets.

CONTESTABILITY   Trusts are generally more difficult for dissatisfied heirs to contest than wills.

DISABILITY   An important advantage of a living trust is the avoidance of a court supervised guardianship in the event you become incapacitated due to stroke, senility, or other form of mental incompetency. One in four Americans will experience some form of disability that lasts more than three months. The average disability lasts over a year. Ordinarily, when a disability occurs, a guardian must be appointed by the court and the guardian must manage your assets through strict court supervised procedures. Many times the guardian appointed by the court is not the person you would have chosen to manage your assets. If your assets are placed in your living trust before your incapacity, the expense and delay of a guardianship is avoided. The trustee of your trust would step in and manage your assets.

OUT-OF-STATE PROPERTIES   If you live in Illinois and own real estate in Florida, upon your death your executor must begin two probate proceedings—one in Illinois to deal with your assets located in Illinois and one in Florida to deal with the transfer of title to the real estate located in Florida. However, if the out-of-state property is placed in your living trust, upon your death such property will not be subject to probate either in Illinois or Florida.

CONTINUATION OF BUSINESS   Living trusts are very useful to business owners. Whether the business is a sole proprietorship or a corporation, the business owner can transfer the business assets to the living trust. If the owner becomes disabled or dies, the successor trustee can step into the owner's shoes and handle the day to day affairs of the business without an interruption in the business. Because many times a business is a primary source of income to the owner and his or her family, after the owner's death or disability it is critical that the business continue to operate and generate the income needed to support the owner's family.

DISADVANTAGES OF A LIVING TRUST

While living trusts offer many advantages, there are some drawbacks to a living trust. While some of those listed below, such as no tax savings, may not be disadvantages over a will, they are disadvantages over doing more extensive estate planning.

NO INCOME
TAX SAVINGS

The living trust does not avoid or save income taxes while you are alive. You have retained control of the assets in the living trust, you receive the benefits of the trust, and you are both the grantor and trustee of the trust. The income earned by the trust assets will be taxed to you. You will be required to report any income earned by the trust on your **U.S. INDIVIDUAL INCOME TAX RETURN (IRS Form 1040)**. (see form 15, p.197.) No separate return has to be filed for the trust.

After your death, the trust will be required to obtain its own taxpayer identification number from the Internal Revenue Service. This is done by filing the **APPLICATION FOR EMPLOYER IDENTIFICATION NUMBER (IRS Form SS-4)** with the District Director of Internal Revenue. (see form 14, p.193.)

The trust will be required to file its own **U.S. INCOME TAX RETURN FOR ESTATES AND TRUSTS (IRS Form 1041)** each year if the trust had "any taxable income" or had "gross income" of $600.00 or more, regardless of the amount of "taxable income" in any one year. (see form 16, p.199.) Thus, even a trust that owns only tax exempt bonds that pay over $600.00 worth of interest during a year will have to file a tax return. On the following page is a chart illustrating how income earned by the trust is reported on your **U.S. INDIVIDUAL INCOME TAX RETURN (IRS FORM 1040)**.

INCOME TAX REPORTING OUTLINE:

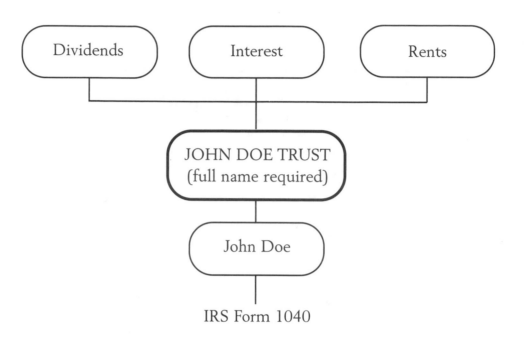

IRS Form 1040

NO ESTATE TAX SAVINGS

At your death, federal estate taxes will be due if the value of your probate and non-probate assets exceeds the amount of the unified credit. Many states also impose their own estate or death taxes. If you are married and the value of the estates of you and your spouse is over the amount of the unified credit, there are special planning techniques that can be used to help eliminate in whole or in part the estate taxes that would be due from you and your spouse's estates.

If you and your spouse's estates are worth more than the amount of the unified credit and you want to avoid estate taxes, then you should consult with an experienced estate tax professional. If the value of your estate exceeds the amount of the unified credit, then your executor will be required to file a federal estate tax return with the IRS. The first four pages of the UNITED STATES ESTATE (AND GENERATION SKIPPING) TAX RETURN (IRS FORM 706) are included in Appendix C. (see form 17, p.207.)

MORE COMPLEX AND EXPENSIVE THAN A WILL

If you hire an attorney to set up a living trust for you, the expense will be greater than for a will. If you create your own living trust, the most complex aspect of the process will be transferring your assets to the trust. Once your assets are transferred to the trust, you will have to keep separate trust records and not mix them with any personal accounts you have, such as joint accounts or pay on death accounts.

NO DEADLINES FOR CLAIMS OF CREDITORS

When a will is probated (or an estate without a will is probated), a deadline is imposed on creditors of the decedent. Creditors are required to present their claim to the executor of the estate within a time period specified by statute. Each state has its own statute establishing this time period. It can range from three months to one year. These statutes also establish the procedures that a creditor must follow to present its claim.

If a creditor does not follow the procedures within the statutory time period, the creditor loses its right to the assets of the estate and is forever prohibited from suing the estate to collect the assets due it. In most states, however, a living trust is not subject to such statutory procedures. Therefore, a creditor can sue the trust or its beneficiaries for amounts due it long after you have died. Even after the trust has terminated and all of the trust assets are distributed to the beneficiaries, creditors can sue the beneficiaries for claims it has against you.

DOES NOT AVOID CREDITOR CLAIMS DURING YOUR LIFE

A revocable living trust does not prevent your creditors from suing you or suing your trust to collect debts during your lifetime. Because you have maintained complete control over the trust assets, the courts treat you as the owner of the assets and can force you to pay trust assets to your creditors. If you know that you owe a creditor money, and you transfer all of your assets to your trust in an attempt to keep them away from your creditor, the courts will view the transfer as a fraudulent conveyance and may force you not only to pay the creditor, but also pay a fine.

DOES NOT ELIMINATE THE NEED FOR A WILL

As was discussed in Chapter 1, even though you have a living trust that is funded with all of your assets during your lifetime, it is important also to have a will. The will can name a guardian for your children, appoint an executor of your probate estate, and provide that no bond be required of your executor. There may be assets that you have forgotten to transfer to your trust, an unexpected inheritance, or a lawsuit that must be filed on behalf of your estate after your death, and a will covers these assets even if the will only provides that such assets pourover to your living trust. Without the will, you will have died intestate, and must follow the probate procedures for intestacy. Intestacy procedures are complex, time consuming, and generally very expensive.

LIVING TRUST VS. OTHER PROBATE ALTERNATIVES

In Chapter 2 other probate alternatives were described. Each of these probate alternatives accomplishes most people's primary goal: avoiding the costs and delay of probate at death. The living trust accomplishes this goal and has the additional advantages discussed above. However, the living trust has a very important advantage over the other probate alternatives: the living trust collects all of your assets in one place. This greatly simplifies the management and investment of your assets and makes it much easier for you to keep track of who you have named as the beneficiaries of your estate.

If a beneficiary dies, or if you decide no longer to include them in your estate, you simply have to amend the trust to remove the beneficiary. You do not have to change every account of which that person is a beneficiary or a joint tenant. Also, if you become incapacitated, the successor trustee can take over the management of your assets and avoid a guardianship. In the case of joint tenancy property, you would have to trust the joint tenant to use the funds for your benefit.

Even though a living trust has some disadvantages, they are greatly outweighed by the many advantages of a living trust, among which are:

- the cost savings of avoiding probate during your life if you become incapacitated;

- the cost savings after your death; and,

- the peace of mind that you gain by knowing that the assets you worked your lifetime to accumulate will pass to your beneficiaries quickly and as you intended after your death.

TYPES OF TRUSTS 4

Before we discuss the living trust in detail, there are a number of other trusts with which you should be familiar. The usefulness of the trusts discussed in this chapter depends upon your particular circumstances and the goals that you want to achieve. Because many of these trusts permanently affect ownership of the property transferred to them, and have significant income, gift, and estate tax implications, it is advisable for you to consult an attorney experienced in preparing such trusts. It is important to remember that all of these trusts are irrevocable and therefore cannot be revised, amended, or cancelled after they are established.

IRREVOCABLE LIFE INSURANCE TRUST

Perhaps one of the most popular types of trusts other than the living trust, is the irrevocable life insurance trust (commonly referred to as an "ILIT"). It is widely used to protect the benefits of a life insurance trust from being subject to estate tax when the insured dies.

When an ILIT is established, an existing life insurance policy is transferred to the trust or money is transferred to the ILIT and the trustee of the trust purchases a life insurance policy on the grantor (the creator) of the trust. Once the insurance policy is transferred to the trust, or money is transferred to the trust to purchase a life insurance policy and pay the annual premiums, the grantor generally cannot reacquire ownership of the policy.

CHILDREN'S TRUST

A children's trust is often established to create a source of funds to pay for the costs of a child or grandchild's college education. The trust is irrevocable and can only continue until the child reaches 21 years of age. Until the child reaches age 21, the trustee can use the assets of the trust for the benefit of the child. When the child attains age 21, the trustee must pay out all of the trust assets to the child.

CRUMMEY TRUST

This trust is named for the gift tax court case in which the Crummey family created trusts and made gifts to them. The Internal Revenue Service argued that because the gifts were made to a trust, they did not qualify as an annual exclusion gift. The Internal Revenue Service lost. As a result of this case, as long as the terms of the trust permit the beneficiary to withdraw the amount of the gift for a certain period time after the gift has been made, the gift will be treated as an annual exclusion gift, and will not be subject to gift tax. Thus, the creator of the trust can transfer money to the beneficiaries of the trust without paying gift tax.

MARITAL QTIP OR QDOT TRUST

Each of these trusts permit an individual to transfer property to his or her spouse either during life or at death, without paying estate tax. The gift or estate tax is not avoided, but deferred until the spouse is no longer a beneficiary of the trust or until the death of the spouse. The terms of these trusts require that all of the income of the trust be paid to the spouse and to no other person. Principal of the trust can be distributed to or for the benefit of the spouse, but to no other person.

A/B Trust

The A/B Trust is a trust that typically involves the creation of two separate trusts. *Trust B* is funded with an amount equal to the federal estate and gift tax unified credit exemption. *Trust A* is funded with the remaining amount of an individual's property. More often than not, Trust A is some form of a marital trust. This trust permits the maximum estate tax savings upon the death of an individual who is survived by a spouse.

Credit Shelter or Bypass Trust

A credit shelter trust and bypass trust are the same type of trust. These trusts are funded with an amount equal to the federal estate and gift tax unified credit exemption. The beneficiaries of this trust commonly are the surviving spouse and children of the grantor.

Generation Skipping Transfer Tax Trust

A generation skipping transfer trust (GST), often referred to as a Grandchildren's Trust, is established for the benefit of grandchildren. The property in such a trust is subject to gift or estate tax only at one generational level. Thus, the property is transferred to the grandchildren without being reduced by tax in their parents' estate.

Charitable Remainder Trust

A charitable remainder trust gives an individual a financial interest in the trust during his or her lifetime, or for a certain number of years. Upon the individual's death or at the end of the term of years, the assets remaining in the trust are transferred to one or more charities named by the grantor when the trust is created.

The financial interest given to an individual may be calculated in various ways. Charitable remainder trusts not only provide gift or estate tax savings, but if created during an individual's lifetime, provide a federal income tax deduction. Charitable remainder trusts are either charitable remainder annuity trusts (CRAT) or charitable remainder unitrusts (CRUT).

GRANTOR RETAINED ANNUITY TRUST

A grantor retained annuity trust (GRAT) is a trust in which the grantor of the trust reserves to himself or herself the right to receive an annuity for a certain number of years. After the term of years ends, the assets remaining in the trust are distributed to the individuals named by the grantor when the trust is created.

PERSONAL RESIDENCE TRUST

A personal residence trust requires the transfer of an individual's residence, typically a second or vacation home, to a trust. This trust is primarily created to achieve gift or estate tax savings. The grantor retains the right to live in the residence for either a number of years or for the remainder of his or her lifetime. If the grantor reserves the right to live in the house for a term of years, he or she may reserve the right to lease the property after the term of years has expired. Because of the many implications that may result from transferring an individual's primary residence to such a trust, a person should consult an attorney knowledgeable in tax, homestead, and real estate before endeavoring to use such a trust.

A thorough discussion of each of these trusts is beyond the scope of this book. Each trust has its advantages, but each trust has disadvantages as well. The most important disadvantage of these trusts is that once established, they cannot be changed or revoked. That means that the property transferred is no longer owned by the grantor. While the grantor may retain a financial interest in the trust property, it is not equivalent to full ownership of the property. Further, once transferred, the grantor generally cannot control or influence the distribution of the trust assets either to himself or to other beneficiaries.

Even after consulting an attorney and tax accountant familiar with the legal and tax implications of these trusts, you should make a list of the advantages and disadvantages of establishing such a trust.

CREATING YOUR LIVING TRUST 5

A living trust is created by a written document that is clear and specific. It does not have to contain fancy legal terms. The living trust document will serve as the road map describing how you want your assets to be distributed during your lifetime and after your death. You need to identify the trustees, the beneficiaries, and the trust assets.

In Chapter 2, the parties to a trust (grantor, trustee, and beneficiary) are described. When you write your trust, it is important to identify each of these parties so that it is absolutely clear who they are. The beneficiary should not be identified as your "spouse" or "Mrs. John Smith." Instead, you should use "my spouse, Mary Smith," to identify your spouse. Often it is helpful to include not only the person's legal name, but something else to clearly identify the person—such as an address or social security number.

In order to create a valid trust, the trust document must be signed by you and the trustee. Although not required in all states, the trust should be notarized by a notary public, particularly if you plan to transfer real estate to the trust. You must also transfer property to the trust when you sign the trust document. This property can be money, securities, real estate, automobiles, personal property and the like.

Chapter 6 describes how your assets can be transferred to your trust. A trust can be created with as little as $10 in it. If you are not ready to transfer all of your assets to the trust, you can simply attach a $10 bill to your signed trust document and your trust will come "alive."

Before you create your living trust, you should take a few moments to complete the ESTATE PLANNING WORKSHEET. (see form 1, p.131.) This worksheet will help you collect all of the information you need to create and fund your living trust. The worksheet will also be helpful to your family because it will identify your assets, which saves your family the time consuming process of collecting such information after your death. If you find that your total assets, including life insurance benefits and retirement plans, exceed the amount of the unified credit, and you wish to minimize your estate taxes, you should seek the advice of an experienced professional.

Four basic living trust forms are included in this book. Forms 4 and 5 are living trusts that can be used by a married individual. Forms 6 and 7 can be used by a single individual. (see Appendix C.) The provisions contained in these forms are the most popular among persons interested in establishing living trusts. Of course, the distribution provisions can be changed to reflect your individual intentions.

THE TRUSTEE

When you create your living trust you will be the initial trustee. It is important to name at least one, and preferably two, alternate trustees. One or both of these trustees will step into your shoes in the event you cannot serve as trustee. Generally, for married couples, the spouse is named as the first alternate trustee. This permits you to maintain total control over your assets. Parents, brothers, sisters or other trusted family members may also be named as alternate trustees. You may also have a friend that you trust and wish to name as trustee. Some people like to name an institution such as a bank or trust company to serve as alternate trustee if all of the persons you name as alternates are unable to serve as trustee. However, you should check the institution's fee schedule. Some charge fees which are outrageously high and some will not accept a trust if it does not have a minimum value.

A trust is a contract or agreement between the grantor and the trustee. It is important that you talk to the alternate trustees and get their permission to name them as trustees. If you did not get their permission and all of the alternates decline to serve, the court would have to appoint an alternate trustee. The person or institution appointed may not be one you would have chosen. If an institution is appointed to serve, the fee it charges will reduce the amount of your assets that pass to your beneficiaries. It takes little time to make certain that you have named alternate trustees who are willing to serve.

If you decide to name two or more individuals to serve as trustee together, to be *co-trustees*, generally all of them must agree before any investments or distributions can be made. Some states require that only the agreement of a majority of the trustees is necessary. Some grantors give one trustee a veto power or a tie-breaking power.

Sometimes a person you want to serve as trustee may have a lot of knowledge about investments and property management, but may not be responsive to the needs of others, namely the trust beneficiaries. In contrast, you may have in mind a person who is very understanding about the needs of beneficiaries, but who has no investment management skills. You can name both of these people as trustees and designate the primary role that each will play as trustee. The investment-wise individual may have the final word with regard to transactions involving the investment of trust property, and the other individual may be given the final word with regard to the nature and timing of distributions to the beneficiaries.

As you decide who to name as alternate trustees, it is important to understand a trustee's duties and powers.

DUTIES OF A TRUSTEE

Each state has laws that impose certain duties on trustees. If the trustee does not fulfill his or her duties, he or she is said to have *breached his or her duty* and he or she can be sued by the grantor or a beneficiary. If the trustee loses the lawsuit, he or she can be made to pay money to the beneficiaries or grantor to recover losses the trust suffered while he or she served. He or she can also be removed from his or her position as trustee.

Possessing and controlling trust assets. A trustee must collect and take possession of trust property as quickly as possible after he or she becomes a trustee. This does not mean that the trustee must take actual physical possession of the trust property. He or she must, however, take whatever steps are necessary to take control of the assets. For instance, the trustee does not have to take actual possession of the stock certificates held by a brokerage firm. Instead, the trustee must make certain that the legal title to the stock is transferred into the name of the trust and that the trustee is authorized to deal with the stocks.

Preserving trust assets. After the trustee has located and taken control of the trust assets, the trustee must preserve and protect the trust assets. The trustee must make certain that the trust assets are not wasting away or in danger of losing value. For instance, if the trust includes interests in a family business, the trustee must make certain that the business is being managed appropriately and that there is no interruption in the business. You certainly would not want to lose business customers, income, or the reputation that the business has developed.

Investing trust assets. The trustee must invest and maintain the trust assets so that they produce income for the benefit of the beneficiaries. A trust is not established with the idea that trust assets will be idle and not produce income that can be given to the beneficiaries. Traditionally, almost every state required that a trustee adhere to the *prudent person rule* with regard to investing trust assets. The prudent person rule requires the trustee to invest, reinvest, supervise and manage trust property using the judgment and care that persons of ordinary prudence, discretion and intelligence would use with regard to their own property.

Trustees are generally authorized to acquire and keep every kind of property (real, personal, and mixed) and every kind of investment (including bonds, stocks, securities, real estate partnerships and the like).

Under the prudent person rule, a trustee should do the following:

- diversify the trust assets among many types of investments such as stocks, bonds, etc.;

- diversify among various industries with his or her stock holdings;

- consider current income as well as long-term increase in value of the asset since the beneficiaries of income and those who will eventually receive trust principal may not be the same; and,

- seek professional advice for initial investment and continuing review of investments.

Under the prudent person rule, a trustee should *not* do the following:

- invest in risky ventures hoping to make a quick fortune;

- lend trust property to him or herself, except at fair value and with the consent of the beneficiary (or all beneficiaries);

- buy assets from the trust except at appraised value;

- continue to hold investments that a prudent person would no longer hold;

- continue to hold investments transferred to the trust without independently investigating their quality; and,

- delegate investment decisions to others. It is acceptable to seek advice from others, but ultimately the trustee must make the actual investment decisions.

While most states still use the prudent person rule, some states (such as Florida) are adopting what is being called the *prudent expert rule*. This requires the trustee to use "the care, skill, prudence and diligence under the circumstances then prevailing that a prudent person acting in a like capacity and familiar with such matters would use in the conduct of an enterprise of a like character and with like aims." This may result in a greater likelihood of a trustee being liable for a bad investment, and in someone being a bit reluctant to serve as a trustee.

With most of the forms in this book, you or your spouse will be serving as trustee or alternatively, will be closely supervising the trustee. Given that, there should be few, if any, problems with regard to the trust investments. In all of the forms included in this book, the trustee is given broad discretion with regard to investment authority. The trustee by state law will be bound by the prudent person rule or the prudent expert rule.

If you wish to restrict the investment power of the trustee you may want to add a provision or do a trust amendment that contains specific investment guidelines for the trustee. These guidelines could limit investments to stock in Fortune 500 companies, bonds with a minimum credit rating, prohibit investment in real estate ventures, etc. However, you must be careful and try to think far off into the future when you limit the trustee's investment power. The trustee needs some degree of flexibility to take into account the changing economic and investment situations.

Example: David established a trust in the early 1980s when certificates of deposit were earning about fifteen percent or more. David limited the trustee's investment power to "certificates of deposit and any other financial instrument backed by the U.S. government with comparable interest rates." Because interest rates on CDs are now yielding only five percent, they would no longer be a good investment.

Informing beneficiaries. The trustee must also inform the trust beneficiaries of the existence of the trust and explain its provisions. To do this, the trustee must understand all of the trust's provisions. Because the trust is a private document between the grantor and the trustee (who usually is the grantor himself), the beneficiaries will often not be aware of the trust's existence until after the grantor dies or becomes incapacitated.

Accounting. The trustee has a responsibility to report to the beneficiaries and keep them informed of all of the trust transactions. This includes reporting all assets received, sold, or exchanged by the trust, income earned, and expenses incurred by the trust and distributions made to beneficiaries. The date, amount, and a short explanation of each transaction should be included in the reports. These reports can be done on a monthly, quarterly, or annual basis. You may include a specific instruction in the trust as to how frequently these reports must be given or you may leave it to the trustee to determine the frequency of such reports.

Keeping trust assets separate. Importantly, the trustee must keep the trust assets separate from his or her own assets. The trust assets must be clearly identified. Titles to bank accounts, stocks, etc., should have the name of the trustee, as trustee, on them. Income earned by the trust assets must be kept separate as well. Failure to do this is called *commingling* and is one of the primary reasons lawsuits are brought against trustees.

Trustees should never borrow assets from the trust, sell assets to the trust, or purchase or lease assets from the trust for his or her own purposes, unless it is at fair value with written consent of all beneficiaries.

Making distributions. Finally, the trustee must make distributions to the trust beneficiaries as provided in the trust document. The trustee is not allowed to substitute his or her judgment for the terms of the trust. If the trust permits the trustee to use his or her discretion in making distributions to the beneficiaries, the trustee must be reasonable in his or her decisions. For instance, it would be inappropriate for a trustee to favor one beneficiary over the other when making distributions simply because the trustee does not like the beneficiary or does not agree with how the beneficiary behaves.

TRUSTEE
POWERS

Each state has specific laws giving trustees powers to administer the trust. As creator of the trust, you can broaden the scope of these powers or you may restrict the powers. For example, you may wish to prohibit the trustee from selling the vacation home you inherited from your parents. The powers often given to trustees under state law include the following:

- investing and selling assets;

- collecting income and rents;

- investing in stocks and real estate;

- opening bank accounts;

- joining in litigation to protect the trust assets; and,

- hiring professionals, such as accountants and attorneys, to assist the trustee in fulfilling his or her duties.

You can grant a trustee special powers, such as the power to distribute funds to beneficiaries before the designated time if the trustee believes that the beneficiary is in need of the funds.

If you wish to limit the type of investments that a trustee can make, you must be very specific in the trust document. If you do not leave clear instructions, the trustee can unknowingly undermine your intentions.

REMOVING A TRUSTEE

Sometimes it is important to be able to remove a trustee without having to involve the court. Generally, the trust document gives the grantor the right to remove the trustee and name an alternate trustee. You may wish to include a provision in the trust giving your beneficiaries or a third party the power to remove a trustee if the trustee is stealing from the trust, is not fulfilling his or her duties under the law, or is not following the terms of the trust document.

A trustee may also voluntarily choose to quit. If your trust does not contain instructions on how a trustee can resign, the trustee must obtain the approval of the court to resign. The beneficiaries cannot simply agree to accept the trustee's resignation.

If your trust does not name an alternate trustee, you or the trust beneficiaries must petition the court to appoint an alternate trustee.

BENEFICIARIES

When you establish your living trust you must decide who will be the beneficiaries of the trust, how much each beneficiary will receive, and when the beneficiaries will receive their gift from the trust.

While you are alive, you will be the primary beneficiary of your living trust. You may also wish to name your spouse and minor children as beneficiaries while you are alive. Then, if you become incapacitated, the successor trustee can make distributions not only for your care but also for the care of your spouse and minor children. This is particularly important if you are the primary income earner. Your trust assets will earn income that can assist your family as it adjusts to the loss of your paycheck.

You may name beneficiaries to receive income only, principal only (principal is the property you transfer to the trust), or both income and principal. After your death, you may wish to give all of trust property to your spouse with the intention that he or she assume your role and provide for himself or herself and your children. If your spouse has established a living trust of his or her own, the trust assets can be distributed directly to his or her living trust.

If you do not have a spouse, or if you believe that your spouse has sufficient assets to take care of himself or herself, and you want to name your children as beneficiaries you have several options available to you.

LUMP SUM DISTRIBUTION

You may wish to distribute all of the trust assets to your children at one time, in a single lump sum, after your death.

DELAYED DISTRIBUTION OF SINGLE TRUST

Most parents want to be certain that there are enough funds available to provide for their children until they reach a certain age. (For example, when the youngest child has completed college.) You can accomplish this by keeping all of the trust property in a single fund and giving the trustee discretion to make distributions to each child as he or she needs funds just as you would do as a parent.

Thus, as medical or tuition bills need to be paid, the trustee can make distributions either directly to the child or to the doctor or college to pay these bills. Generally, such discretionary distributions are limited to food, clothing, shelter, health care, education and special events such as weddings. When the youngest child reaches the age you specify, the remaining trust property can be divided equally among the children and distributed to them. The trust will then terminate.

DELAYED
DISTRIBUTION
OF SEPARATE
TRUSTS

Alternatively, the trust can immediately separate into equal shares after your death, one for each child. The trustee can make distributions to the child for the same reasons described above. Such distributions would be entirely within the discretion of the trustee. The trustee can also make periodic distributions to the child at scheduled intervals—monthly, quarterly or annually. This provides the beneficiary with a regular income. Of course, you can combine the two methods and provide a regular income and—to the extent the regular income does not fulfill the needs of the child—the trustee can make additional distributions to the child.

As long as the trustee alone has the decision-making power with regard to when distributions (other than the periodic distributions) will be made and for what purpose, the creditors of the child cannot touch the trust property.

STAGGERED
DISTRIBUTIONS

You may also provide that distributions of principal be staggered to your children. For example, your living trust may provide that distributions be made to your child quarterly and that the trustee may make additional distributions to the child if he or she is in need. Instead of distributing all of the trust property at once, you can provide, for example, that one-third of the trust property be distributed to the child at age twenty-five, one-third at age thirty and the remaining trust property at age thirty-five. This allows the trust to terminate over time while not sacrificing the needs of the child. You can decide on the ages and percentages as you create your living trust.

Whichever method of distribution you use you should be careful to avoid making distributions contingent on the happening of a certain event. For instance, you should not provide that distributions will be made when a child gets married, graduates from a particular college, has a child, etc. These restrictions may keep a child from ever receiving the trust property.

NOTE: *Children are different from each other and even from their parents. Do not put restrictions in your trust that force your child to live up to expectations that cannot be changed after you have died.*

RULE AGAINST
PERPETUITIES

If you decide to keep the property in trust for the benefit of your children or other beneficiaries, you should be aware of a rule governing the length of time that property can be held in trust. This rule is called the *rule against perpetuities.* The rule prohibits a trust grantor from controlling the distribution of trust property for too long.

To prevent trusts from extending several generations and keeping family wealth tied up for extremely long periods of time, the rule against perpetuities states that a trust cannot keep property for longer than the life of any person living when the trust was created plus twenty-one years. At that time, the full ownership rights in the trust property must be given to the beneficiaries. Most people do not have to concern themselves with this rule, but most trust documents contain a clause to make sure that the rule against perpetuities is not violated.

DEATH OF A
BENEFICIARY
BEFORE
DISTRIBUTION

What happens if a beneficiary dies before you do or dies before his or her share of the trust is completely distributed to him or her? Most people would like their grandchildren to be provided for and inherit the property their children would have received. Lawyers commonly use either the phrase *per capita* or *per stirpes* in the clause specifying how the property will be distributed.

PER CAPITA

Per capita distributions are *pro rata* or *share and share alike* distributions. That means that all of the surviving descendants, regardless of generation, get equal shares of the trust property.

Example: Michael has four grown children: George, Tom, Judy and Karen. Karen has three children and she dies before Michael. At Michael's death, the trust property is to be distributed per capita. The trust property will be distributed in six equal shares—one for each living child of Michael and one for each of Karen's children.

PER STIRPES   Per stirpes distributions are by representation. This means that if one of your children dies before you do, the amount that beneficiary would have received is divided equally among that beneficiary's direct descendants.

Example: Same facts as above, but at Michael's death the trust property is divided into four equal shares—one for each of his children and one to be subdivided among Karen's three children.

All of the above examples and discussion apply not only to your children, but to any beneficiaries that you name. Remember, the living trust identifies who you want to receive your property, how much, and when. You can design the living trust any way you want to make sure that your intentions are carried out.

SPECIFIC GIFTS   You may chose to leave certain assets to selected beneficiaries. For instance, you may want your oldest child to receive the vacation home that has been in your family. Or you may want your daughter to receive your jewelry. You can include these specific gifts in your living trust.

Sometimes the list of specific gifts may be lengthy. Rather than include all of the specific gifts in your trust you may leave a written memorandum in addition to your living trust that lists the specific items of your tangible personal property to be distributed. Your living trust must, however, refer to this memorandum. Forms included in this book refer to the memorandum. If you choose not to leave specific gifts, you do not need to complete the memorandum. If you wish to change the specific gifts, you can simply change the memorandum and do not have to sign an entire new trust document. A MEMORANDUM OF DISPOSITION OF TANGIBLE PERSONAL PROPERTY with instructions is included in Appendix C. (see form 8, p.181.) This memorandum should not be used for real estate, stocks, bonds, or anything other than tangible personal items. Such specific gifts should be included in your living trust document.

CHARITABLE BENEFICIARIES

If you would like to leave a gift to your church or some other charitable organization, you can include a provision in your trust giving such organization a specified dollar amount or a percentage of the assets in the trust. Remember, your living trust acts as a will substitute, so any gifts you would have included in your will you can include in your trust.

SPECIAL CIRCUMSTANCES

There may be special circumstances that require your living trust to contain unique provisions. For instance, you may wish to provide for a disabled or special needs child or you may have a child who is financially irresponsible and needs more restrictions on his or her share. You may have children from two marriages and wish to provide for them differently. Your parents may depend on you for support and would require continued financial assistance after your death.

With the help of an experienced professional, your living trust can be designed to address such special circumstances. The forms contained in this book provide the most common and basic trust alternatives. You should not expect to use these forms for such circumstances.

GIFTS TO PETS

Except in California and Tennessee, you cannot leave property to your pets. This is because a pet is property, and property cannot own other property. If you wish to have a pet cared for after your death, you should make arrangements with a person you trust and leave them money for that purpose. Otherwise you might be able to sign up for a life care contract with an animal shelter or veterinarian.

SIGNING YOUR LIVING TRUST

Now that you have designed your living trust by choosing your alternate trustees, your beneficiaries, and the distribution pattern of trust property, you must sign the trust document and fund the trust. You should sign the trust document as both the grantor and trustee. Three witnesses should watch you sign the trust document and sign the document themselves (most states only require two witnesses, but a few require three). All of this should be done in the presence of a notary public who should sign and notarize the living trust (notary requirements may also vary from state to state, but your notary should know how to modify the forms to meet these requirements). To get started, you should fund the trust with $10 by attaching a $10 bill to the last page of the trust document. Now you are ready to transfer assets to your trust. Later the $10 can be deposited into the trust bank account.

AMENDING YOUR LIVING TRUST

After you have signed your living trust, events may occur that make you want to change your living trust. For example, a successor trustee may die or change his or her mind about serving as trustee, you may wish to add or remove a beneficiary, or you may wish to change the requirements for distributions of trust assets. Your living trust can be easily amended to reflect these changes. You do not have to draft an entire new living trust. Instead, you can do an amendment to the trust that only makes the change that you desire. An AMENDMENT TO LIVING TRUST is included in Appendix C. (see form 9, p.183.) A filled-in sample is in Appendix B.

If you wish to cancel your living trust in the future, you can use a REVOCATION OF LIVING TRUST for this purpose. (see form 10, p.185.) When the trust is canceled, you will have to *unfund* your trust and transfer all of the assets out of the trust and back to yourself in your individual name or into joint accounts or other arrangements as discussed in Chapter 2.

FAMILY LIMITED PARTNERSHIPS

One of the increasing popular ways to avoid probate is the family limited partnership. There are many tax and non-tax advantages associated with family limited partnerships. The most common objectives of family limited partnerships are protection of assets from future creditors, consolidation of asset ownership and management, family wealth accumulation, and flexibility.

A limited partnership is similar to a corporation in that its assets are owned by various individuals who have an ownership interest in the limited partnership. Each individual owner is called a *partner*. There are two different categories of partners: limited partners and general partners. The basic, and very important difference between these two categories of partners is that in the event of a lawsuit against the partnership, the limited partner's exposure to loss is limited to his or her investment in the partnership—the money or property that the limited partner contributed to the partnership. A general partner, however, may lose not only his or her investment in the partnership, but all of his or her other assets as well.

Some of the features of a limited partnership include the following:

ASSET
PROTECTION

In the event of a lawsuit against a partner individually, all of the partner's investment assets, including real estate, would be exposed to seizure by the suing party. If these assets are owned by a family limited partnership, creditors could not reach the assets themselves. Instead, creditors could only attach the limited partnership interest.

A properly constructed family partnership would prevent a limited partner from causing the termination of the partnership. This protects the underlying assets from a creditor-forced distribution. The creditor of a limited partner may obtain a charging order that gives the creditor the right to the income portion of the limited partner's interest. However, the general partner may decide not to authorize distribution of income to the limited partners. Therefore, a creditor may have a responsibility for federal income tax liability attributable to the limited partnership interest, yet have limited or no rights to receive actual distributions from the partnership.

Since the creditor may be responsible for the liability of paying taxes on "phantom" income, and yet not acquire partnership assets or take part in partnership management (which is usually vested in the general partner), creditors generally are not interested in obtaining limited partnership interests. This protects the partnership's assets and preserves them for distribution to family members in the future.

CONSOLIDATION OF ASSET OWNERSHIP AND MANAGEMENT

All of the investment assets are brought under the ownership of one entity—the limited partnership. Family members are not given fractional interests in stock, real estate, and the like. Consolidation of the investments reduces the need for more than one money manager and more than one investment account and it likely results in a reduction of fees. The general partner is typically vested with the authority to manage the partnership's affairs, which include employing investment advisors and money managers.

FAMILY WEALTH ACCUMULATION

Family partnership agreements are often drafted with buy-sell provisions to help make certain that the assets will remain in the family. If a family member attempts to assign his or her interest in the partnership to a non-family member, the partnership agreement may provide that the other partners or the partnership have the right to acquire the assigned partnership interest on the same terms as the proposed assignment. This permits the wealth generated by the investments to accrue to the benefit of the family. This often becomes important when there exists a fear of protecting one's children from the consequences of divorce in a community property state, such as Texas.

FLEXIBILITY

The limited partnership agreement is a flexible document. If all of the partners agree, the partnership agreement may be amended or terminated. In contrast, an irrevocable trust generally cannot be amended or terminated without participation by a court and a guardian ad litem or a lawyer. A partnership may generally be terminated without adverse tax consequences, but there may be severe tax consequences when a corporation is terminated.

Additionally, a limited partnership provides greater investment flexibility because of the operation of the business judgment rule. The prudent person rule, which applies to trustees, is a stricter standard than the business judgment rule, which applies to managing partners of a partnership.

Example: Joe and Kathy transfer their property to a family limited partnership. The partnership agreement provides that the income will be paid to Joe and Kathy during their lifetimes in such amounts determined by the general partner. Joe and Kathy set up a trust, which they control, to be the general partner. Joe and Kathy pay all of the income to themselves each year. When Joe is involved in an automobile accident and is sued, no income is paid to Joe until the lawsuit is settled.

Family limited partnerships provide many benefits. However, they must be set up carefully to make certain that the benefits are enjoyed by the partners. Consultation with an expert in this field of planning is a must.

FUNDING YOUR LIVING TRUST 6

The primary purpose for creating your living trust is to avoid probate during your lifetime (such as during an incapacity) and after your death. In order to accomplish this, you must transfer legal title to your property to the trust and thereby transform it into non-probate property.

HOW MUCH PROPERTY TO TRANSFER

There is no rule telling you how much or which property you should transfer to the trust. Obviously, the more property transferred to the trust, the less is subject to the expense and delay of probate after your death. Often, it is advisable to keep some cash in a JTWROS checking account with a bank. Grocery stores, department stores, and the like are not familiar with checks drawn on trust accounts and signed by trustees. Rather than deal with the hassles caused by a store clerk who hesitates or refuses to accept a trust check, it is advisable to keep at least one bank account outside of the trust. However, if possible and practical, you should use some form of joint tenancy or POD account to avoid subjecting the property to probate at your death.

How Title Is Held for Trust Assets

Most property transferred to your living trust must be retitled in the name of the trust. The basic title that is recommended for use in holding all assets in the trust is as follows:

[YOUR NAME], trustee, [YOUR NAME] Trust, dated _____, _____.

Example:

JOHN DOE, trustee, JOHN DOE Trust, dated January 23, 2002.

Some institutions may require slightly different wording. However, the name of the trust, the name of the trustee, and the date the trust was created are normally all that is required.

Whenever you execute documents on behalf of your living trust and transact trust business, you should sign your name:

[YOUR NAME], TRUSTEE

How to Transfer Property to a Living Trust

PERSONAL PROPERTY
You can transfer personal belongings such as furniture, antiques, artwork, clothing, jewelry, etc., to the trust by signing an **ASSIGNMENT OF PERSONAL PROPERTY**. (see form 11, p.187.) This form should be notarized.

AUTOMOBILES
Automobiles have title certificates that must be changed. You can contact your local government agency that handles motor vehicle registrations to obtain the correct forms to accomplish this. Also, contact your automobile insurance company to make sure that the owner on your policy is changed. Such a transfer should not affect your insurance rates, but you should verify this with your agent.

REAL ESTATE
Real estate can be transferred to the living trust by executing a new deed. This deed will depict you as the grantor of the property and you

in your capacity as trustee, as the grantee of the property. Each state has different forms of deeds and the form of deed that is used is often very important. It would be advisable to contact an attorney who is familiar with real estate transfers to determine your state's deed requirements.

If your house is subject to a mortgage, the approval of the mortgage company is generally required. Often the mortgage company will ask for a copy of the trust to make certain that you are the owner of all of the assets in the trust and that you will continue to be responsible for future mortgage payments. It is important to contact your fire and casualty insurance company to change the policy to reflect the trust as the new owner of your home.

In some states there is a homestead exemption for real estate taxes on your home. This exemption can result in significant real estate tax savings over the years. Once your homestead property is transferred to your trust, you no longer own the property, the trust does. Trusts generally do not qualify for the homestead exemption. However, many states recognize that the living trust is simply your "alter ego" and will permit the homestead exemption to continue. Prior to transferring your homestead to your trust you should check with the local taxing authorities to make certain that the homestead exemption will continue and what, if any, forms you must complete to protect the homestead exemption.

Whenever you acquire an additional piece of real estate, generally all that you need to do is tell the title company to prepare and record title to the real estate in the name of your living trust. The title company may wish to see a copy of your living trust to make certain that the trustee has the power to own real estate and that the trustee has the power to pay make mortgage payments, pay real estate taxes, etc. If this is the case, you need only show the title company a copy of the first page of the trust, the pages that contain the powers of the trustee, and the signature page. None of the other provisions of the trust are relevant to the title company. The identity of the trust beneficiaries, and the amounts to which they are entitled, are a private matter and the title company is not entitled to see such information.

BANK ACCOUNTS

Checking and savings accounts, and other accounts at financial institutions should be retitled as follows:

[YOUR NAME], trustee, [YOUR NAME] Trust, dated _____, _____.

The transfer of bank accounts or accounts with other insured institutions like credit unions or savings & loans are accomplished quite easily. Make a copy of the first page of your living trust, the pages that contain the powers of the trustee, and the signature page and give these to the financial institution. Tell the manager or appropriate official to transfer your accounts, certificates of deposit, and safe deposit boxes into the name of your living trust. Be sure to ask whether the transfer of the certificate of deposit into the name of your trust will result in a charge or penalty for early withdrawal because of the name change. Typically, the financial institution will not assess any charge, but it is important to ask before making the transfer.

> *Warning:* Checking accounts are a type of asset that should not be put into your living trust. Unless you are keeping a large balance in the household account, your checking account should be held as you hold it now. Why? Often when you deal with cashiers at retail stores they will be confused when they see a check in the name of a trust. A manager may be called to review the check and you may have to go through an unnecessary explanation.

The delay and inconvenience of the situation above is far outweighed by keeping a checking account in your name individually funded with enough money to take care of your anticipated monthly expenses. The remainder of your assets can be kept in accounts in the name of your living trust. You can make transfers of cash to your checking account on a monthly basis, or more frequently as you are comfortable.

REGISTERED STOCKS AND BONDS

Your stock broker can work with you to re-register the stocks and bonds that you now own. You may need to complete a stock transfer power of attorney and surrender your stock certificates to the broker so he or she can have new certificates issued to your trust. As you acquire stocks in the future, simply have them titled in the name of the trust (as described on the previous page).

Bonds should also be re-registered in the name of the trust. Again, your stock broker can assist you with this or you can contact the issuing institution directly to get the appropriate forms.

Sometimes stocks and bonds are held in a *street name* or custodian account with your broker. The broker often collects all interest and dividends on the stocks and bonds and disposes of them according to your instructions, (i.e. pays them out directly to you or deposits them into some sort of money market account). These street name accounts can also be registered in the name of the trust.

If you have a brokerage account that holds your stocks and bonds in *street name*, the only thing you need to do is to have your broker change that account into the name of your living trust. All of your stocks and bonds in that account will then belong to your trust.

LIFE INSURANCE The beneficiary designations on your life insurance policies should be changed to make your trust the beneficiary. The beneficiary designation should read:

The Then Acting Trustee of the [YOUR NAME] Trust, dated _____, ____.

RETIREMENT PLANS Because of the specific and complex tax rules governing tax qualified retirement plans such as 401(k), pensions, profit-sharing plans, IRAs, Keoghs, etc., you should consult with a tax professional to determine whether your trust should be named as the beneficiary of such plans.

Do not hesitate to contact professionals to assist you with the property transfers. Your stock broker and banker should be willing to help with these transfers with no additional charge to you. Do not let them drag their feet; keep after them to get the assets transferred.

If you are having trouble with the real estate transfers, or if you own real estate outside of your state of residence, you should contact an attorney who can assist you. The charge for this service should be nominal. Often, the fee paid to an attorney is well worth it because it can save you a lot of frustration and time. More than likely, there will be a recording or document fee that is charged by the county when a new deed is filed. This fee covers the cost of entering the new deed in the county land records. You should not have to pay documentary stamp fees (transfer fees) on a deed to your own trust.

Once you have initially funded your living trust, you must keep separate records for the trust property. As you acquire property in the future, title it directly in the name of the trust. As you sell trust property, keep the proceeds in a special trust bank account. As the grantor of the trust, you can distribute trust property to yourself at any time with little or no additional effort, so there is no reason to allow the proceeds to end up outside the trust. There is much to be gained by keeping the property in the trust, so you should take the extra time to make certain that the goal of your living trust—probate avoidance—is met.

GLOSSARY

A

administrator (administratrix if female). A person appointed by the court to oversee distribution of the property of someone who died (either without a will, or if the person designated in the will is unable to serve).

annual exclusion. The amount of property a person can give to another person per year that is not counted against the lifetime unified credit.

annuity trust. Charitable remainder trust that provides the donor a fixed annual income

assets. Money and real or personal property owned by a person or organization.

B

beneficial interest. Right to enjoy or profit from property held in trust; the person with the beneficial interest is the beneficiary.

beneficiary. Person who is named to receive some benefit or money from a legal document such as a trust, life insurance policy or will.

bequest. Gift of personal property left in a will.

bond. Monetary guarantee that, should a trustee steal trust funds, compensation will be awarded up to the bond's limit.

bypass trust.   Trust typically created by a married couple to contain property that will not be included, for estate tax purposes, in the estate of the surviving spouse. The surviving spouse receives income from the trust but not the principal.

C

charitable lead trust. Trust that donates to a charity income from trust assets while reserving the assets for later distribution to other beneficiaries. Compare with charitable remainder trust.

charitable remainder trust. Trust that pays income from trust assets to the donor or beneficiaries while reserving the assets for later contribution to a charity. Compare with charitable lead trust.

children's trust.   A trust set up to hold property given to children. Usually it provides that the children will not receive their property until they reach a higher age than the age of majority.

codicil. A written charge or amendment to a will.

community property.   Property acquired during marriage that was not a gift to or inheritance of one spouse or specifically kept separate.

contingent interest.   Interest in property that is dependent on the occurrence of a future event, such as a college graduation, not on the passage of time.

credit estate tax.   State tax on the assets of someone who has died. Applies only in some states and only to estates that are required to pay federal estate taxes. Estate does not pay double taxes but instead, by paying a credit estate tax, rebates part of the federal estate tax owed back to the state.

creditor.   Person or corporation to whom money is due.

credit shelter trust.   Another name for bypass trust.

D

decedent.   Person who has died.

descendant.   A child, grandchild, great-grandchild, etc.

donee.   Recipient of a gift, trust or power left in a trust; beneficiary of a trust.

donor.   Person or corporation that gives a gift to or confers a power on another; creator of a trust.

E

estate.   All property, real or personal, that a person owns.

estate tax.   Type of death tax based on the decedent's right to transfer property; not a tax on the property itself.

executor.   Person or corporation appointed in a will or by a court to settle the estate of a deceased person (female gender, executrix).

family trust.   Another name for a bypass trust.

federal estate tax.   Federal tax assessed against the assets of a person who has died if the value of the taxable assets exceeds 675,000.

fiduciary.   Person in a position of trust and confidence; a person who has a duty to act primarily for the benefit of another. A trustee or executor acts as a fiduciary.

future interest.   Interest in property that cannot be possessed or enjoyed until a specified period of time passes or a future event (for example, a 21st birthday) occurs.

G

generation-skipping trust.   Trust designed to skip one generation of estate taxes because the trust leaves the principal to the grantor's grandchildren, not the grantor's children.

gift. Voluntary lifetime or at-death transfer of property, made without compensation.

gift tax. Tax on lifetime transfers of property given without consideration or for less consideration than the property is worth.

grantor. Another term for creator of a trust. See also donor, settlor, trustor.

grantor trust. Living trust in which the grantor maintains enough control over the assets so that the trust income received is taxed to the grantor, not to the trust or to the trust's beneficiaries.

gross estate. Property owned by a decedent at death. Value before debts are paid.

guardian. Person or corporation appointed by a court to handle the affairs or property of another who is unable to do so because of incapacity.

H

heir. Person or corporation designated to inherit property from someone who has died.

I

incapacitated/incompetent. One who is unable to manage his or her own affairs either temporarily or permanently.

income. All financial gains from investments, work or business.

income beneficiary. Beneficiary of a trust who receives only the income generated by the trust assets.

inheritance tax. Tax imposed on property received by beneficiaries from the estate of a decedent.

insurance trust. Trust that owns and manages a life insurance policy and designates its beneficiaries.

intestate. Not leaving a valid will.

irrevocable trust. Trust that cannot be changed or canceled after it is created.

J

joint tenancy with right of survivorship. Form of ownership in which property is equally shared by all owners and is automatically transferred to the surviving owners when one of them dies.

L

living (or inter vivos) trust. A revocable trust separate from a will that may be funded or unfunded during the settlor's lifetime. It is commonly used to avoid probate and provide a means for the management of assets during incompetency or incapacity.

living will. A separate document in which a person, while competent to do so, expresses a wish that his or her life not be prolonged by artificial life support systems if his or her medical condition becomes hopeless.

P

per capita. Will or trust distribution plan that requires that all living descendants of the grantor, regardless of generation, receive an equal share of the grantor's estate.

personal property. Property that is movable, not land or things attached to land.

personal representative. Person named in a will or appointed by a court to settle an estate. Also called PR. *See also* **executor**.

per stirpes. Will or trust distribution plan that requires that descendants of a deceased beneficiary, as a group, inherit equal shares of the amount the deceased beneficiary would have received had he or she lived. (For example, if your child predeceases you, any grandchildren descended from that child would receive equal shares of your deceased child's inheritance.)

pourover will. Will provision that distributes money or property to a trust that already exists.

power of attorney. Legal document whereby one person authorizes another to make medical and financial decisions should illness or incapacitation occur.

present interest. Right to use property immediately. Compare with future interest.

principal. Property in a trust; also called corpus.

probate. Legal process of establishing the validity of a deceased person's last will and testament; commonly refers to the process and laws for settling an estate.

Q

QTIP (qualified terminable interest property) trust. Trust that qualifies for the unlimited marital deduction and postpones payment of any estate taxes owed until both spouses have died. The surviving spouse receives trust income for life but has little or no legal right to the trust's principal.

R

real property. Property that is immovable, such as land, buildings and whatever else is attached to or growing on land.

residual beneficiary. Person who receives remaining property that has not been given away in a trust or will, or person who receives property only after the original beneficiary has died.

S

Section 2503(c) trust. Trust that allows a grantor to make gifts of $10,000 a year to a trust for the future benefit of minor children without the grantor incurring gift taxes.

settlor. Another term for creator of a trust. *See also* **grantor, donor.**

spendthrift clause. Provision included in some trusts that prohibits the beneficiary from giving or selling to others the beneficiary's rights to the trust's assets or income.

standby trust. Living trust that takes effect if a grantor becomes ill or incapacitated or dies. The grantor's assets are transferred to the trust and managed by the designated trustee.

successor trustee. Person who takes over the rights and responsibilities of an original trustee.

T

tenancy by entirety. Form of spousal ownership in which property is equally shared and automatically transferred to the surviving spouse. While both spouses are living, ownership of the property can be altered only by divorce or mutual agreement.

tenancy in common. Way of jointly owning property in which each person's share passes to his or her heirs or beneficiaries, but the ownership shares need not be equal.

testamentary trust. Trust established in a person's will.

testate. Dying with a valid will.

title. Ownership of property, or the document that shows ownership.

Totten trust. Revocable trust created by the owner of a bank account (checking, savings or other) for the future benefit of another.

trust. Real or personal property held by one party (the trustee) for the benefit of another (the beneficiary).

trust B. Another name for bypass trust.

trustee. Person who holds and/or manages money or property for the benefit of another.

U

unified credit.   The federal credit against estate taxes that is allowed to each person or estate.

unlimited marital deduction.   Allows a spouse to transfer all property to his or her spouse without federal estate tax.

W

will.   Legal document that declares how a person wishes property to be distributed to heirs or beneficiaries after death. Can only be enforced through a probate court.

APPENDIX A
TAX EXPLANATIONS

The following pages contain explanations of the state death taxes and the federal estate tax. If you do not understand these, you may want to see an attorney.

Explanation of State Death Taxes Including
State Death Tax Credit Table

STATE DEATH TAXES

Each state imposes some form of death tax on a decedent's estate. There are three types of state death taxes: the pick-up tax, the estate tax, and the inheritance tax.

The Pick-Up Tax

The federal government permits a limited credit against federal estate taxes for death taxes paid to the states. The amount of this state tax credit is calculated through a formula established by the federal government. A chart illustrating how this credit is calculated follows. Several states have a death tax that is equal to the maximum state tax credit that the federal government permits. This is referred to as a "pick-up" tax. The following states have pick-up taxes:

Alabama	Florida	Missouri	Texas
Alaska	Georgia	Nevada	Utah
Arizona	Hawaii	New Mexico	Vermont
Arkansas	Idaho	North Dakota	Virginia
California	Illinois	Oregon	Washington
Colorado	Maine	Rhode Island	West Virginia
District of	Minnesota	South Carolina	Wisconsin
Columbia			Wyoming

State Estate Tax

The states listed below impose an estate tax on their residents. The estate tax is calculated in the same manner as the federal estate tax. It is a tax on the value of the assets owned by the decedent at the date of his or her death. Often the estate tax imposed by a state is much more than the state death tax credit that the federal government allows. Estate tax states are:

Massachusetts	Ohio
Mississippi	Oklahoma
New York	

State Inheritance Tax

Several states impose an inheritance tax. This type of tax is levied directly on the beneficiaries who receive the assets. Often the amount of the inheritance tax depends upon the relationship of the beneficiary to the decedent. Spouses, children, grandchildren and parents are often taxed at a lower rate than sisters, brothers, nieces, nephews and nonrelatives. The following states use the inheritance tax system:

Connecticut	Louisiana	New Jersey
Delaware	Maryland	North Carolina
Indiana	Michigan	Pennsylvania
Iowa	Montana	South Dakota
Kansas	Nebraska	Tennessee
Kentucky	New Hampshire	

No matter which type of tax that a state imposes, you need to be aware of the tax and the potential impact of that tax on your estate. You can obtain specific information on your state's form of tax and the rate of tax by contacting the state treasurer or comptroller or the state tax department.

STATE DEATH TAX CREDIT

Adjustable Taxable Estate[1]		Credit =	+ %	Of Excess Over
At Least	But Less Than			
$ 0	$ 40,000	$ 0	0	$ 0
40,000	90,000	0	.8	40,000
90,000	140,000	400	1.6	90,000
140,000	240,000	1,200	2.4	140,000
240,000	440,000	3,600	3.2	240,000
440,000	640,000	10,000	4.0	440,000
640,000	840,000	18,000	4.8	640,000
840,000	1,040,000	27,600	5.6	840,000
1,040,000	1,540,000	38,800	6.4	1,040,000
1,540,000	2,040,000	70,800	7.2	1,540,000
2,040,000	2,540,000	106,800	8.0	2,040,000
2,540,000	3,040,000	146,800	8.8	2,540,000
3,040,000	3,540,000	190,800	9.6	3,040,000
3,540,000	4,040,000	238,800	10.4	3,540,000
4,040,000	5,040,000	290,800	11.2	4,040,000
5,040,000	6,040,000	402,800	12.0	5,040,000
6,040,000	7,040,000	522,800	12.8	6,040,000
7,040,000	8,040,000	650,800	13.6	7,040,000
8,040,000	9,040,000	786,800	14.4	8,040,000
9,040,000	10,040,000	930,800	15.2	9,040,000
10,040,000	* * * * *	1,082,800	16.0	10,040,000

[1] The adjusted taxable estate is the taxable estate reduced by $60,000.

Explanation of Federal Estate Taxes Including
Federal Estate and Gift Schedule

FEDERAL ESTATE TAX

As discussed throughout the text, all property owned by you at your death, probate and non-probate, is subject to the federal estate tax at your death. The federal estate tax applies to all estates. However, the law grants you a unified credit and your estate does not have to pay tax on an amount up to that credit. In June, 2001, President Bush signed a new tax law that contains among its provisions, drastic changes to the estate and gift tax law. Under the new law, the estate tax will be completely repealed by the year 2010. The new law also reduces the highest estate and gift tax rates. The following table sets forth the increase in the unified credit and the decrease in the estate and gift tax rate.

Calendar Year	Estate and Gift Tax Unified Credit Amount	Highest Estate & Gift Tax Rate
2002	$1 million	50%
2003	$1 million	49%
2004	$1.5 million	48%
2005	$1.5 million	47%
2006	$2 million	46%
2007	$2 million	45%
2008	$2 million	45%
2009	$3.5 million	45%
2010	N/A	Replaced by top individual income tax rate (gifts only)

The gift tax is not repealed. Instead, there is a new $1 million lifetime exemption for gifts beginning in 2002. In 2010, the maximum gift tax rate on gifts in excess of $1 million will be 35%.

Under the current law, when an individual inherits property and later sells it, the person does not have to pay capital gains tax on the appreciation that occurred prior to the death of the person from whom they inherited the property. The heir was able to "step up" the basis of the asset to the value at the date of the decedent's death. Capital gain was calculated, therefore, from the date of death until the date of sale.

In 2010, however, with the repeal of the estate tax, the step-up in basis rules would change for property inherited from a decedent. A decedent's estate would be permitted to increase the basis of assets transferred to heirs by up to a total of $1.3 million. The basis of property transferred to a surviving spouse could be increased by $3.0 million. Thus, the basis of property transferred to a surviving spouse could be increased by a total of $4.3 million. What does this mean? For anyone who has an estate in excess of $1.3 million, there will still be a tax that will eventually be paid—a capital gains tax—by the beneficiary. The headaches will come when executors, trustees, beneficiaries and their accountants will have to determine the decedent's basis in assets to make the proper "step-up," and later when a beneficiary sells assets that did not receive a step-up in basis upon the decedent's death.

APPENDIX B
SAMPLE FILLED-IN FORMS

This appendix contains samples of some of the forms in Appendix C. These are to demonstrate the way you can fill them in. The form numbers correspond to the form numbers in Appendix C.

TABLE OF FORMS

<u>   John Smith   </u>   **LIVING TRUST**

THIS AGREEMENT OF TRUST is entered into at <u>Dallas</u>, State of <u>Texas</u>, this <u>4th</u> day of <u>March</u>, <u>2002</u>, by and between _____, as Grantor and Trustee. This Trust, as from time to time amended, shall be known as the "<u>John Smith</u>
LIVING TRUST dated <u>March 4</u>, <u>2002</u>."

ARTICLE I

My Spouse. My spouse is: <u>Jane Smith</u>.

My Children. My Children are: <u>Joseph Smith, Jennifer Smith, and</u>

<u>John Smith, Jr.</u>.

ARTICLE II

FUNDING

Initial Funding. I hereby transfer to Trustee the sum of Ten Dollars ($10.00).

Additional Funding. From time to time the trust may be funded with additional property by me or by any other person in any manner. All property transferred, assigned, conveyed or delivered to the Trustee shall be held, administered and distributed by the Trustee in accordance with the terms of this Trust Agreement.

ARTICLE III

ADMINISTRATION OF TRUST DURING MY LIFETIME

Distributions of Income. While I am living, the Trustee shall distribute the trust's net income as directed in writing by me from time to time. In default of such direction, the Trustee shall pay to or expend on behalf of me all of the trust's net income from the Trust quarterly or more frequently.

Distributions of Principal. The Trustee shall pay to or expend for my benefit such part or all of the principal of the trust as I may request, from time to time. In default of such direction, the Trustee shall pay to or expend for my benefit so much of the principal of the trust as the Trustee, determines to be necessary or advisable for my health, maintenance and support.

Use of Residential Property. If any real property used by me for residential purposes (whether on a full-time or part-time basis, including recreational property) becomes part of the trust estate, I shall have the right to use and occupy such property without rental or other accounting to the trust estate.

Distributions to My Spouse and Children. The Trustee shall pay to or expend for the benefit of my spouse and minor Children so much of the principal of the trust as the Trustee, in his/her sole discretion, determines to be necessary for the education, health, maintenance and support of my spouse and Children. The Trustee shall make such discretionary distributions only after conferring with me. The trust distributions do not need to be equal.

ARTICLE IV

ADMINISTRATION OF TRUST UPON MY DEATH

Payment of Expenses, Claims and Taxes. Upon my death, the Trustee shall, upon the request of the Executor of my estate, pay such part or all of the expenses of the last illness, funeral, and burial, legally enforceable claims against me or my estate and estate administration expenses. The Trustee may also pay any estate, inheritance, or succession taxes, state, federal and foreign, or any other taxes together with interest and penalties thereon that are payable by reason of my death.

ARTICLE V

DISTRIBUTION OF TRUST TO MY SPOUSE AND CHILDREN

Tangible Personal Property. The Trustee shall distribute my tangible personal property in accordance with any written, signed and dated memorandum prepared by me. Any tangible personal property which is not disposed of by memorandum shall be distributed to my spouse or if my spouse is not alive in equal shares to my surviving Children.

Specific Bequest. The Trustee shall distribute the following property to the named individuals:

$10,000.00   to   my brother, Peter Smith

$10,000.00   to   Humane Society

If any of the individuals named does not survive me, the gift to that person will lapse and the property will pass as provided below.

Distribution to My Spouse. If my spouse survives me, the Trustee shall distribute the remaining trust estate to my spouse outright or, if my spouse so chooses, to the Living Trust dated _July 4_, _2001_, established by my spouse. If my spouse does not survive me, the Trustee shall distribute the trust estate as provided in the next paragraph.

Distribution to My Children. The Trustee shall divide the remaining trust estate, including any additions to the Trust by reason of my death, into separate equal shares as follows: one share for each Child of mine who is then living, and one share for the then living descendants, collectively, of each deceased Child of mine with one or more descendants then living. The Trustee shall distribute the share for each Child to such Child outright. The share for the descendants of each deceased Child, shall be distributed, per stirpes, to those descendants living at my death.

Contingent Distribution. If my spouse, my Children and their descendants and all of my descendants are deceased, the trust estate then remaining shall be distributed, to the following individuals in the amounts specified:

| 50% | to my brother, Peter Smith |
| 50% | to my wife's sister, Sally Jones |

ARTICLE VI

THE TRUSTEE

Successor Trustees. During my lifetime, if I cannot serve as Trustee, I will appoint a successor Trustee. If I do not appoint a successor trustee, or after my death, the successor trustee shall be my spouse, or if my spouse is not able to serve, the successor trustee(s) shall be John Smith, Jr. . If the successor trustee fails or ceases to serve, Peter Smith shall be successor trustee. If all successor trustees fail or cease to serve, a majority in number of the income beneficiaries of the trust at that time shall appoint a successor trustee. Any appointment under this section shall be by a signed, acknowledged instrument delivered to the successor trustee.

Removal of Trustee. During my life, I may remove a trustee at any time for any reason. After my death or if I am incapacitated and unable to remove the trustee, my spouse may remove the trustee. If my spouse is not alive or is unable to exercise this power, John Smith, Jr. shall have the power to remove a trustee.

Resignation of Trustee. A Trustee may resign as to any one or more of the trusts created hereunder by giving written notice to all co-trustees then serving, if any, the current income beneficiaries, the successor trustee if identified in this Trust Agreement, and to those persons, if any, authorized in this Trust Agreement to appoint the successor trustee. Notice shall be delivered at least thirty (30) days prior to the date of resignation.

Trustee's Fees. The Trustee shall be entitled to reasonable fees commensurate with the Trustee's duties and responsibilities, taking into account the value and nature of the trust estate and the time and work involved. The Trustee shall be reimbursed for reasonable costs and expenses incurred in connection with fiduciary duties.

Bond. The Trustee shall not be required to furnish bond or other security.

Liability of Trustee. A Trustee shall only be liable for willful misconduct or gross negligence, and shall not be liable for breach of fiduciary duty by virtue of mistake or error in judgment.

Incapacity of Individual Trustee. This Section shall apply in the event a Trustee becomes unable to discharge the duties of Trustee by reason of accident, physical or mental illness or deterioration, or other cause, and does not resign. Upon certification by two medical doctors that each has examined the Trustee and has concluded that the Trustee is unable to discharge such duties, the Trustee shall cease to serve, as if the Trustee had resigned, effective the date of the certification.

ARTICLE VII

TRUST ADMINISTRATION

Trustee Powers: Investment and Management of Trust Estate. Subject to any limitation stated elsewhere in this instrument, the Trustee shall have, with respect to each trust established hereunder, all of the powers granted to trustees by common law and by applicable statutes as amended from time to time. In addition, the trustee shall have the following powers:

(a) **Retain Property.** To retain any property received from any source, regardless of lack of diversification, risk, or nonproductivity.

(b) **Invest.** To invest the trust estate in any kind of property, without being limited by any law dealing with the character, risk, productivity, diversification, wasting nature of, or otherwise concerning, investments by trustees.

(c) **Sell.** By public offering or private negotiation, to sell, exchange, assign, transfer, or otherwise dispose of all or any real or personal trust property and give options for these purposes, for such price and on such terms, with such covenants of warranty and such security for deferred payment as the Trustee deems proper. To partition between the trust and any other owner, as the Trustee deems proper, any property in which the trust owns an undivided interest.

(d) **Lease.** To lease trust property for terms within or extending beyond the term of the trust, for any purpose.

(e) **Real Estate.** To operate, maintain, repair, rehabilitate, alter, erect, improve, or remove any improvements on real estate; to subdivide real estate; to grant easements, give consents, and enter into contracts relating to real estate or its use; and to release or dedicate any interest in real estate.

(f) **Borrow.** To borrow money for any purpose; to encumber or hypothecate trust property by mortgage, deed of trust, or otherwise; and to maintain, prepay, renew, or extend any indebtedness upon such terms as the Trustee deems appropriate.

(g) **Loans.** To lend money to any person or entity, including, but not limited to, a beneficiary hereunder, upon such terms and with such security as the Trustee deems advisable.

(h) **Securities.** To engage in all actions necessary to the effective administration of securities including, but not limited to, the authority to: vote securities in person or by proxy; engage in a voting trust or voting agreement; exercise any options, rights, or privileges pertaining to any trust property; and consent to or participate in mergers, consolidations, sales of assets, recapitalizations, reorganizations, dissolutions, or other alterations of corporate structure affecting securities held by the Trustee.

(i) **Business Powers.** To enter into, carry on, and expand or acquire additional interests in (through the investment or loan of trust funds) any business activity, in sole proprietorship, general or limited partnership, joint venture, corporate or other form (and to convert from one form to another), including, but not limited to, any business interest which may be contributed to the trust, to employ agents and confer upon them the authority to manage and operate such business activity without liability for the acts of any such agents or for any loss, liability or indebtedness of such business, if the agents are selected and retained with reasonable care; and to sell, liquidate, or otherwise terminate any business interest, including, but not limited to, the fulfillment of any agreement for the disposition of any such business interest.

(j) **Litigation.** To commence or defend at the expense of the trust such litigation with respect to the trust estate as the Trustee deems advisable.

(k) **Claims.** To collect, pay, contest, compromise, settle, renew, or abandon any claims or demands of or against the trust estate, on whatever terms the Trustee deems advisable.

(l) **Additional Property.** To receive from any source additional property which is acceptable to the Trustee, and add it to the trust estate.

(m) **Agents.** To employ attorneys, auditors, brokers, investment advisors, depositaries, and agents with or without discretionary powers, to employ a trust company or bank with trust powers as agent for the purpose of performing any delegable duties of the administration, and to pay all expenses and fees so incurred.

(n) **Nominee.** To hold securities and other property in bearer form or in the name of a Trustee or nominee with or without disclosure of any fiduciary relationship.

(o) **Miscellaneous Powers.** Generally, to do and perform any and all acts, things, or deeds which an individual could do with respect to property and which, in the judgment of the Trustee, may be necessary or proper for the investment, management, protection and promotion of the property of the trust estate.

(p) **Tax Elections.** Unless otherwise expressly directed hereunder, to exercise any tax option, allocation or election permitted by law as the Trustee determines in the Trustee's sole discretion.

(q) **Division and Distribution.** To make all allocations, distributions, or divisions contemplated by this instrument; to allocate, distribute and divide different kinds or disproportionate shares of property or undivided interests in property among the beneficiaries or trusts, in cash or in kind, or both, without regard to the income tax basis of specific property allocated to any beneficiary or trust, even though shares may as a result be composed differently, and to determine the value of any property so allocated, divided or distributed.

(r) **Reliance.** To rely upon any notice, certificate, affidavit, or other document or evidence believed by the Trustee to be genuine and accurate, in making any payment or distribution. The Trustee shall incur no liability for a disbursement or distribution made in good faith and without actual notice or knowledge of a changed condition or status affecting any person's interest in the trust or any other matter.

Court Supervision. The Trustee shall not be required to qualify before or be appointed by any court; nor shall the Trustee be required to obtain the order or approval of any court in the exercise of any power or discretion.

Periodic Accounting. The Trustee shall make reports at least annually to those beneficiaries who may receive current distributions, such reports to reflect the property held in trust, the receipts, disbursements, and distributions made during the accounting period, and such other information as may be necessary to convey the condition of and changes to the trust estate.

Beneficiary Under Disability. Where a beneficiary is under the disability of minority or, in the Trustee's opinion, any other legal, physical or mental disability, a parent, custodian or guardian who, entirely in the Trustee's discretion, is acceptable to the Trustee may, in carrying out the provisions of this Trust Agreement, act and receive notice in the beneficiary's place, and sign any instrument for the beneficiary.

Spendthrift Trusts. All trusts created under this Trust Agreement are spendthrift trusts. No beneficiary may anticipate, by assignment or otherwise, a beneficial interest in the principal or income of the trusts created hereunder; nor may any beneficiary sell, transfer, encumber, or in any way charge an interest in trust income or principal prior to actually receiving it. Neither the income nor the principal of any trust established hereunder shall be subject to any execution, garnishment, attachment, bankruptcy, claims for alimony or support, other legal proceeding of any character, legal sequestration, levy or sale, or in any other event or manner be applicable or subject, voluntarily or involuntarily, to the payment of a beneficiary's debts. The Trustee shall make distributions to or for each beneficiary according to the terms hereof, notwithstanding any purported sale, assignment, hypothecation, transfer, attachment, or judicial process.

Limitation on Distributions.

(a) **Support Obligation.** Any other provision of this Trust Agreement notwithstanding, no distribution shall be made which discharges, in whole or in part, the Trustee's legal obligations, from time to time existing, to support, educate or otherwise provide for any of the trust beneficiaries. When determining these legal obligations, the existence of the trust estate and funds made available by it shall not be taken into consideration.

(b) **Distribution to Trustee/Beneficiary.** Notwithstanding anything to the contrary in this Trust Agreement, no Trustee shall have the authority to make discretionary distributions to that person as beneficiary, except to the extent the distributions are for the beneficiary's health, maintenance, support or education. If the Trustee is otherwise in this Trust Agreement authorized to make a distribution beyond that standard, the distributions shall be so limited.

Rule Against Perpetuities. Every trust created hereunder (or through the exercise of a power of appointment granted in this Trust Agreement) must vest not later than twenty-one (21) years after my death and descendants living at the time the trust created hereunder first becomes irrevocable. If a trust is not vested within that period, it will terminate as of the maximum vesting date. In the event of termination, the Trustee shall distribute each trust to its income beneficiaries determined at the time of distribution in the proportions to which they are entitled to receive income.

Out-of-State Properties. If the Trustee must act in a jurisdiction in which a person or entity serving as Trustee is unable or unwilling to act, the other or others serving as Trustee may act in that jurisdiction. If no Trustee is able or willing to act, the Trustee may appoint an ancillary trustee for that jurisdiction and may confer upon the ancillary trustee such rights, powers, discretions and duties, exercisable without court order, to act with respect to such matters as the Trustee deems proper. The ancillary trustee shall be responsible to the Trustee for any property it administers. The Trustee may pay the ancillary trustee reasonable compensation for services and may absolve the ancillary trustee from any requirement to furnish bond or other security.

ARTICLE VIII

AMENDMENT AND REVOCATION OF TRUST

I may amend, revoke or modify this Trust Agreement in whole or in part by an instrument signed and acknowledged by me and delivered to the Trustee. Amendment or modification of the Trust Agreement shall be effective immediately upon delivery of the instrument to the Trustee, except that changes affecting the Trustee's duties, liabilities, or compensation shall not be effective without the Trustee's written consent. On my death, this Trust Agreement may no longer be amended or modified, and the trust created hereunder shall become irrevocable.

ARTICLE IX

MISCELLANEOUS PROVISIONS

Applicable Law. The validity, construction, and administration of each trust created hereunder shall be governed by the laws of the State of __Texas_____.

Adoption. For purposes of this Trust Agreement, a person shall be regarded as having been legally adopted by another only if the adoption is by court proceedings, the finality of which is not being contested by the adopting person.

Survival. Any person must survive by thirty (30) days for a gift made in this Trust Agreement which directly or indirectly requires such person's survival of another to be effective.

Education. "Education" shall include preparatory, collegiate, postgraduate, professional and vocational education; specialized formal or informal training in music, the stage, handicrafts, the arts or sports or athletic endeavors, whether by private instruction or otherwise; and any other activity, including foreign or domestic travel, which tends to develop the talents and potential of the beneficiary, regardless of age. Education shall also include all tuition, board, lodging fees, books and equipment, travel expenses and other expenses incidental thereto.

Executor. "Executor" shall include personal representative, executrix, administrator and administratrix.

Health. "Health" shall include medical, dental, hospital and nursing care expenses, and other expenses of invalidism, and distributions for the "health" of a beneficiary may, in the discretion of the Trustee include any part or all of the costs of purchasing or maintaining hospital or medical insurance and disability income insurance coverage for such beneficiary and/or any person in whom such beneficiary has an insurable interest.

Binding Agreement. This agreement shall extend to and be binding upon the heirs, executors, administrators, successors and assigns of the parties.

Use of Words. As used in this instrument, the masculine, feminine, and neuter gender, and the singular or plural of any word includes the others unless the context indicates otherwise.

Unenforceable Provision. If any provision of this Trust Agreement is unenforceable, the remaining provisions shall be given effect, unless to do so would produce an unreasonable result.

Titles, Headings, and Captions. All titles, headings, and captions used in this Trust Agreement have been included for convenience only and should not be construed in interpreting this instrument.

IN WITNESS WHEREOF, I as Grantor and Trustee have hereunto set my hand, on the day and year first above written in multiple originals.

Wanda Watcher	_John Smith_
Witness	Grantor
Ned Neighbor	_John Smith_
Witness	Trustee

STATE OF _Texas_ §

§

COUNTY OF _Dallas_ §

BEFORE ME, the undersigned authority, on this day personally appeared _John Smith_ , Grantor and Trustee, known to me to be the person whose name is subscribed to the foregoing instrument and acknowledged to me that he/she executed the same for the purposes and consideration therein expressed.

GIVEN UNDER MY HAND AND SEAL OF OFFICE this _4th_ day of _March_ , _2002_ .

C.U. Sine

Notary Public

My Commission Expires:

This page intentionally left blank.

<u>   John Smith   </u> **LIVING TRUST**

THIS AGREEMENT OF TRUST is entered into at <u>Dallas   </u>, State of <u>Texas   </u>, this <u>4th</u> day of <u>March   </u>, <u>2002   </u>, by and between <u>   </u>, as Grantor and Trustee. This Trust, as from time to time amended, shall be known as the "<u>   John Smith   </u>" LIVING TRUST dated <u> March 4   </u>, <u>2002 </u>."

ARTICLE I

My Spouse. My Spouse is: <u>Jane Smith   </u>.

My Children. My Children are: <u>Joseph Smith, Jennifer Smith, and   </u>

<u>John Smith, Jr.   </u>.

ARTICLE II

FUNDING

Initial Funding. I hereby transfer to Trustee the sum of Ten Dollars ($10.00).

Additional Funding. From time to time the trust may be funded with additional property by me or by any other person in any manner. All property transferred, assigned, conveyed or delivered to the Trustee shall be held, administered and distributed by the Trustee in accordance with the terms of this Trust Agreement.

ARTICLE III

ADMINISTRATION OF TRUST DURING MY LIFETIME

Distributions of Income. While I am living, the Trustee shall distribute the trust's net income as directed in writing by me from time to time. In default of such direction, the Trustee shall pay to or expend on behalf of me all of the trust's net income from the Trust quarterly or more frequently.

Distributions of Principal. The Trustee shall pay to or expend for my benefit such part or all of the principal of the trust as I may request, from time to time. In default of such direction, the Trustee shall pay to or expend for my benefit so much of the principal of the trust as the Trustee, determines to be necessary or advisable for my health, maintenance and support.

Use of Residential Property. If any real property used by me for residential purposes (whether on a full-time or part-time basis, including recreational property) becomes part of the trust estate, I shall have the right to use and occupy such property without rental or other accounting to the trust estate.

Distributions to My Spouse and Children. The Trustee shall pay to or expend for the benefit of my spouse and minor Children so much of the principal of the trust as the Trustee, in his/her sole discretion, determines to be necessary for the education, health, maintenance and support of my spouse and Children. The Trustee shall make such discretionary distributions only after conferring with me. The trust distributions do not need to be equal.

ARTICLE IV

ADMINISTRATION OF TRUST UPON MY DEATH

Payment of Expenses, Claims and Taxes. Upon my death, the Trustee shall, upon the request of the Executor of my estate, pay such part or all of the expenses of the last illness, funeral, and burial, legally enforceable claims against me or my estate and estate administration expenses. The Trustee may also pay any estate, inheritance, or succession taxes, state, federal and foreign, or any other taxes together with interest and penalties thereon that are payable by reason of my death.

ARTICLE V

DISTRIBUTIONS OF TRUST TO MY SPOUSE AND CHILDREN

Tangible Personal Property. The Trustee shall distribute my tangible personal property in accordance with any written, signed and dated memorandum prepared by me. Any tangible personal property which is not disposed of by memorandum shall be distributed to my spouse or if my spouse is not alive in equal shares to my surviving Children.

Specific Bequest. The Trustee shall distribute the following property to the named individuals:

$10,000.00	to	Peter Smith
$10,000.00	to	Sally Jones

If any of the individuals named does not survive me, the gift to that person will lapse and the property will pass as provided below.

Distribution to My Spouse. If my spouse survives me, the Trustee shall distribute the remaining trust estate to my spouse outright or, if my spouse so chooses, to the Living Trust dated ___March 4___, ___2002___, established by my spouse. If my spouse does not survive me, the Trustee shall distribute the trust estate as provided in the next paragraph.

Division of Trust Estate for My Children. The Trustee shall divide the remaining trust estate, including any additions to the Trust by reason of my death, into separate equal shares as follows: one share for each Child of mine who is then living, and one share for the then living descendants, collectively, of each deceased Child of mine with one or more descendants then living. The Trustee shall administer a share for each Child in a separate trust, and a share for the Descendants of each deceased Child, pursuant to the provisions of Article VI, following.

ARTICLE VI

TRUSTS FOR CHILDREN AND DESCENDANTS

Separate Trust for Child. Each trust for the benefit of a Child shall be administered and distributed upon the following terms:

(a) **Distributions to Child.** The Trustee shall distribute to the Child all of the trust's net income quarterly or more frequently and so much of the principal of the trust as the Trustee deems necessary to provide for the Child's health, maintenance, education and support.

When the Child attains age ___25___, the Trustee shall distribute to the Child ___50%___ of the value of the then remaining trust estate.

When the Child attains age ___30___, the Trustee shall distribute to the Child the remaining trust estate.

(b) **Termination of Trust.** If not earlier terminated by distribution of the entire trust estate under the foregoing provisions, the trust shall terminate upon the death of the Child. The Trustee shall distribute the remaining trust estate to the Child's then living descendants, pursuant to the limitation described in subsection (c) hereof. If there are no descendants of the Child then living, the Trustee shall distribute the remaining trust estate to my then living descendants, per stirpes.

(c) **Distribution to Descendants of a Deceased Child.** Property which is to be distributed under this subsection to the descendants of a deceased Child shall be distributed, per stirpes, to those descendants living at the event causing the distribution hereunder.

Contingent Distribution. If my spouse, my Children and their descendants and all of my descendants are deceased, the trust estate then remaining shall be distributed, to the following individuals in the amounts specified:

___50%___	to _my brother, Peter Smith_
___50%___	to _my wife's sister, Sally Jones_

ARTICLE VII

THE TRUSTEE

Successor Trustees. During my lifetime, if I cannot serve as Trustee, I will appoint a successor Trustee. If I do not appoint a successor trustee, or after my death, the successor trustee shall be my spouse, or if I am not married or my spouse is not able to serve, the successor trustee(s) shall be: John Smith, Jr. . If the successor trustee fails or ceases to serve, Peter Smith shall be successor trustee. If all successor trustees fail or cease to serve, a majority in number of the income beneficiaries of the trust at that time shall appoint a successor trustee.

Any appointment under this Section shall be by a signed, acknowledged instrument delivered to the successor trustee.

Removal of Trustee. During my life, I may remove a trustee at any time for any reason. After my death or if I am incapacitated and unable to remove the trustee, my spouse may remove the trustee. If my spouse is not alive or is unable to exercise this power, John Smith, Jr. shall have the power to remove a trustee.

Resignation of Trustee. A Trustee may resign as to any one or more of the trusts created hereunder by giving written notice to all co-trustees then serving, if any, the current income beneficiaries, the successor trustee if identified in this Trust Agreement, and to those persons, if any, authorized in this Trust Agreement to appoint the successor trustee. Notice shall be delivered at least thirty (30) days prior to the date of resignation.

Trustee's Fees. The Trustee shall be entitled to reasonable fees commensurate with the Trustee's duties and responsibilities, taking into account the value and nature of the trust estate and the time and work involved. The Trustee shall be reimbursed for reasonable costs and expenses incurred in connection with fiduciary duties.

Bond. The Trustee shall not be required to furnish bond or other security.

Liability of Trustee. A Trustee shall only be liable for willful misconduct or gross negligence, and shall not be liable for breach of fiduciary duty by virtue of mistake or error in judgment.

Incapacity of Individual Trustee. This Section shall apply in the event a Trustee becomes unable to discharge the duties of Trustee by reason of accident, physical or mental illness or deterioration, or other cause, and does not resign. Upon certification by two medical doctors that each has examined the Trustee and has concluded that the Trustee is unable to discharge such duties, the Trustee shall cease to serve, as if the Trustee had resigned, effective the date of the certification.

ARTICLE VIII

TRUST ADMINISTRATION

Trustee Powers: Investment and Management of Trust Estate. Subject to any limitation stated elsewhere in this instrument, the Trustee shall have, with respect to each trust established hereunder, all of the powers granted to trustees by common law and by applicable statutes as amended from time to time. In addition, the trustee shall have the following powers:

(a) **Retain Property.** To retain any property received from any source, regardless of lack of diversification, risk, or nonproductivity.

(b) **Invest.** To invest the trust estate in any kind of property, without being limited by any law dealing with the character, risk, productivity, diversification, wasting nature of, or otherwise concerning, investments by trustees.

(c) **Sell.** By public offering or private negotiation, to sell, exchange, assign, transfer, or otherwise dispose of all or any real or personal trust property and give options for these purposes, for such price and on such terms, with such covenants of warranty and such security for deferred payment as the Trustee deems proper. To partition between the trust and any other owner, as the Trustee deems proper, any property in which the trust owns an undivided interest.

(d) **Lease.** To lease trust property for terms within or extending beyond the term of the trust, for any purpose.

(e) **Real Estate.** To operate, maintain, repair, rehabilitate, alter, erect, improve, or remove any improvements on real estate; to subdivide real estate; to grant easements, give consents, and enter into contracts relating to real estate or its use; and to release or dedicate any interest in real estate.

(f) **Borrow.** To borrow money for any purpose; to encumber or hypothecate trust property by mortgage, deed of trust, or otherwise; and to maintain, prepay, renew, or extend any indebtedness upon such terms as the Trustee deems appropriate.

(g) **Loans.** To lend money to any person or entity, including, but not limited to, a beneficiary hereunder, upon such terms and with such security as the Trustee deems advisable.

(h) **Securities.** To engage in all actions necessary to the effective administration of securities including, but not limited to, the authority to: vote securities in person or by proxy; engage in a voting trust or voting agreement; exercise any options, rights, or privileges pertaining to any trust property; and consent to or participate in mergers,

consolidations, sales of assets, recapitalizations, reorganizations, dissolutions, or other alterations of corporate structure affecting securities held by the Trustee.

(i) **Business Powers.** To enter into, carry on, and expand or acquire additional interests in (through the investment or loan of trust funds) any business activity, in sole proprietorship, general or limited partnership, joint venture, corporate or other form (and to convert from one form to another), including, but not limited to, any business interest which may be contributed to the trust, to employ agents and confer upon them the authority to manage and operate such business activity without liability for the acts of any such agents or for any loss, liability or indebtedness of such business, if the agents are selected and retained with reasonable care; and to sell, liquidate, or otherwise terminate any business interest, including, but not limited to, the fulfillment of any agreement for the disposition of any such business interest.

(j) **Litigation.** To commence or defend at the expense of the trust such litigation with respect to the trust estate as the Trustee deems advisable.

(k) **Claims.** To collect, pay, contest, compromise, settle, renew, or abandon any claims or demands of or against the trust estate, on whatever terms the Trustee deems advisable.

(l) **Additional Property.** To receive from any source additional property which is acceptable to the Trustee, and add it to the trust estate.

(m) **Agents.** To employ attorneys, auditors, brokers, investment advisors, depositaries, and agents with or without discretionary powers, to employ a trust company or bank with trust powers as agent for the purpose of performing any delegable duties of the administration, and to pay all expenses and fees so incurred.

(n) **Nominee.** To hold securities and other property in bearer form or in the name of a Trustee or nominee with or without disclosure of any fiduciary relationship.

(o) **Miscellaneous Powers.** Generally, to do and perform any and all acts, things, or deeds which an individual could do with respect to property and which, in the judgment of the Trustee, may be necessary or proper for the investment, management, protection and promotion of the property of the trust estate.

(p) **Tax Elections.** Unless otherwise expressly directed hereunder, to exercise any tax option, allocation or election permitted by law as the Trustee determines in the Trustee's sole discretion.

(q) **Division and Distribution.** To make all allocations, distributions, or divisions contemplated by this instrument; to allocate, distribute and divide different kinds or disproportionate shares of property or undivided interests in property among the beneficiaries or trusts, in cash or in kind, or both, without regard to the income tax basis of specific property allocated to any beneficiary or trust, even though shares may as a result be composed differently, and to determine the value of any property so allocated, divided or distributed.

(r) **Reliance.** To rely upon any notice, certificate, affidavit, or other document or evidence believed by the Trustee to be genuine and accurate, in making any payment or distribution. The Trustee shall incur no liability for a disbursement or distribution made in good faith and without actual notice or knowledge of a changed condition or status affecting any person's interest in the trust or any other matter.

Court Supervision. The Trustee shall not be required to qualify before or be appointed by any court; nor shall the Trustee be required to obtain the order or approval of any court in the exercise of any power or discretion.

Periodic Accounting. The Trustee shall make reports at least annually to those beneficiaries who may receive current distributions, such reports to reflect the property held in trust, the receipts, disbursements, and distributions made during the accounting period, and such other information as may be necessary to convey the condition of and changes to the trust estate.

Beneficiary Under Disability. Where a beneficiary is under the disability of minority or, in the Trustee's opinion, any other legal, physical or mental disability, a parent, custodian or guardian who, entirely in the Trustee's discretion, is acceptable to the Trustee may, in carrying out the provisions of this Trust Agreement, act and receive notice in the beneficiary's place, and sign any instrument for the beneficiary.

Spendthrift Trusts. All trusts created under this Trust Agreement are spendthrift trusts. No beneficiary may anticipate, by assignment or otherwise, a beneficial interest in the principal or income of the trusts created hereunder; nor may any beneficiary sell, transfer, encumber, or in any way charge an interest in trust income or principal prior to actually receiving it. Neither the income nor the principal of any trust established hereunder shall be subject to any execution, garnishment, attachment, bankruptcy, claims for alimony or support, other legal proceeding of any character, legal sequestration, levy or sale, or in any other event or manner be applicable or subject, voluntarily or involuntarily, to the payment of a beneficiary's debts. The Trustee shall make distributions to or for each beneficiary according to the terms hereof, notwithstanding any purported sale, assignment, hypothecation, transfer, attachment, or judicial process.

Limitation on Distributions.

(a) **Support Obligation.** Any other provision of this Trust Agreement notwithstanding, no distribution shall be made which discharges, in whole or in part, the Trustee's legal obligations, from time to time existing, to support, educate or otherwise provide for any of the trust beneficiaries. When determining these legal obligations, the existence of the trust estate and funds made available by it shall not be taken into consideration.

(b) **Distribution to Trustee/Beneficiary.** Notwithstanding anything to the contrary in this Trust Agreement, no Trustee shall have the authority to make discretionary distributions to that person as beneficiary, except to the extent the distributions are for the beneficiary's health, maintenance, support or education. If the Trustee is otherwise in this Trust Agreement authorized to make a distribution beyond that standard, the distributions shall be so limited.

Rule Against Perpetuities. Every trust created hereunder (or through the exercise of a power of appointment granted in this Trust Agreement) must vest not later than twenty-one (21) years after my death and descendants living at the time the trust created hereunder first becomes irrevocable. If a trust is not vested within that period, it will terminate as of the maximum vesting date. In the event of termination, the Trustee shall distribute each trust to its income beneficiaries determined at the time of distribution in the proportions to which they are entitled to receive income.

Out-of-State Properties. If the Trustee must act in a jurisdiction in which a person or entity serving as Trustee is unable or unwilling to act, the other or others serving as Trustee may act in that jurisdiction. If no Trustee is able or willing to act, the Trustee may appoint an ancillary trustee for that jurisdiction and may confer upon the ancillary trustee such rights, powers, discretions and duties, exercisable without court order, to act with respect to such matters as the Trustee deems proper. The ancillary trustee shall be responsible to the Trustee for any property it administers. The Trustee may pay the ancillary trustee reasonable compensation for services and may absolve the ancillary trustee from any requirement to furnish bond or other security.

ARTICLE IX

AMENDMENT AND REVOCATION OF TRUST

I may amend, revoke or modify this Trust Agreement in whole or in part by an instrument signed and acknowledged by me and delivered to the Trustee. Amendment or modification of the Trust Agreement shall be effective immediately upon delivery of the instrument to the Trustee, except that changes affecting the Trustee's duties, liabilities, or compensation shall not be effective without the Trustee's written consent. On my death, this Trust Agreement may no longer be amended or modified, and the trust created hereunder shall become irrevocable.

ARTICLE X

MISCELLANEOUS PROVISIONS

Applicable Law. The validity, construction, and administration of each trust created hereunder shall be governed by the laws of the State of ___Texas___.

Adoption. For purposes of this Trust Agreement, a person shall be regarded as having been legally adopted by another only if the adoption is by court proceedings, the finality of which is not being contested by the adopting person.

Survival. Any person must survive by thirty (30) days for a gift made in this Trust Agreement which directly or indirectly requires such person's survival of another to be effective.

Education. "Education" shall include preparatory, collegiate, postgraduate, professional and vocational education; specialized formal or informal training in music, the stage, handicrafts, the arts or sports or athletic endeavors, whether by private instruction or otherwise; and any other activity, including foreign or domestic travel, which tends to develop the talents and potential of the beneficiary, regardless of age. Education shall also include all tuition, board, lodging fees, books and equipment, travel expenses and other expenses incidental thereto.

Executor. "Executor" shall include personal representative, executrix, administrator and administratrix.

Health. "Health" shall include medical, dental, hospital and nursing care expenses, and other expenses of invalidism, and distributions for the "health" of a beneficiary may, in the discretion of the Trustee include any part or all of the costs of purchasing or maintaining hospital or medical insurance and disability income insurance coverage for such beneficiary and/or any person in whom such beneficiary has an insurable interest.

Binding Agreement. This agreement shall extend to and be binding upon the heirs, executors, administrators, successors and assigns of the parties.

Use of Words. As used in this instrument, the masculine, feminine, and neuter gender, and the singular or plural of any word includes the others unless the context indicates otherwise.

Unenforceable Provision. If any provision of this Trust Agreement is unenforceable, the remaining provisions shall be given effect, unless to do so would produce an unreasonable result.

Titles, Headings, and Captions. All titles, headings, and captions used in this Trust Agreement have been included for convenience only and should not be construed in interpreting this instrument.

IN WITNESS WHEREOF, I as Grantor and Trustee have hereunto set my hand, on the day and year first above written in multiple originals.

Sigmund Signature
Witness

John Smith
Grantor

Victor Verify
Witness

John Smith
Trustee

STATE OF ___Texas___ §

§

COUNTY OF ___Dallas___ §

BEFORE ME, the undersigned authority, on this day personally appeared ___John Smith___, Grantor and Trustee, known to me to be the person whose name is subscribed to the foregoing instrument and acknowledged to me that he/she executed the same for the purposes and consideration therein expressed.

GIVEN UNDER MY HAND AND SEAL OF OFFICE this 4th day of ___March___, ___2002___.

C.U. Sine
Notary Public
My Commission Expires:

_____ John Smith _____ **LIVING TRUST**

THIS AGREEMENT OF TRUST is entered into at _Dallas_____, State of _Texas_____, this _4th_ day of _March_____, _2002___, by and between _____, as Grantor and Trustee. This Trust, as from time to time amended, shall be known as the "_John Smith_____ LIVING TRUST dated _March 4_____, _2002___."

ARTICLE I

My Children. My Children are: Joseph Smith, Jennifer Smith, and

John Smith, Jr. .

ARTICLE II

FUNDING

Initial Funding. I hereby transfer to Trustee the sum of Ten Dollars ($10.00).

Additional Funding. From time to time the trust may be funded with additional property by me or by any other person in any manner. All property transferred, assigned, conveyed or delivered to the Trustee shall be held, administered and distributed by the Trustee in accordance with the terms of this Trust Agreement.

ARTICLE III

ADMINISTRATION OF TRUST DURING MY LIFETIME

Distributions of Income. While I am living, the Trustee shall distribute the trust's net income as directed in writing by me from time to time. In default of such direction, the Trustee shall pay to or expend on behalf of me all of the trust's net income from the Trust quarterly or more frequently.

Distributions of Principal. The Trustee shall pay to or expend for my benefit such part or all of the principal of the trust as I may request, from time to time. In default of such direction, the Trustee shall pay to or expend for my benefit so much of the principal of the trust as the Trustee, determines to be necessary or advisable for my health, maintenance and support.

Use of Residential Property. If any real property used by me for residential purposes (whether on a full-time or part-time basis, including recreational property) becomes part of the trust estate, I shall have the right to use and occupy such property without rental or other accounting to the trust estate.

Distributions to My Children. The Trustee shall pay to or expend for the benefit of my minor children so much of the principal of the trust as the Trustee, in his/her sole discretion, determines to be necessary for the education, health, maintenance and support of my children. The Trustee shall make such discretionary distributions only after conferring with me. The trust distributions do not need to be equal.

ARTICLE IV

ADMINISTRATION OF TRUST UPON MY DEATH

Payment of Expenses, Claims and Taxes. Upon my death, the Trustee shall, upon the request of the Executor of my estate, pay such part or all of the expenses of the last illness, funeral, and burial, legally enforceable claims against me or my estate and estate administration expenses. The Trustee may also pay any estate, inheritance, or succession taxes, state, federal and foreign, or any other taxes together with interest and penalties thereon that are payable by reason of my death.

ARTICLE V

DISTRIBUTION OF TRUST TO MY CHILDREN

Tangible Personal Property. The Trustee shall distribute my tangible personal property in accordance with any written, signed and dated memorandum prepared by me. Any tangible personal property which is not disposed of by memorandum shall be distributed in equal shares to my surviving Children.

Specific Bequest. The Trustee shall distribute the following property to the named individuals:

$10,000.00	to	Peter Smith
$10,000.00	to	Sally Jones

If any of the individuals named does not survive me, the gift to that person will lapse and the property will pass as provided below.

Distribution to My Children. The Trustee shall divide the remaining trust estate, including any additions to the Trust by reason of my death, into separate equal shares as follows: one share for each Child of mine who is then living, and one share for the then living descendants, collectively, of each deceased Child of mine with one or more descendants then living. The Trustee shall distribute the share for each Child to such Child outright. The share for the descendants of each deceased Child, shall be distributed, per stirpes, to those descendants living at the my death.

Contingent Distribution. If my Children and their descendants and all of my descendants are deceased, the trust estate then remaining shall be distributed, to the following individuals in the amounts specified:

50%	to	Peter Smith
50%	to	Sally Jones

ARTICLE VI

THE TRUSTEE

Successor Trustees. During my lifetime, if I cannot serve as Trustee, I will appoint a successor Trustee. If I do not appoint a successor trustee, or after my death, the successor trustee shall be John Smith, Jr. . If John Smith, Jr. is not able to serve, the successor trustee(s) shall be Peter Smith . If the successor trustee fails or ceases to serve, Joseph Smith shall be successor trustee. If all successor trustees fail or cease to serve, a majority in number of the income beneficiaries of the trust at that time shall appoint a successor trustee. Any appointment under this section shall be by a signed, acknowledged instrument delivered to the successor trustee.

Removal of Trustee. During my life, I may remove a trustee at any time for any reason. After my death or if I am incapacitated and unable to remove the trustee, John Smith, Jr. may remove the trustee. If John Smith, Jr. is not alive or is unable to exercise this power, Peter Smith shall have the power to remove a trustee.

Resignation of Trustee. A Trustee may resign as to any one or more of the trusts created hereunder by giving written notice to all co-trustees then serving, if any, the current income beneficiaries, the successor trustee if identified in this Trust Agreement, and to those persons, if any, authorized in this Trust Agreement to appoint the successor trustee. Notice shall be delivered at least thirty (30) days prior to the date of resignation.

Trustee's Fees. The Trustee shall be entitled to reasonable fees commensurate with the Trustee's duties and responsibilities, taking into account the value and nature of the trust estate and the time and work involved. The Trustee shall be reimbursed for reasonable costs and expenses incurred in connection with fiduciary duties.

Bond. The Trustee shall not be required to furnish bond or other security.

Liability of Trustee. A Trustee shall only be liable for willful misconduct or gross negligence, and shall not be liable for breach of fiduciary duty by virtue of mistake or error in judgment.

Incapacity of Individual Trustee. This Section shall apply in the event a Trustee becomes unable to discharge the duties of Trustee by reason of accident, physical or mental illness or deterioration, or other cause, and does not resign. Upon certification by two medical doctors that each has examined the Trustee and has concluded that the Trustee is unable to discharge such duties, the Trustee shall cease to serve, as if the Trustee had resigned, effective the date of the certification.

ARTICLE VII

TRUST ADMINISTRATION

Trustee Powers: Investment and Management of Trust Estate. Subject to any limitation stated elsewhere in this instrument, the Trustee shall have, with respect to each trust established hereunder, all of the powers granted to trustees by common law and by applicable statutes as amended from time to time. In addition, the trustee shall have the following powers:

(a) **Retain Property.** To retain any property received from any source, regardless of lack of diversification, risk, or nonproductivity.

(b) **Invest.** To invest the trust estate in any kind of property, without being limited by any law dealing with the character, risk, productivity, diversification, wasting nature of, or otherwise concerning, investments by trustees.

(c) **Sell.** By public offering or private negotiation, to sell, exchange, assign, transfer, or otherwise dispose of all or any real or personal trust property and give options for these purposes, for such price and on such terms, with such covenants of warranty and such security for deferred payment as the Trustee deems proper. To partition between the trust and any other owner, as the Trustee deems proper, any property in which the trust owns an undivided interest.

(d) **Lease.** To lease trust property for terms within or extending beyond the term of the trust, for any purpose.

(e) **Real Estate.** To operate, maintain, repair, rehabilitate, alter, erect, improve, or remove any improvements on real estate; to subdivide real estate; to grant easements, give consents, and enter into contracts relating to real estate or its use; and to release or dedicate any interest in real estate.

(f) **Borrow.** To borrow money for any purpose; to encumber or hypothecate trust property by mortgage, deed of trust, or otherwise; and to maintain, prepay, renew, or extend any indebtedness upon such terms as the Trustee deems appropriate.

(g) **Loans.** To lend money to any person or entity, including, but not limited to, a beneficiary hereunder, upon such terms and with such security as the Trustee deems advisable.

(h) **Securities.** To engage in all actions necessary to the effective administration of securities including, but not limited to, the authority to: vote securities in person or by proxy; engage in a voting trust or voting agreement; exercise any options, rights, or privileges pertaining to any trust property; and consent to or participate in mergers, consolidations, sales of assets, recapitalizations, reorganizations, dissolutions, or other alterations of corporate structure affecting securities held by the Trustee.

(i) **Business Powers.** To enter into, carry on, and expand or acquire additional interests in (through the investment or loan of trust funds) any business activity, in sole proprietorship, general or limited partnership, joint venture, corporate or other form (and to convert from one form to another), including, but not limited to, any business interest which may be contributed to the trust, to employ agents and confer upon them the authority to manage and operate such business activity without liability for the acts of any such agents or for any loss, liability or indebtedness of such business, if the agents are selected and retained with reasonable care; and to sell, liquidate, or otherwise terminate any business interest, including, but not limited to, the fulfillment of any agreement for the disposition of any such business interest.

(j) **Litigation.** To commence or defend at the expense of the trust such litigation with respect to the trust estate as the Trustee deems advisable.

(k) **Claims.** To collect, pay, contest, compromise, settle, renew, or abandon any claims or demands of or against the trust estate, on whatever terms the Trustee deems advisable.

(l) **Additional Property.** To receive from any source additional property which is acceptable to the Trustee, and add it to the trust estate.

(m) **Agents.** To employ attorneys, auditors, brokers, investment advisors, depositaries, and agents with or without discretionary powers, to employ a trust company or bank with trust powers as agent for the purpose of performing any delegable duties of the administration, and to pay all expenses and fees so incurred.

(n) **Nominee.** To hold securities and other property in bearer form or in the name of a Trustee or nominee with or without disclosure of any fiduciary relationship.

(o) **Miscellaneous Powers.** Generally, to do and perform any and all acts, things, or deeds which an individual could do with respect to property and which, in the judgment of the Trustee, may be necessary or proper for the investment, management, protection and promotion of the property of the trust estate.

(p) **Tax Elections.** Unless otherwise expressly directed hereunder, to exercise any tax option, allocation or election permitted by law as the Trustee determines in the Trustee's sole discretion.

(q) **Division and Distribution.** To make all allocations, distributions, or divisions contemplated by this instrument; to allocate, distribute and divide different kinds or disproportionate shares of property or undivided interests in property among the beneficiaries or trusts, in cash or in kind, or both, without regard to the income tax basis of specific property allocated to any beneficiary or trust, even though shares may as a result be composed differently, and to determine the value of any property so allocated, divided or distributed.

(r) **Reliance.** To rely upon any notice, certificate, affidavit, or other document or evidence believed by the Trustee to be genuine and accurate, in making any payment or distribution. The Trustee shall incur no liability for a disbursement or distribution made in good faith and without actual notice or knowledge of a changed condition or status affecting any person's interest in the trust or any other matter.

Court Supervision. The Trustee shall not be required to qualify before or be appointed by any court; nor shall the Trustee be required to obtain the order or approval of any court in the exercise of any power or discretion.

Periodic Accounting. The Trustee shall make reports at least annually to those beneficiaries who may receive current distributions, such reports to reflect the property held in trust, the receipts, disbursements, and distributions made during the accounting period, and such other information as may be necessary to convey the condition of and changes to the trust estate.

Beneficiary Under Disability. Where a beneficiary is under the disability of minority or, in the Trustee's opinion, any other legal, physical or mental disability, a parent, custodian or guardian who, entirely in the Trustee's discretion, is acceptable to the Trustee may, in carrying out the provisions of this Trust Agreement, act and receive notice in the beneficiary's place, and sign any instrument for the beneficiary.

Spendthrift Trusts. All trusts created under this Trust Agreement are spendthrift trusts. No beneficiary may anticipate, by assignment or otherwise, a beneficial interest in the principal or income of the trusts created hereunder; nor may any beneficiary sell, transfer, encumber, or in any way charge an interest in trust income or principal prior to actually receiving it. Neither the income nor the principal of any trust established hereunder shall be subject to any execution, garnishment, attachment, bankruptcy, claims for alimony or support, other legal proceeding of any character, legal sequestration, levy or sale, or in any other event or manner be applicable or subject, voluntarily or involuntarily, to the payment of a beneficiary's debts. The Trustee shall make distributions to or for each beneficiary according to the terms hereof, notwithstanding any purported sale, assignment, hypothecation, transfer, attachment, or judicial process.

Limitation on Distributions.

(a) **Support Obligation.** Any other provision of this Trust Agreement notwithstanding, no distribution shall be made which discharges, in whole or in part, the Trustee's legal obligations, from time to time existing, to support, educate or otherwise provide for any of the trust beneficiaries. When determining these legal obligations, the existence of the trust estate and funds made available by it shall not be taken into consideration.

(b) **Distribution to Trustee/Beneficiary.** Notwithstanding anything to the contrary in this Trust Agreement, no Trustee shall have the authority to make discretionary distributions to that person as beneficiary, except to the extent the distributions are for the beneficiary's health, maintenance, support or education. If the Trustee is otherwise in this Trust Agreement authorized to make a distribution beyond that standard, the distributions shall be so limited.

Rule Against Perpetuities.
Every trust created hereunder (or through the exercise of a power of appointment granted in this Trust Agreement) must vest not later than twenty-one (21) years after my death and descendants living at the time the trust created hereunder first becomes irrevocable. If a trust is not vested within that period, it will terminate as of the maximum vesting date. In the event of termination, the Trustee shall distribute each trust to its income beneficiaries determined at the time of distribution in the proportions to which they are entitled to receive income.

Out-of-State Properties.
If the Trustee must act in a jurisdiction in which a person or entity serving as Trustee is unable or unwilling to act, the other or others serving as Trustee may act in that jurisdiction. If no Trustee is able or willing to act, the Trustee may appoint an ancillary trustee for that jurisdiction and may confer upon the ancillary trustee such rights, powers, discretions and duties, exercisable without court order, to act with respect to such matters as the Trustee deems proper. The ancillary trustee shall be responsible to the Trustee for any property it administers. The Trustee may pay the ancillary trustee reasonable compensation for services and may absolve the ancillary trustee from any requirement to furnish bond or other security.

ARTICLE VIII

AMENDMENT AND REVOCATION OF TRUST

I may amend, revoke or modify this Trust Agreement in whole or in part by an instrument signed and acknowledged by me and delivered to the Trustee. Amendment or modification of the Trust Agreement shall be effective immediately upon delivery of the instrument to the Trustee, except that changes affecting the Trustee's duties, liabilities, or compensation shall not be effective without the Trustee's written consent. On my death, this Trust Agreement may no longer be amended or modified, and the trust created hereunder shall become irrevocable.

ARTICLE IX

MISCELLANEOUS PROVISIONS

Applicable Law. The validity, construction, and administration of each trust created hereunder shall be governed by the laws of the State of __Texas__.

Adoption. For purposes of this Trust Agreement, a person shall be regarded as having been legally adopted by another only if the adoption is by court proceedings, the finality of which is not being contested by the adopting person.

Survival. Any person must survive by thirty (30) days for a gift made in this Trust Agreement which directly or indirectly requires such person's survival of another to be effective.

Education. "Education" shall include preparatory, collegiate, postgraduate, professional and vocational education; specialized formal or informal training in music, the stage, handicrafts, the arts or sports or athletic endeavors, whether by private instruction or otherwise; and any other activity, including foreign or domestic travel, which tends to develop the talents and potential of the beneficiary, regardless of age. Education shall also include all tuition, board, lodging fees, books and equipment, travel expenses and other expenses incidental thereto.

Executor. "Executor" shall include personal representative, executrix, administrator and administratrix.

Health. "Health" shall include medical, dental, hospital and nursing care expenses, and other expenses of invalidism, and distributions for the "health" of a beneficiary may, in the discretion of the Trustee include any part or all of the costs of purchasing or maintaining hospital or medical insurance and disability income insurance coverage for such beneficiary and/or any person in whom such beneficiary has an insurable interest.

Binding Agreement. This agreement shall extend to and be binding upon the heirs, executors, administrators, successors and assigns of the parties.

Use of Words. As used in this instrument, the masculine, feminine, and neuter gender, and the singular or plural of any word includes the others unless the context indicates otherwise.

Unenforceable Provision. If any provision of this Trust Agreement is unenforceable, the remaining provisions shall be given effect, unless to do so would produce an unreasonable result.

Titles, Headings, and Captions. All titles, headings, and captions used in this Trust Agreement have been included for convenience only and should not be construed in interpreting this instrument.

IN WITNESS WHEREOF, I as Grantor and Trustee have hereunto set my hand, on the day and year first above written in multiple originals.

Ned Neighbor

Witness

John Smith

Grantor

Ingrid Neighbor

Witness

John Smith

Trustee

STATE OF __Texas__ §

§

COUNTY OF __Dallas__ §

BEFORE ME, the undersigned authority, on this day personally appeared __John Smith__, Grantor and Trustee, known to me to be the person whose name is subscribed to the foregoing instrument and acknowledged to me that he/she executed the same for the purposes and consideration therein expressed.

GIVEN UNDER MY HAND AND SEAL OF OFFICE this _4th_ day of _March_, _2002_.

C.U. Sine

Notary Public

My Commission Expires:

This page intentionally left blank.

__John Smith__ LIVING TRUST

THIS AGREEMENT OF TRUST is entered into at __Dallas__, State of __Texas__, this __4th__ day of __March__, __2002__, by and between __John Smith__, as Grantor and Trustee. This Trust, as from time to time amended, shall be known as the "__John Smith__ LIVING TRUST dated __March 4__, __2002__."

ARTICLE I

My Children. My Children are: __Joseph Smith, Jennifer Smith, and__ __John Smith, Jr.__ .

ARTICLE II

FUNDING

Initial Funding. I hereby transfer to Trustee the sum of Ten Dollars ($10.00).

Additional Funding. From time to time the trust may be funded with additional property by me or by any other person in any manner. All property transferred, assigned, conveyed or delivered to the Trustee shall be held, administered and distributed by the Trustee in accordance with the terms of this Trust Agreement.

ARTICLE III

ADMINISTRATION OF TRUST DURING MY LIFETIME

Distributions of Income. While I am living, the Trustee shall distribute the trust's net income as directed in writing by me from time to time. In default of such direction, the Trustee shall pay to or expend on behalf of me all of the trust's net income from the Trust quarterly or more frequently.

Distributions of Principal. The Trustee shall pay to or expend for my benefit such part or all of the principal of the trust as I may request, from time to time. In default of such direction, the Trustee shall pay to or expend for my benefit so much of the principal of the trust as the Trustee, determines to be necessary or advisable for my health, maintenance and support.

Use of Residential Property. If any real property used by me for residential purposes (whether on a full-time or part-time basis, including recreational property) becomes part of the trust estate, I shall have the right to use and occupy such property without rental or other accounting to the trust estate.

Distributions to My Children. The Trustee shall pay to or expend for the benefit of my minor Children so much of the principal of the trust as the Trustee, in his/her sole discretion, determines to be necessary for the education, health, maintenance and support of my Children. The Trustee shall make such discretionary distributions only after conferring with me. The trust distributions do not need to be equal.

ARTICLE IV

ADMINISTRATION OF TRUST UPON MY DEATH

Payment of Expenses, Claims and Taxes. Upon my death, the Trustee shall, upon the request of the Executor of my estate, pay such part or all of the expenses of the last illness, funeral, and burial, legally enforceable claims against me or my estate and estate administration expenses. The Trustee may also pay any estate, inheritance, or succession taxes, state, federal and foreign, or any other taxes together with interest and penalties thereon that are payable by reason of my death.

ARTICLE V

DISTRIBUTION OF TRUST TO MY CHILDREN

Tangible Personal Property. The Trustee shall distribute my tangible personal property in accordance with any written, signed and dated memorandum prepared by me. Any tangible personal property which is not disposed of by memorandum shall be distributed in equal shares to my surviving Children.

Specific Bequest. The Trustee shall distribute the following property to the named individuals:

$10,000.00	to	Peter Smith
$25,000.00	to	Sally Jones

If any of the individuals named does not survive me, the gift to that person will lapse and the property will pass as provided below.

Division of Trust Estate for My Children. The Trustee shall divide the remaining trust estate, including any additions to the Trust by reason of my death, into separate equal shares as follows: one share for each Child of mine who is then living, and one share for the then living descendants, collectively, of each deceased Child of mine with one or more descendants then living. The Trustee shall administer a share for each Child in a separate trust, and a share for the Descendants of each deceased Child, pursuant to the provisions of Article VI, following.

ARTICLE VI

TRUSTS FOR CHILDREN AND DESCENDANTS

Separate Trust for Child. Each trust for the benefit of a Child shall be administered and distributed upon the following terms:

(a) **Distributions to Child.** The Trustee shall distribute to the Child all of the trust's net income quarterly or more frequently and so much of the principal of the trust as the Trustee deems necessary to provide for the Child's health, maintenance, education and support.

When the Child attains age _25_, the Trustee shall distribute to the Child _50%_ of the value of the then remaining trust estate.

When the Child attains age _30_, the Trustee shall distribute to the Child the remaining trust estate.

(b) **Termination of Trust.** If not earlier terminated by distribution of the entire trust estate under the foregoing provisions, the trust shall terminate upon the death of the Child. The Trustee shall distribute the remaining trust estate to the Child's then living descendants, pursuant to the limitation described in subsection (c) hereof. If there are no descendants of the Child then living, the Trustee shall distribute the remaining trust estate to my then living descendants, per stirpes.

(c) **Distribution to Descendants of a Deceased Child.** Property which is to be distributed under this subsection to the descendants of a deceased Child shall be distributed, per stirpes, to those descendants living at the event causing the distribution hereunder.

Contingent Distribution. If my spouse, my Children and their descendants and all of my descendants are deceased, the trust estate then remaining shall be distributed, to the following individuals in the amounts specified:

_50%_	to _Peter Smith_
_50%_	to _Sally Jones_

ARTICLE VII

THE TRUSTEE

Successor Trustees. During my lifetime, if I cannot serve as Trustee, I will appoint a successor Trustee. If I do not appoint a successor trustee, or after my death, the successor trustee shall be _Peter Smith_. If

_____Peter Smith_____ is not able to serve, the successor trustee(s) shall be ____John Smith, Jr._____.
If the successor trustee fails or ceases to serve, __Joseph Smith_____ shall be successor trustee. If all successor trustees fail or cease to serve, a majority in number of the income beneficiaries of the trust at that time shall appoint a successor trustee. Any appointment under this section shall be by a signed, acknowledged instrument delivered to the successor trustee.

Removal of Trustee. During my life, I may remove a trustee at any time for any reason. After my death or if I am incapacitated and unable to remove the trustee, __Peter Smith_____ _____ may remove the trustee. If _____Peter Smith_____is not alive or is unable to exercise this power, __John Smith, Jr._____ shall have the power to remove a trustee.

Resignation of Trustee. A Trustee may resign as to any one or more of the trusts created hereunder by giving written notice to all co-trustees then serving, if any, the current income beneficiaries, the successor trustee if identified in this Trust Agreement, and to those persons, if any, authorized in this Trust Agreement to appoint the successor trustee. Notice shall be delivered at least thirty (30) days prior to the date of resignation.

Trustee's Fees. The Trustee shall be entitled to reasonable fees commensurate with the Trustee's duties and responsibilities, taking into account the value and nature of the trust estate and the time and work involved. The Trustee shall be reimbursed for reasonable costs and expenses incurred in connection with fiduciary duties.

Bond. The Trustee shall not be required to furnish bond or other security.

Liability of Trustee. A Trustee shall only be liable for willful misconduct or gross negligence, and shall not be liable for breach of fiduciary duty by virtue of mistake or error in judgment.

Incapacity of Individual Trustee. This Section shall apply in the event a Trustee becomes unable to discharge the duties of Trustee by reason of accident, physical or mental illness or deterioration, or other cause, and does not resign. Upon certification by two medical doctors that each has examined the Trustee and has concluded that the Trustee is unable to discharge such duties, the Trustee shall cease to serve, as if the Trustee had resigned, effective the date of the certification.

ARTICLE VIII

TRUST ADMINISTRATION

Trustee Powers: Investment and Management of Trust Estate. Subject to any limitation stated elsewhere in this instrument, the Trustee shall have, with respect to each trust established hereunder, all of the powers granted to trustees by common law and by applicable statutes as amended from time to time. In addition, the trustee shall have the following powers:

(a) **Retain Property.** To retain any property received from any source, regardless of lack of diversification, risk, or nonproductivity.

(b) **Invest.** To invest the trust estate in any kind of property, without being limited by any law dealing with the character, risk, productivity, diversification, wasting nature of, or otherwise concerning, investments by trustees.

(c) **Sell.** By public offering or private negotiation, to sell, exchange, assign, transfer, or otherwise dispose of all or any real or personal trust property and give options for these purposes, for such price and on such terms, with such covenants of warranty and such security for deferred payment as the Trustee deems proper. To partition between the trust and any other owner, as the Trustee deems proper, any property in which the trust owns an undivided interest.

(d) **Lease.** To lease trust property for terms within or extending beyond the term of the trust, for any purpose.

(e) **Real Estate.** To operate, maintain, repair, rehabilitate, alter, erect, improve, or remove any improvements on real estate; to subdivide real estate; to grant easements, give consents, and enter into contracts relating to real estate or its use; and to release or dedicate any interest in real estate.

(f) **Borrow.** To borrow money for any purpose; to encumber or hypothecate trust property by mortgage, deed of trust, or otherwise; and to maintain, prepay, renew, or extend any indebtedness upon such terms as the Trustee deems appropriate.

(g) **Loans.** To lend money to any person or entity, including, but not limited to, a beneficiary hereunder, upon such terms and with such security as the Trustee deems advisable.

(h) **Securities.** To engage in all actions necessary to the effective administration of securities including, but not limited to, the authority to: vote securities in person or by proxy; engage in a voting trust or voting agreement; exercise any options, rights, or privileges pertaining to any trust property; and consent to or participate in mergers,

consolidations, sales of assets, recapitalizations, reorganizations, dissolutions, or other alterations of corporate structure affecting securities held by the Trustee.

(i) **Business Powers.** To enter into, carry on, and expand or acquire additional interests in (through the investment or loan of trust funds) any business activity, in sole proprietorship, general or limited partnership, joint venture, corporate or other form (and to convert from one form to another), including, but not limited to, any business interest which may be contributed to the trust, to employ agents and confer upon them the authority to manage and operate such business activity without liability for the acts of any such agents or for any loss, liability or indebtedness of such business, if the agents are selected and retained with reasonable care; and to sell, liquidate, or otherwise terminate any business interest, including, but not limited to, the fulfillment of any agreement for the disposition of any such business interest.

(j) **Litigation.** To commence or defend at the expense of the trust such litigation with respect to the trust estate as the Trustee deems advisable.

(k) **Claims.** To collect, pay, contest, compromise, settle, renew, or abandon any claims or demands of or against the trust estate, on whatever terms the Trustee deems advisable.

(l) **Additional Property.** To receive from any source additional property which is acceptable to the Trustee, and add it to the trust estate.

(m) **Agents.** To employ attorneys, auditors, brokers, investment advisors, depositaries, and agents with or without discretionary powers, to employ a trust company or bank with trust powers as agent for the purpose of performing any delegable duties of the administration, and to pay all expenses and fees so incurred.

(n) **Nominee.** To hold securities and other property in bearer form or in the name of a Trustee or nominee with or without disclosure of any fiduciary relationship.

(o) **Miscellaneous Powers.** Generally, to do and perform any and all acts, things, or deeds which an individual could do with respect to property and which, in the judgment of the Trustee, may be necessary or proper for the investment, management, protection and promotion of the property of the trust estate.

(p) **Tax Elections.** Unless otherwise expressly directed hereunder, to exercise any tax option, allocation or election permitted by law as the Trustee determines in the Trustee's sole discretion.

(q) **Division and Distribution.** To make all allocations, distributions, or divisions contemplated by this instrument; to allocate, distribute and divide different kinds or disproportionate shares of property or undivided interests in property among the beneficiaries or trusts, in cash or in kind, or both, without regard to the income tax basis of specific property allocated to any beneficiary or trust, even though shares may as a result be composed differently, and to determine the value of any property so allocated, divided or distributed.

(r) **Reliance.** To rely upon any notice, certificate, affidavit, or other document or evidence believed by the Trustee to be genuine and accurate, in making any payment or distribution. The Trustee shall incur no liability for a disbursement or distribution made in good faith and without actual notice or knowledge of a changed condition or status affecting any person's interest in the trust or any other matter.

Court Supervision. The Trustee shall not be required to qualify before or be appointed by any court; nor shall the Trustee be required to obtain the order or approval of any court in the exercise of any power or discretion.

Periodic Accounting. The Trustee shall make reports at least annually to those beneficiaries who may receive current distributions, such reports to reflect the property held in trust, the receipts, disbursements, and distributions made during the accounting period, and such other information as may be necessary to convey the condition of and changes to the trust estate.

Beneficiary Under Disability. Where a beneficiary is under the disability of minority or, in the Trustee's opinion, any other legal, physical or mental disability, a parent, custodian or guardian who, entirely in the Trustee's discretion, is acceptable to the Trustee may, in carrying out the provisions of this Trust Agreement, act and receive notice in the beneficiary's place, and sign any instrument for the beneficiary.

Spendthrift Trusts. All trusts created under this Trust Agreement are spendthrift trusts. No beneficiary may anticipate, by assignment or otherwise, a beneficial interest in the principal or income of the trusts created hereunder; nor may any beneficiary sell, transfer, encumber, or in any way charge an interest in trust income or principal prior to actually receiving it. Neither the income nor the principal of any trust established hereunder shall be subject to any execution, garnishment, attachment, bankruptcy, claims for alimony or support, other legal proceeding of any character, legal sequestration, levy or sale, or in any other event or manner be applicable or subject, voluntarily or involuntarily, to the payment of a beneficiary's debts. The Trustee shall make distributions to or for each beneficiary according to the terms hereof, notwithstanding any purported sale, assignment, hypothecation, transfer, attachment, or judicial process.

Limitation on Distributions.

(a) **Support Obligation.** Any other provision of this Trust Agreement notwithstanding, no distribution shall be made which discharges, in whole or in part, the Trustee's legal obligations, from time to time existing, to support, educate or otherwise provide for any of the trust beneficiaries. When determining these legal obligations, the existence of the trust estate and funds made available by it shall not be taken into consideration.

(b) **Distribution to Trustee/Beneficiary.** Notwithstanding anything to the contrary in this Trust Agreement, no Trustee shall have the authority to make discretionary distributions to that person as beneficiary, except to the extent the distributions are for the beneficiary's health, maintenance, support or education. If the Trustee is otherwise in this Trust Agreement authorized to make a distribution beyond that standard, the distributions shall be so limited.

Rule Against Perpetuities. Every trust created hereunder (or through the exercise of a power of appointment granted in this Trust Agreement) must vest not later than twenty-one (21) years after my death and descendants living at the time the trust created hereunder first becomes irrevocable. If a trust is not vested within that period, it will terminate as of the maximum vesting date. In the event of termination, the Trustee shall distribute each trust to its income beneficiaries determined at the time of distribution in the proportions to which they are entitled to receive income.

Out-of-State Properties. If the Trustee must act in a jurisdiction in which a person or entity serving as Trustee is unable or unwilling to act, the other or others serving as Trustee may act in that jurisdiction. If no Trustee is able or willing to act, the Trustee may appoint an ancillary trustee for that jurisdiction and may confer upon the ancillary trustee such rights, powers, discretions and duties, exercisable without court order, to act with respect to such matters as the Trustee deems proper. The ancillary trustee shall be responsible to the Trustee for any property it administers. The Trustee may pay the ancillary trustee reasonable compensation for services and may absolve the ancillary trustee from any requirement to furnish bond or other security.

ARTICLE IX

AMENDMENT AND REVOCATION OF TRUST

I may amend, revoke or modify this Trust Agreement in whole or in part by an instrument signed and acknowledged by me and delivered to the Trustee. Amendment or modification of the Trust Agreement shall be effective immediately upon delivery of the instrument to the Trustee, except that changes affecting the Trustee's duties, liabilities, or compensation shall not be effective without the Trustee's written consent. On my death, this Trust Agreement may no longer be amended or modified, and the trust created hereunder shall become irrevocable.

ARTICLE X

MISCELLANEOUS PROVISIONS

Applicable Law. The validity, construction, and administration of each trust created hereunder shall be governed by the laws of the State of _Texas_____.

Adoption. For purposes of this Trust Agreement, a person shall be regarded as having been legally adopted by another only if the adoption is by court proceedings, the finality of which is not being contested by the adopting person.

Survival. Any person must survive by thirty (30) days for a gift made in this Trust Agreement which directly or indirectly requires such person's survival of another to

be effective.

Education. "Education" shall include preparatory, collegiate, postgraduate, professional and vocational education; specialized formal or informal training in music, the stage, handicrafts, the arts or sports or athletic endeavors, whether by private instruction or otherwise; and any other activity, including foreign or domestic travel, which tends to develop the talents and potential of the beneficiary, regardless of age. Education shall also include all tuition, board, lodging fees, books and equipment, travel expenses and other expenses incidental thereto.

Executor. "Executor" shall include personal representative, executrix, administrator and administratrix.

Health. "Health" shall include medical, dental, hospital, and nursing care expenses, and other expenses of invalidism, and distributions for the "health" of a beneficiary may, in the discretion of the Trustee include any part or all of the costs of purchasing or maintaining hospital or medical insurance and disability income insurance coverage for such beneficiary and/or any person in whom such beneficiary has an insurable interest.

Binding Agreement. This agreement shall extend to and be binding upon the heirs, executors, administrators, successors and assigns of the parties.

Use of Words. As used in this instrument, the masculine, feminine, and neuter gender, and the singular or plural of any word includes the others unless the context indicates otherwise.

Unenforceable Provision. If any provision of this Trust Agreement is unenforceable, the remaining provisions shall be given effect, unless to do so would produce an unreasonable result.

Titles, Headings, and Captions. All titles, headings, and captions used in this Trust Agreement have been included for convenience only and should not be construed in interpreting this instrument.

IN WITNESS WHEREOF, I as Grantor and Trustee have hereunto set my hand, on the day and year first above written in multiple originals.

Ned Neighbor
_____
Witness

John Smith
_____
Grantor

Nancy Neighbor
_____
Witness

John Smith
_____
Trustee

STATE OF ___Texas_____ §
                                                                         §
COUNTY OF ___Dallas_____ §

BEFORE ME, the undersigned authority, on this day personally appeared ___John Smith_____, Grantor and Trustee, known to me to be the person whose name is subscribed to the foregoing instrument and acknowledged to me that he/she executed the same for the purposes and consideration therein expressed.

GIVEN UNDER MY HAND AND SEAL OF OFFICE this __4th__ day of __March_____, __2002____.

C.U. Sine
_____
Notary Public
My Commission Expires:

AMENDMENT
TO
THE <u>John Smith</u> **LIVING TRUST**

Dated <u>March 4</u>, <u>2002</u>

This Amendment to THE <u>John Smith</u> LIVING TRUST, dated <u>March 4</u>, <u>2002</u> (the "Trust"), by <u>John Smith</u> _____, as Grantor and as Trustee. Pursuant to the power of amendment reserved by me in Article <u>V</u> of the Trust, Grantor hereby amends the Trust as follows:

ITEM 1.

Grantor hereby deletes the following paragraph of the Trust in its entirety, and substitutes in its place the following:

Deleted paragraph:

Contingent Distribution. If my spouse, my Children and their descendants and all of my descendants are deceased, the trust estate then remaining shall be distributed, to the following individuals in the amounts specified:

<u>50%</u>	to	<u>Peter Smith</u>
<u>50%</u>	to	<u>Sally Jones</u>

Replacement paragraph:

Contingent Distribution. If my spouse, my Children and their descendants and all of my descendants are deceased, the trust estate then remaining shall be distributed, to the following individuals in the amounts specified:

<u>40%</u>	to	<u>Peter Smith</u>
<u>60%</u>	to	<u>Sally Jones</u>

ITEM 2.

Grantor hereby adds the following paragraph to the Trust:

IN WITNESS WHEREOF, __John Smith__ has hereunder caused his/her name to be subscribed as Grantor and as Trustee of this Amendment to THE __John Smith__ LIVING TRUST, dated __July 4__, __2002__, at the City of __Dallas__, County of __Dallas__, State of __Texas__, on this __1st__ day of __September__, __2002__.

__Ned Neighbor__
Witness

__Nancy Neighbor__
Witness

__John Smith__
Grantor

__John Smith__
Trustee

THE STATE OF __Texas__ §

§

COUNTY OF __Dallas__ §

BEFORE ME, the undersigned authority, a Notary Public in and for said County and State, on this day personally appeared __John Smith__, known to me to be the person whose name is subscribed to the annexed or foregoing instrument, and acknowledged to me that he/she executed the same for the purposes and consideration therein expressed and in the capacities therein stated.

GIVEN UNDER MY HAND AND SEAL OF OFFICE, this the __1st__ day of __September__, __2002__.

__C.U. Sine__
Notary Public
My commission expires:

REVOCATION OF

THE _____John Smith_____LIVING TRUST

On __July 1_____, __2002___, I, ___John Smith_____,
as trustee and grantor, executed a certain trust agreement, wherein I reserved the right at any time
or times to amend or revoke the trust agreement in whole or in part by an instrument in writing
delivered to the trustee.

Pursuant to the right reserved to me under the trust agreement, I hereby revoke the trust
agreement in its entirety and direct that the trust property held thereunder be conveyed by the
trustee to me.

IN WITNESS WHEREOF, I have signed this revocation this __1st_____ day of
__September_____, __2002____.

_Ned Neighbor______   **_John Smith_**_____
Witness   Grantor

_Nancy Neighbor______
Witness

STATE OF __Texas_____ §

                                                      §

COUNTY OF __Dallas_____ §

I, __C.U. Sine_____, Notary Public, hereby certify that
__John Smith_____, personally known to me to be the same per-
son whose name is signed to the foregoing instrument, appeared before me this day in person and
acknowledged that he/she signed the instrument as his/her free and voluntary act, for the uses
and purposes therein set forth.

Given under my hand and official seal this __1st__ day of __September_____, __2002____.

_C.U. Sine______
Notary Public
My commission expires:

APPENDIX C
BLANK FORMS

The following pages contain forms that can be used to prepare a living trust and a pourover will to assign personal property to the trust and file taxes. The forms should only be used by persons who have read this book, who do not have any complications in their legal affairs, and who understand the forms they are using.

The forms may be used right out of the book or they may be photocopied or retyped. Each form is numbered in the upper right corner. Be sure you have the correct form number. If there is anything you do not understand, be sure to consult an attorney.

The following is a list of the forms contained in this appendix, along with the page number where each form begins:

TABLE OF FORMS

ESTATE PLANNING WORKSHEET

I. FAMILY INFORMATION

Date _____

Husband

_____
Name

Wife

_____
Name

_____
Address

_____
Address

_____
Phone Number

_____
Phone Number

_____
Birth Date

_____
Birth Date

_____
Employer

_____
Employer

_____
Address/Phone Number

_____
Address/Phone Number

Children	Birth Date	Social Security Number
1. _____	_____	_____
2. _____	_____	_____
3. _____	_____	_____

Grandchildren/Other dependents	Birth Date	Social Security Number
1. _____	_____	_____
2. _____	_____	_____
3. _____	_____	_____

II. IMPORTANT FAMILY ADVISORS
(include name, address and phone number)

Lawyer _____

Accountant_____

Bank Officer_____

Clergy _____

Doctor_____

Insurance agent_____

Stockbroker_____

III. FINANCIAL INFORMATION

A.   ASSETS

Real estate (land, homes, business property, condos, co-ops, etc.):

Address	Ownership (sole, joint, etc.)	Value/Equity	Mortgage Balance
_____	_____	_____	_____
_____	_____	_____	_____
_____	_____	_____	_____

Cash (checking and savings accounts, money market accounts, CDs, etc.):

Type	Bank	Account Number	Balance
_____	_____	_____	_____
_____	_____	_____	_____
_____	_____	_____	_____

Investments (stocks, bonds, mutual fund shares, etc.):

Description	Company	Number of Shares	Market Value
_____	_____	_____	_____
_____	_____	_____	_____
_____	_____	_____	_____

Personal Property

(only list assets of significant value such as jewelry, antiques, artwork, collectibles, etc.):

Description and Value

_____

_____

_____

Retirement plans (IRAs, 401Ks, pension plans, Keoghs, etc.):

Type	Name of PlanBeneficiary	Current	Value
_____	_____	_____	_____
_____	_____	_____	_____
_____	_____	_____	_____

Life Insurance:

Insured	Company/ Policy Number	Beneficiary	Death Benefit Whole Life or Term
_____	_____	_____	_____
_____	_____	_____	_____
_____	_____	_____	_____

Debts owed to you:

Name and Address of Person who owes you	Amount Owed
_____	_____
_____	_____
_____	_____

B. DEBTS

Type	Company/Person Owed	Amount Owed	When Due	Secured by
Mortgages	_____	_____	_____	_____
Installment Loans	_____	_____	_____	_____
Education loans	_____	_____	_____	_____
Personal loans	_____	_____	_____	_____
Other debts	_____	_____	_____	_____

C. NET WORTH

	Husband	Wife	Joint
ASSETS			
Real estate	_____	_____	_____
Cash	_____	_____	_____
Investments	_____	_____	_____
Personal Property	_____	_____	_____
Retirement plans	_____	_____	_____
Life insurance	_____	_____	_____
Debts owed you	_____	_____	_____
Total assets	_____	_____	_____
DEBTS			
Mortgages	_____	_____	_____
Installment loans	_____	_____	_____
Education loans	_____	_____	_____
Personal loans	_____	_____	_____
Other debts	_____	_____	_____
Total liabilities	_____	_____	_____
NET WORTH	_____	_____	_____
(assets minus debts)			

IV. WILL INFORMATION

Executor(s)   _____
(Include alternates)   _____

_____

Guardian(s) for Minor   _____
Children   _____
(Include alternates)   _____

_____

_____

Minor Beneficiaries   _____

_____

_____

Other Beneficiaries
_____

_____

_____

Charitable Beneficiaries
_____

_____

_____

Alternate Beneficiaries
_____

_____

_____

V. TRUST INFORMATION

Trustee(s)
_____

(Include alternates)
_____

_____

Minor Beneficiaries
_____

_____

_____

Other Beneficiaries
_____

_____

_____

Charitable Beneficiaries
_____

_____

Alternate Beneficiaries
_____

_____

This page intentionally left blank.

LAST WILL AND TESTAMENT

OF

_____

I, _____, a resident of

_____ County, State of _____,

do hereby make, publish and declare this to be my Last Will and Testament and revoke any prior

wills and codicils.

FIRST: My Spouse is _____ and my

Children are: _____

_____ and

any other children born to or adopted by me after the date of this Will.

SECOND: I direct that all of my just debts, taxes and funeral expenses be paid out of my

estate as soon after my death as is practical.

THIRD: I give my interest in all of my tangible personal property (including, but not lim-

ited to, my jewelry, clothing, books, china, crystal, silverware, furniture and furnishings, objects of

art, and automobiles), to my spouse. If my spouse is not alive, I give such property to my Children

who survive me in shares of substantially equal value to be divided as they agree. If none of my

Children survive me, I give such property to _____

_____.

FOURTH: I give the rest, remainder and residue of my estate, real and personal, where-

soever situate, now owned or hereafter acquired by me, to the Trustee of my Living Trust, dated

_____, _____, to be added to the trust, subject to its terms as now

provided and as amended from time to time.

FIFTH: If I am the surviving natural parent of my Children, I appoint

_____ as

guardian of the person of each of my minor Children.

SIXTH: I hereby, nominate, constitute and appoint _____

_____to serve as executor of my Last Will and

Testament, to serve without bond or surety. In the event _____

_____is unable or unwilling to serve for any reason, then

I nominate, constitute and appoint _____

_____as alternate executor also to serve without bond or

137

other surety. I give my executor the fullest power in all matters including the power to sell or convey real or personal property or any interest therein without court order.

IN WITNESS WHEREOF, I have signed and published this my Last Will and Testament this _____ day of _____, _____.

_____

We, the undersigned persons, of lawful age, have on this _____ day of _____, _____, at the request of _____, _____witnessed his/her signature to the foregoing Will in the presence of each of us; and we have, at the same time and in his/her presence and in the presence of each other, subscribed our names hereto as attesting witnesses.

_____   ADDRESS: _____
WITNESS   _____

_____   ADDRESS: _____
WITNESS   _____

_____   ADDRESS: _____
WITNESS   _____

LAST WILL AND TESTAMENT

OF

_____

I,_____, a resident of
_____ County, State of _____, do hereby
make, publish and declare this to be my Last Will and Testament and revoke any prior wills and
codicils.

FIRST: My Children are: _____
_____and any
other children born to or adopted by me after the date of this Will.

SECOND: I direct that all of my just debts, taxes and funeral expenses be paid out of my
estate as soon after my death as is practical.

THIRD: I give my interest in all of my tangible personal property (including, but not limited to, my jewelry, clothing, books, china, crystal, silverware, furniture and furnishings, objects of
art, and automobiles), to my Children who survive me in shares of substantially equal value to be
divided as they agree. If none of my Children survive me, I give such property to
_____.

FOURTH: I give the rest, remainder and residue of my estate, real and personal, where-
soever situate, now owned or hereafter acquired by me, to the Trustee of my Living Trust, dated
_____,   , to be added to the trust, subject to its terms as now provided
and as amended from time to time.

FIFTH: If I am the surviving natural parent of my Children, I appoint
_____
as guardian of the person of each of my minor Children.

SIXTH: I hereby, nominate, constitute and appoint _____
_____to serve as executor of my Last Will and
Testament, to serve without bond or surety. In the event _____
_____is unable or unwilling to serve for any reason, then I
nominate, constitute and appoint _____
_____as alternate executor also to serve without bond or other
surety. I give my executor the fullest power in all matters including the power to sell or convey
real or personal property or any interest therein without court order.

IN WITNESS WHEREOF, I have signed and published this my Last Will and Testament this _____ day of _____, _____.

_____

We, the undersigned persons, of lawful age, have on this _____ day of _____, _____, at the request of _____, _____witnessed his/her signature to the foregoing Will in the presence of each of us; and we have, at the same time and in his/her presence and in the presence of each other, subscribed our names hereto as attesting witnesses.

_____   ADDRESS: _____

WITNESS   _____

_____   ADDRESS: _____

WITNESS   _____

_____   ADDRESS: _____

WITNESS   _____

_____ LIVING TRUST

THIS AGREEMENT OF TRUST is entered into at _____, State of _____, this _____ day of _____, _____, by and between _____, as Grantor and Trustee. This Trust, as from time to time amended, shall be known as the "_____ LIVING TRUST dated _____, _____."

ARTICLE I

My Spouse. My spouse is: _____.

My Children. My Children are: _____

_____.

ARTICLE II

FUNDING

Initial Funding. I hereby transfer to Trustee the sum of Ten Dollars ($10.00).

Additional Funding. From time to time the trust may be funded with additional property by me or by any other person in any manner. All property transferred, assigned, conveyed or delivered to the Trustee shall be held, administered and distributed by the Trustee in accordance with the terms of this Trust Agreement.

ARTICLE III

ADMINISTRATION OF TRUST DURING MY LIFETIME

Distributions of Income. While I am living, the Trustee shall distribute the trust's net income as directed in writing by me from time to time. In default of such direction, the Trustee shall pay to or expend on behalf of me all of the trust's net income from the Trust quarterly or more frequently.

Distributions of Principal. The Trustee shall pay to or expend for my benefit such part or all of the principal of the trust as I may request, from time to time. In default of such direction, the Trustee shall pay to or expend for my benefit so much of the principal of the trust as the Trustee, determines to be necessary or advisable for my health, maintenance and support.

Use of Residential Property. If any real property used by me for residential purposes (whether on a full-time or part-time basis, including recreational property) becomes part of the trust estate, I shall have the right to use and occupy such property without rental or other accounting to the trust estate.

Distributions to My Spouse and Children. The Trustee shall pay to or expend for the benefit of my spouse and minor Children so much of the principal of the trust as the Trustee, in his/her sole discretion, determines to be necessary for the education, health, maintenance and support of my spouse and Children. The Trustee shall make such discretionary distributions only after conferring with me. The trust distributions do not need to be equal.

ARTICLE IV

ADMINISTRATION OF TRUST UPON MY DEATH

Payment of Expenses, Claims and Taxes. Upon my death, the Trustee shall, upon the request of the Executor of my estate, pay such part or all of the expenses of the last illness, funeral, and burial, legally enforceable claims against me or my estate and estate administration expenses. The Trustee may also pay any estate, inheritance, or succession taxes, state, federal and foreign, or any other taxes together with interest and penalties thereon that are payable by reason of my death.

ARTICLE V

DISTRIBUTION OF TRUST TO MY SPOUSE AND CHILDREN

Tangible Personal Property. The Trustee shall distribute my tangible personal property in accordance with any written, signed and dated memorandum prepared by me. Any tangible personal property which is not disposed of by memorandum shall be distributed to my spouse or if my spouse is not alive in equal shares to my surviving Children.

Specific Bequest. The Trustee shall distribute the following property to the named individuals:

_____ to _____

_____ to _____

If any of the individuals named does not survive me, the gift to that person will lapse and the property will pass as provided below.

Distribution to My Spouse. If my spouse survives me, the Trustee shall distribute the remaining trust estate to my spouse outright or, if my spouse so chooses, to the Living Trust dated _____, _____, established by my spouse. If my spouse does not survive me, the Trustee shall distribute the trust estate as provided in the next paragraph.

Distribution to My Children. The Trustee shall divide the remaining trust estate, including any additions to the Trust by reason of my death, into separate equal shares as follows: one share for each Child of mine who is then living, and one share for the then living descendants, collectively, of each deceased Child of mine with one or more descendants then living. The Trustee shall distribute the share for each Child to such Child outright. The share for the descendants of each deceased Child, shall be distributed, per stirpes, to those descendants living at my death.

Contingent Distribution. If my spouse, my Children and their descendants and all of my descendants are deceased, the trust estate then remaining shall be distributed, to the following individuals in the amounts specified:

_____ to_____

_____ to_____

ARTICLE VI

THE TRUSTEE

Successor Trustees. During my lifetime, if I cannot serve as Trustee, I will appoint a successor Trustee. If I do not appoint a successor trustee, or after my death, the successor trustee shall be my spouse, or if my spouse is not able to serve, the successor trustee(s) shall be _____. If the successor trustee fails or ceases to serve, _____ shall be successor trustee. If all successor trustees fail or cease to serve, a majority in number of the income beneficiaries of the trust at that time shall appoint a successor trustee. Any appointment under this section shall be by a signed, acknowledged instrument delivered to the successor trustee

Removal of Trustee. During my life, I may remove a trustee at any time for any reason. After my death or if I am incapacitated and unable to remove the trustee, my spouse may remove the trustee. If my spouse is not alive or is unable to exercise this power, _____ shall have the power to remove a trustee.

Resignation of Trustee. A Trustee may resign as to any one or more of the trusts created hereunder by giving written notice to all co-trustees then serving, if any, the current income beneficiaries, the successor trustee if identified in this Trust Agreement, and to those persons, if any, authorized in this Trust Agreement to appoint the successor trustee. Notice shall be delivered at least thirty (30) days prior to the date of resignation.

Trustee's Fees. The Trustee shall be entitled to reasonable fees commensurate with the Trustee's duties and responsibilities, taking into account the value and nature of the trust estate and the time and work involved. The Trustee shall be reimbursed for reasonable costs and expenses incurred in connection with fiduciary duties.

Bond. The Trustee shall not be required to furnish bond or other security.

Liability of Trustee. A Trustee shall only be liable for willful misconduct or gross negligence, and shall not be liable for breach of fiduciary duty by virtue of mistake or error in judgment.

Incapacity of Individual Trustee. This Section shall apply in the event a Trustee becomes unable to discharge the duties of Trustee by reason of accident, physical or mental illness or deterioration, or other cause, and does not resign. Upon certification by two medical doctors that each has examined the Trustee and has concluded that the Trustee is unable to discharge such duties, the Trustee shall cease to serve, as if the Trustee had resigned, effective the date of the certification.

ARTICLE VII

TRUST ADMINISTRATION

Trustee Powers: Investment and Management of Trust Estate. Subject to any limitation stated elsewhere in this instrument, the Trustee shall have, with respect to each trust established hereunder, all of the powers granted to trustees by common law and by applicable statutes as amended from time to time. In addition, the trustee shall have the following powers:

(a) **Retain Property.** To retain any property received from any source, regardless of lack of diversification, risk, or nonproductivity.

(b) **Invest.** To invest the trust estate in any kind of property, without being limited by any law dealing with the character, risk, productivity, diversification, wasting nature of, or otherwise concerning, investments by trustees.

(c) **Sell.** By public offering or private negotiation, to sell, exchange, assign, transfer, or otherwise dispose of all or any real or personal trust property and give options for these purposes, for such price and on such terms, with such covenants of warranty and such security for deferred payment as the Trustee deems proper. To partition between the trust and any other owner, as the Trustee deems proper, any property in which the trust owns an undivided interest.

(d) **Lease.** To lease trust property for terms within or extending beyond the term of the trust, for any purpose.

(e) **Real Estate.** To operate, maintain, repair, rehabilitate, alter, erect, improve, or remove any improvements on real estate; to subdivide real estate; to grant easements, give consents, and enter into contracts relating to real estate or its use; and to release or dedicate any interest in real estate.

(f) **Borrow.** To borrow money for any purpose; to encumber or hypothecate trust property by mortgage, deed of trust, or otherwise; and to maintain, prepay, renew, or extend any indebtedness upon such terms as the Trustee deems appropriate.

(g) **Loans.** To lend money to any person or entity, including, but not limited to, a beneficiary hereunder, upon such terms and with such security as the Trustee deems advisable.

(h) **Securities.** To engage in all actions necessary to the effective administration of securities including, but not limited to, the authority to: vote securities in person or by proxy; engage in a voting trust or voting agreement; exercise any options, rights, or privileges pertaining to any trust property; and consent to or participate in mergers, consolidations, sales of assets, recapitalizations, reorganizations, dissolutions, or other alterations of corporate structure affecting securities held by the Trustee.

(i) **Business Powers.** To enter into, carry on, and expand or acquire additional interests in (through the investment or loan of trust funds) any business activity, in sole proprietorship, general or limited partnership, joint venture, corporate or other form (and to convert from one form to another), including, but not limited to, any business interest which may be contributed to the trust, to employ agents and confer upon them the authority to manage and operate such business activity without liability for the acts of any such agents or for any loss, liability or indebtedness of such business, if the agents are selected and retained with reasonable care; and to sell, liquidate, or otherwise terminate any business interest, including, but not limited to, the fulfillment of any agreement for the disposition of any such business interest.

(j) **Litigation.** To commence or defend at the expense of the trust such litigation with respect to the trust estate as the Trustee deems advisable.

(k) **Claims.** To collect, pay, contest, compromise, settle, renew, or abandon any claims or demands of or against the trust estate, on whatever terms the Trustee deems advisable.

(l) **Additional Property.** To receive from any source additional property which is acceptable to the Trustee, and add it to the trust estate.

(m) **Agents.** To employ attorneys, auditors, brokers, investment advisors, depositaries, and agents with or without discretionary powers, to employ a trust company or bank with trust powers as agent for the purpose of performing any delegable duties of the administration, and to pay all expenses and fees so incurred.

(n) **Nominee.** To hold securities and other property in bearer form or in the name of a Trustee or nominee with or without disclosure of any fiduciary relationship.

(o) **Miscellaneous Powers.** Generally, to do and perform any and all acts, things, or deeds which an individual could do with respect to property and which, in the judgment of the Trustee, may be necessary or proper for the investment, management, protection and promotion of the property of the trust estate.

(p) **Tax Elections.** Unless otherwise expressly directed hereunder, to exercise any tax option, allocation or election permitted by law as the Trustee determines in the Trustee's sole discretion.

(q) **Division and Distribution.** To make all allocations, distributions, or divisions contemplated by this instrument; to allocate, distribute and divide different kinds or disproportionate shares of property or undivided interests in property among the beneficiaries or trusts, in cash or in kind, or both, without regard to the income tax basis of specific property allocated to any beneficiary or trust, even though shares may as a result be composed differently, and to determine the value of any property so allocated, divided or distributed.

(r) **Reliance.** To rely upon any notice, certificate, affidavit, or other document or evidence believed by the Trustee to be genuine and accurate, in making any payment or distribution. The Trustee shall incur no liability for a disbursement or distribution made in good faith and without actual notice or knowledge of a changed condition or status affecting any person's interest in the trust or any other matter.

Court Supervision. The Trustee shall not be required to qualify before or be appointed by any court; nor shall the Trustee be required to obtain the order or approval of any court in the exercise of any power or discretion.

Periodic Accounting. The Trustee shall make reports at least annually to those beneficiaries who may receive current distributions, such reports to reflect the property held in trust, the receipts, disbursements, and distributions made during the accounting period, and such other information as may be necessary to convey the condition of and changes to the trust estate.

Beneficiary Under Disability. Where a beneficiary is under the disability of minority or, in the Trustee's opinion, any other legal, physical or mental disability, a parent, custodian or guardian who, entirely in the Trustee's discretion, is acceptable to the Trustee may, in carrying out the provisions of this Trust Agreement, act and receive notice in the beneficiary's place, and sign any instrument for the beneficiary.

Spendthrift Trusts. All trusts created under this Trust Agreement are spendthrift trusts. No beneficiary may anticipate, by assignment or otherwise, a beneficial interest in the principal or income of the trusts created hereunder; nor may any beneficiary sell, transfer, encumber, or in any way charge an interest in trust income or principal prior to actually receiving it. Neither the income nor the principal of any trust established hereunder shall be subject to any execution, garnishment, attachment, bankruptcy, claims for alimony or support, other legal proceeding of any character, legal sequestration, levy or sale, or in any other event or manner be applicable or subject, voluntarily or involuntarily, to the payment of a beneficiary's debts. The Trustee shall make distributions to or for each beneficiary according to the terms hereof, notwithstanding any purported sale, assignment, hypothecation, transfer, attachment, or judicial process.

Limitation on Distributions.

(a) **Support Obligation.** Any other provision of this Trust Agreement notwithstanding, no distribution shall be made which discharges, in whole or in part, the Trustee's legal obligations, from time to time existing, to support, educate or otherwise provide for any of the trust beneficiaries. When determining these legal obligations, the existence of the trust estate and funds made available by it shall not be taken into consideration.

(b) **Distribution to Trustee/Beneficiary.** Notwithstanding anything to the contrary in this Trust Agreement, no Trustee shall have the authority to make discretionary distributions to that person as beneficiary, except to the extent the distributions are for the beneficiary's health, maintenance, support or education. If the Trustee is otherwise in this Trust Agreement authorized to make a distribution beyond that standard, the distributions shall be so limited.

Rule Against Perpetuities. Every trust created hereunder (or through the exercise of a power of appointment granted in this Trust Agreement) must vest not later than twenty-one (21) years after my death and descendants living at the time the trust created hereunder first becomes irrevocable. If a trust is not vested within that period, it will terminate as of the maximum vesting date. In the event of termination, the Trustee shall distribute each trust to its income beneficiaries determined at the time of distribution in the proportions to which they are entitled to receive income.

Out-of-State Properties. If the Trustee must act in a jurisdiction in which a person or entity serving as Trustee is unable or unwilling to act, the other or others serving as Trustee may act in that jurisdiction. If no Trustee is able or willing to act, the Trustee may appoint an ancillary trustee for that jurisdiction and may confer upon the ancillary trustee such rights, powers, discretions and duties, exercisable without court order, to act with respect to such matters as the Trustee deems proper. The ancillary trustee shall be responsible to the Trustee for any property it administers. The Trustee may pay the ancillary trustee reasonable compensation for services and may absolve the ancillary trustee from any requirement to furnish bond or other security.

ARTICLE VIII

AMENDMENT AND REVOCATION OF TRUST

I may amend, revoke or modify this Trust Agreement in whole or in part by an instrument signed and acknowledged by me and delivered to the Trustee. Amendment or modification of the Trust Agreement shall be effective immediately upon delivery of the instrument to the Trustee, except that changes affecting the Trustee's duties, liabilities, or compensation shall not be effective without the Trustee's written consent. On my death, this Trust Agreement may no longer be amended or modified, and the trust created hereunder shall become irrevocable.

ARTICLE IX

MISCELLANEOUS PROVISIONS

Applicable Law. The validity, construction, and administration of each trust created hereunder shall be governed by the laws of the State of _____.

Adoption. For purposes of this Trust Agreement, a person shall be regarded as having been legally adopted by another only if the adoption is by court proceedings, the finality of which is not being contested by the adopting person.

Survival. Any person must survive by thirty (30) days for a gift made in this Trust Agreement which directly or indirectly requires such person's survival of another to be effective.

Education. "Education" shall include preparatory, collegiate, postgraduate, professional and vocational education; specialized formal or informal training in music, the stage, handicrafts, the arts or sports or athletic endeavors, whether by private instruction or otherwise; and any other activity, including foreign or domestic travel, which tends to develop the talents and potential of the beneficiary, regardless of age. Education shall also include all tuition, board, lodging fees, books and equipment, travel expenses and other expenses incidental thereto.

Executor. "Executor" shall include personal representative, executrix, administrator and administratrix.

Health. "Health" shall include medical, dental, hospital and nursing care expenses, and other expenses of invalidism, and distributions for the "health" of a beneficiary may, in the discretion of the Trustee include any part or all of the costs of purchasing or maintaining hospital or medical insurance and disability income insurance coverage for such beneficiary and/or any person in whom such beneficiary has an insurable interest.

Binding Agreement. This agreement shall extend to and be binding upon the heirs, executors, administrators, successors and assigns of the parties.

Use of Words. As used in this instrument, the masculine, feminine, and neuter gender, and the singular or plural of any word includes the others unless the context indicates otherwise.

Unenforceable Provision. If any provision of this Trust Agreement is unenforceable, the remaining provisions shall be given effect, unless to do so would produce an unreasonable result.

Titles, Headings, and Captions. All titles, headings, and captions used in this Trust Agreement have been included for convenience only and should not be construed in interpreting this instrument.

IN WITNESS WHEREOF, I as Grantor and Trustee have hereunto set my hand, on the day and year first above written in multiple originals.

_____   _____

Witness   Grantor

_____   _____

Witness   Trustee

STATE OF _____ §

                                            §

COUNTY OF _____ §

BEFORE ME, the undersigned authority, on this day personally appeared _____, Grantor and Trustee, known to me to be the person whose name is subscribed to the foregoing instrument and acknowledged to me that he/she executed the same for the purposes and consideration therein expressed.

GIVEN UNDER MY HAND AND SEAL OF OFFICE this ____ day of _____, _____.

_____

Notary Public

My Commission Expires:

This page intentionally left blank.

_____ LIVING TRUST

THIS AGREEMENT OF TRUST is entered into at _____, State of _____, this _____ day of _____, _____, by and between _____, as Grantor and Trustee. This Trust, as from time to time amended, shall be known as the "_____ LIVING TRUST dated _____, _____."

ARTICLE I

My Spouse. My Spouse is: _____.

My Children. My Children are: _____

_____ .

ARTICLE II

FUNDING

Initial Funding. I hereby transfer to Trustee the sum of Ten Dollars ($10.00).

Additional Funding. From time to time the trust may be funded with additional property by me or by any other person in any manner. All property transferred, assigned, conveyed or delivered to the Trustee shall be held, administered and distributed by the Trustee in accordance with the terms of this Trust Agreement.

ARTICLE III

ADMINISTRATION OF TRUST DURING MY LIFETIME

Distributions of Income. While I am living, the Trustee shall distribute the trust's net income as directed in writing by me from time to time. In default of such direction, the Trustee shall pay to or expend on behalf of me all of the trust's net income from the Trust quarterly or more frequently.

Distributions of Principal. The Trustee shall pay to or expend for my benefit such part or all of the principal of the trust as I may request, from time to time. In default of such direction, the Trustee shall pay to or expend for my benefit so much of the principal of the trust as the Trustee, determines to be necessary or advisable for my health, maintenance and support.

Use of Residential Property. If any real property used by me for residential purposes (whether on a full-time or part-time basis, including recreational property) becomes part of the trust estate, I shall have the right to use and occupy such property without rental or other accounting to the trust estate.

Distributions to My Spouse and Children. The Trustee shall pay to or expend for the benefit of my spouse and minor Children so much of the principal of the trust as the Trustee, in his/her sole discretion, determines to be necessary for the education, health, maintenance and support of my spouse and Children. The Trustee shall make such discretionary distributions only after conferring with me. The trust distributions do not need to be equal.

ARTICLE IV

ADMINISTRATION OF TRUST UPON MY DEATH

Payment of Expenses, Claims and Taxes. Upon my death, the Trustee shall, upon the request of the Executor of my estate, pay such part or all of the expenses of the last illness, funeral, and burial, legally enforceable claims against me or my estate and estate administration expenses. The Trustee may also pay any estate, inheritance, or succession taxes, state, federal and foreign, or any other taxes together with interest and penalties thereon that are payable by reason of my death.

ARTICLE V

DISTRIBUTIONS OF TRUST TO MY SPOUSE AND CHILDREN

Tangible Personal Property. The Trustee shall distribute my tangible personal property in accordance with any written, signed and dated memorandum prepared by me. Any tangible personal property which is not disposed of by memorandum shall be distributed to my spouse or if my spouse is not alive in equal shares to my surviving Children.

Specific Bequest. The Trustee shall distribute the following property to the named individuals:

_____ to _____

_____ to _____

If any of the individuals named does not survive me, the gift to that person will lapse and the property will pass as provided below.

Distribution to My Spouse. If my spouse survives me, the Trustee shall distribute the remaining trust estate to my spouse outright or, if my spouse so chooses, to the Living Trust dated _____, _____, established by my spouse. If my spouse does not survive me, the Trustee shall distribute the trust estate as provided in the next paragraph.

Division of Trust Estate for My Children. The Trustee shall divide the remaining trust estate, including any additions to the Trust by reason of my death, into separate equal shares as follows: one share for each Child of mine who is then living, and one share for the then living descendants, collectively, of each deceased Child of mine with one or more descendants then living. The Trustee shall administer a share for each Child in a separate trust, and a share for the Descendants of each deceased Child, pursuant to the provisions of Article VI, following.

ARTICLE VI

TRUSTS FOR CHILDREN AND DESCENDANTS

Separate Trust for Child. Each trust for the benefit of a Child shall be administered and distributed upon the following terms:

(a) **Distributions to Child.** The Trustee shall distribute to the Child all of the trust's net income quarterly or more frequently and so much of the principal of the trust as the Trustee deems necessary to provide for the Child's health, maintenance, education and support.

When the Child attains age _____, the Trustee shall distribute to the Child _____ of the value of the then remaining trust estate.

When the Child attains age _____, the Trustee shall distribute to the Child the remaining trust estate.

(b) **Termination of Trust.** If not earlier terminated by distribution of the entire trust estate under the foregoing provisions, the trust shall terminate upon the death of the Child. The Trustee shall distribute the remaining trust estate to the Child's then living descendants, pursuant to the limitation described in subsection (c) hereof. If there are no descendants of the Child then living, the Trustee shall distribute the remaining trust estate to my then living descendants, per stirpes.

(c) **Distribution to Descendants of a Deceased Child.** Property which is to be distributed under this subsection to the descendants of a deceased Child shall be distributed, per stirpes, to those descendants living at the event causing the distribution hereunder.

Contingent Distribution. If my spouse, my Children and their descendants and all of my descendants are deceased, the trust estate then remaining shall be distributed, to the following individuals in the amounts specified:

_____ to_____

_____ to_____

ARTICLE VII

THE TRUSTEE

Successor Trustees. During my lifetime, if I cannot serve as Trustee, I will appoint a successor Trustee. If I do not appoint a successor trustee, or after my death, the successor trustee shall be my spouse, or if I am not married or my spouse is not able to serve, the successor trustee(s) shall be:_____. If the successor trustee fails or ceases to serve, _____ shall be successor trustee. If all successor trustees fail or cease to serve, a majority in number of the income beneficiaries of the trust at that time shall appoint a successor trustee.

Any appointment under this Section shall be by a signed, acknowledged instrument delivered to the successor trustee.

Removal of Trustee. During my life, I may remove a trustee at any time for any reason. After my death or if I am incapacitated and unable to remove the trustee, my spouse may remove the trustee. If my spouse is not alive or is unable to exercise this power, _____ _____ shall have the power to remove a trustee.

Resignation of Trustee. A Trustee may resign as to any one or more of the trusts created hereunder by giving written notice to all co-trustees then serving, if any, the current income beneficiaries, the successor trustee if identified in this Trust Agreement, and to those persons, if any, authorized in this Trust Agreement to appoint the successor trustee. Notice shall be delivered at least thirty (30) days prior to the date of resignation.

Trustee's Fees. The Trustee shall be entitled to reasonable fees commensurate with the Trustee's duties and responsibilities, taking into account the value and nature of the trust estate and the time and work involved. The Trustee shall be reimbursed for reasonable costs and expenses incurred in connection with fiduciary duties.

Bond. The Trustee shall not be required to furnish bond or other security.

Liability of Trustee. A Trustee shall only be liable for willful misconduct or gross negligence, and shall not be liable for breach of fiduciary duty by virtue of mistake or error in judgment.

Incapacity of Individual Trustee. This Section shall apply in the event a Trustee becomes unable to discharge the duties of Trustee by reason of accident, physical or mental illness or deterioration, or other cause, and does not resign. Upon certification by two medical doctors that each has examined the Trustee and has concluded that the Trustee is unable to discharge such duties, the Trustee shall cease to serve, as if the Trustee had resigned, effective the date of the certification.

ARTICLE VIII

TRUST ADMINISTRATION

Trustee Powers: Investment and Management of Trust Estate. Subject to any limitation stated elsewhere in this instrument, the Trustee shall have, with respect to each trust established hereunder, all of the powers granted to trustees by common law and by applicable statutes as amended from time to time. In addition, the trustee shall have the following powers:

(a) **Retain Property.** To retain any property received from any source, regardless of lack of diversification, risk, or nonproductivity.

(b) **Invest.** To invest the trust estate in any kind of property, without being limited by any law dealing with the character, risk, productivity, diversification, wasting nature of, or otherwise concerning, investments by trustees.

(c) **Sell.** By public offering or private negotiation, to sell, exchange, assign, transfer, or otherwise dispose of all or any real or personal trust property and give options for these purposes, for such price and on such terms, with such covenants of warranty and such security for deferred payment as the Trustee deems proper. To partition between the trust and any other owner, as the Trustee deems proper, any property in which the trust owns an undivided interest.

(d) **Lease.** To lease trust property for terms within or extending beyond the term of the trust, for any purpose.

(e) **Real Estate.** To operate, maintain, repair, rehabilitate, alter, erect, improve, or remove any improvements on real estate; to subdivide real estate; to grant easements, give consents, and enter into contracts relating to real estate or its use; and to release or dedicate any interest in real estate.

(f) **Borrow.** To borrow money for any purpose; to encumber or hypothecate trust property by mortgage, deed of trust, or otherwise; and to maintain, prepay, renew, or extend any indebtedness upon such terms as the Trustee deems appropriate.

(g) **Loans.** To lend money to any person or entity, including, but not limited to, a beneficiary hereunder, upon such terms and with such security as the Trustee deems advisable.

(h) **Securities.** To engage in all actions necessary to the effective administration of securities including, but not limited to, the authority to: vote securities in person or by proxy; engage in a voting trust or voting agreement; exercise any options, rights, or privileges pertaining to any trust property; and consent to or participate in mergers,

consolidations, sales of assets, recapitalizations, reorganizations, dissolutions, or other alterations of corporate structure affecting securities held by the Trustee.

(i) **Business Powers.** To enter into, carry on, and expand or acquire additional interests in (through the investment or loan of trust funds) any business activity, in sole proprietorship, general or limited partnership, joint venture, corporate or other form (and to convert from one form to another), including, but not limited to, any business interest which may be contributed to the trust, to employ agents and confer upon them the authority to manage and operate such business activity without liability for the acts of any such agents or for any loss, liability or indebtedness of such business, if the agents are selected and retained with reasonable care; and to sell, liquidate, or otherwise terminate any business interest, including, but not limited to, the fulfillment of any agreement for the disposition of any such business interest.

(j) **Litigation.** To commence or defend at the expense of the trust such litigation with respect to the trust estate as the Trustee deems advisable.

(k) **Claims.** To collect, pay, contest, compromise, settle, renew, or abandon any claims or demands of or against the trust estate, on whatever terms the Trustee deems advisable.

(l) **Additional Property.** To receive from any source additional property which is acceptable to the Trustee, and add it to the trust estate.

(m) **Agents.** To employ attorneys, auditors, brokers, investment advisors, depositaries, and agents with or without discretionary powers, to employ a trust company or bank with trust powers as agent for the purpose of performing any delegable duties of the administration, and to pay all expenses and fees so incurred.

(n) **Nominee.** To hold securities and other property in bearer form or in the name of a Trustee or nominee with or without disclosure of any fiduciary relationship.

(o) **Miscellaneous Powers.** Generally, to do and perform any and all acts, things, or deeds which an individual could do with respect to property and which, in the judgment of the Trustee, may be necessary or proper for the investment, management, protection and promotion of the property of the trust estate.

(p) **Tax Elections.** Unless otherwise expressly directed hereunder, to exercise any tax option, allocation or election permitted by law as the Trustee determines in the Trustee's sole discretion.

(q) **Division and Distribution.** To make all allocations, distributions, or divisions contemplated by this instrument; to allocate, distribute and divide different kinds or disproportionate shares of property or undivided interests in property among the beneficiaries or trusts, in cash or in kind, or both, without regard to the income tax basis of specific property allocated to any beneficiary or trust, even though shares may as a result be composed differently, and to determine the value of any property so allocated, divided or distributed.

(r) **Reliance.** To rely upon any notice, certificate, affidavit, or other document or evidence believed by the Trustee to be genuine and accurate, in making any payment or distribution. The Trustee shall incur no liability for a disbursement or distribution made in good faith and without actual notice or knowledge of a changed condition or status affecting any person's interest in the trust or any other matter.

Court Supervision. The Trustee shall not be required to qualify before or be appointed by any court; nor shall the Trustee be required to obtain the order or approval of any court in the exercise of any power or discretion.

Periodic Accounting. The Trustee shall make reports at least annually to those beneficiaries who may receive current distributions, such reports to reflect the property held in trust, the receipts, disbursements, and distributions made during the accounting period, and such other information as may be necessary to convey the condition of and changes to the trust estate.

Beneficiary Under Disability. Where a beneficiary is under the disability of minority or, in the Trustee's opinion, any other legal, physical or mental disability, a parent, custodian or guardian who, entirely in the Trustee's discretion, is acceptable to the Trustee may, in carrying out the provisions of this Trust Agreement, act and receive notice in the beneficiary's place, and sign any instrument for the beneficiary.

Spendthrift Trusts. All trusts created under this Trust Agreement are spendthrift trusts. No beneficiary may anticipate, by assignment or otherwise, a beneficial interest in the principal or income of the trusts created hereunder; nor may any beneficiary sell, transfer, encumber, or in any way charge an interest in trust income or principal prior to actually receiving it. Neither the income nor the principal of any trust established hereunder shall be subject to any execution, garnishment, attachment, bankruptcy, claims for alimony or support, other legal proceeding of any character, legal sequestration, levy or sale, or in any other event or manner be applicable or subject, voluntarily or involuntarily, to the payment of a beneficiary's debts. The Trustee shall make distributions to or for each beneficiary according to the terms hereof, notwithstanding any purported sale, assignment, hypothecation, transfer, attachment, or judicial process.

Limitation on Distributions.

(a) **Support Obligation.** Any other provision of this Trust Agreement notwithstanding, no distribution shall be made which discharges, in whole or in part, the Trustee's legal obligations, from time to time existing, to support, educate or otherwise provide for any of the trust beneficiaries. When determining these legal obligations, the existence of the trust estate and funds made available by it shall not be taken into consideration.

(b) **Distribution to Trustee/Beneficiary.** Notwithstanding anything to the contrary in this Trust Agreement, no Trustee shall have the authority to make discretionary distributions to that person as beneficiary, except to the extent the distributions are for the beneficiary's health, maintenance, support or education. If the Trustee is otherwise in this Trust Agreement authorized to make a distribution beyond that standard, the distributions shall be so limited.

Rule Against Perpetuities. Every trust created hereunder (or through the exercise of a power of appointment granted in this Trust Agreement) must vest not later than twenty-one (21) years after my death and descendants living at the time the trust created hereunder first becomes irrevocable. If a trust is not vested within that period, it will terminate as of the maximum vesting date. In the event of termination, the Trustee shall distribute each trust to its income beneficiaries determined at the time of distribution in the proportions to which they are entitled to receive income.

Out-of-State Properties. If the Trustee must act in a jurisdiction in which a person or entity serving as Trustee is unable or unwilling to act, the other or others serving as Trustee may act in that jurisdiction. If no Trustee is able or willing to act, the Trustee may appoint an ancillary trustee for that jurisdiction and may confer upon the ancillary trustee such rights, powers, discretions and duties, exercisable without court order, to act with respect to such matters as the Trustee deems proper. The ancillary trustee shall be responsible to the Trustee for any property it administers. The Trustee may pay the ancillary trustee reasonable compensation for services and may absolve the ancillary trustee from any requirement to furnish bond or other security.

ARTICLE IX

AMENDMENT AND REVOCATION OF TRUST

I may amend, revoke or modify this Trust Agreement in whole or in part by an instrument signed and acknowledged by me and delivered to the Trustee. Amendment or modification of the Trust Agreement shall be effective immediately upon delivery of the instrument to the Trustee, except that changes affecting the Trustee's duties, liabilities, or compensation shall not be effective without the Trustee's written consent. On my death, this Trust Agreement may no longer be amended or modified, and the trust created hereunder shall become irrevocable.

ARTICLE X

MISCELLANEOUS PROVISIONS

Applicable Law. The validity, construction, and administration of each trust created hereunder shall be governed by the laws of the State of _____.

Adoption. For purposes of this Trust Agreement, a person shall be regarded as having been legally adopted by another only if the adoption is by court proceedings, the finality of which is not being contested by the adopting person.

Survival. Any person must survive by thirty (30) days for a gift made in this Trust Agreement which directly or indirectly requires such person's survival of another to be effective.

Education. "Education" shall include preparatory, collegiate, postgraduate, professional and vocational education; specialized formal or informal training in music, the stage, handicrafts, the arts or sports or athletic endeavors, whether by private instruction or otherwise; and any other activity, including foreign or domestic travel, which tends to develop the talents and potential of the beneficiary, regardless of age. Education shall also include all tuition, board, lodging fees, books and equipment, travel expenses and other expenses incidental thereto.

Executor. "Executor" shall include personal representative, executrix, administrator and administratrix.

Health. "Health" shall include medical, dental, hospital and nursing care expenses, and other expenses of invalidism, and distributions for the "health" of a beneficiary may, in the discretion of the Trustee include any part or all of the costs of purchasing or maintaining hospital or medical insurance and disability income insurance coverage for such beneficiary and/or any person in whom such beneficiary has an insurable interest.

Binding Agreement. This agreement shall extend to and be binding upon the heirs, executors, administrators, successors and assigns of the parties.

Use of Words. As used in this instrument, the masculine, feminine, and neuter gender, and the singular or plural of any word includes the others unless the context indicates otherwise.

Unenforceable Provision. If any provision of this Trust Agreement is unenforceable, the remaining provisions shall be given effect, unless to do so would produce an unreasonable result.

Titles, Headings, and Captions. All titles, headings, and captions used in this Trust Agreement have been included for convenience only and should not be construed in interpreting this instrument.

IN WITNESS WHEREOF, I as Grantor and Trustee have hereunto set my hand, on the day and year first above written in multiple originals.

_____   _____
Witness   Grantor

_____   _____
Witness   Trustee

STATE OF _____ §
                                 §
COUNTY OF _____ §

BEFORE ME, the undersigned authority, on this day personally appeared _____, Grantor and Trustee, known to me to be the person whose name is subscribed to the foregoing instrument and acknowledged to me that he/she executed the same for the purposes and consideration therein expressed.

GIVEN UNDER MY HAND AND SEAL OF OFFICE this _____ day of _____, _____.

                              _____
                              Notary Public
                              My Commission Expires:

_____ LIVING TRUST

THIS AGREEMENT OF TRUST is entered into at _____, State of _____, this _____ day of _____, _____, by and between _____, as Grantor and Trustee. This Trust, as from time to time amended, shall be known as the "_____ LIVING TRUST dated _____, _____."

ARTICLE I

My Children. My Children are: _____

_____ .

ARTICLE II

FUNDING

Initial Funding. I hereby transfer to Trustee the sum of Ten Dollars ($10.00).

Additional Funding. From time to time the trust may be funded with additional property by me or by any other person in any manner. All property transferred, assigned, conveyed or delivered to the Trustee shall be held, administered and distributed by the Trustee in accordance with the terms of this Trust Agreement.

ARTICLE III

ADMINISTRATION OF TRUST DURING MY LIFETIME

Distributions of Income. While I am living, the Trustee shall distribute the trust's net income as directed in writing by me from time to time. In default of such direction, the Trustee shall pay to or expend on behalf of me all of the trust's net income from the Trust quarterly or more frequently.

Distributions of Principal. The Trustee shall pay to or expend for my benefit such part or all of the principal of the trust as I may request, from time to time. In default of such direction, the Trustee shall pay to or expend for my benefit so much of the principal of the trust as the Trustee, determines to be necessary or advisable for my health, maintenance and support.

Use of Residential Property. If any real property used by me for residential purposes (whether on a full-time or part-time basis, including recreational property) becomes part of the trust estate, I shall have the right to use and occupy such property without rental or other accounting to the trust estate.

Liability of Trustee. A Trustee shall only be liable for willful misconduct or gross negligence, and shall not be liable for breach of fiduciary duty by virtue of mistake or error in judgment.

Incapacity of Individual Trustee. This Section shall apply in the event a Trustee becomes unable to discharge the duties of Trustee by reason of accident, physical or mental illness or deterioration, or other cause, and does not resign. Upon certification by two medical doctors that each has examined the Trustee and has concluded that the Trustee is unable to discharge such duties, the Trustee shall cease to serve, as if the Trustee had resigned, effective the date of the certification.

ARTICLE VII

TRUST ADMINISTRATION

Trustee Powers: Investment and Management of Trust Estate. Subject to any limitation stated elsewhere in this instrument, the Trustee shall have, with respect to each trust established hereunder, all of the powers granted to trustees by common law and by applicable statutes as amended from time to time. In addition, the trustee shall have the following powers:

(a) **Retain Property.** To retain any property received from any source, regardless of lack of diversification, risk, or nonproductivity.

(b) **Invest.** To invest the trust estate in any kind of property, without being limited by any law dealing with the character, risk, productivity, diversification, wasting nature of, or otherwise concerning, investments by trustees.

(c) **Sell.** By public offering or private negotiation, to sell, exchange, assign, transfer, or otherwise dispose of all or any real or personal trust property and give options for these purposes, for such price and on such terms, with such covenants of warranty and such security for deferred payment as the Trustee deems proper. To partition between the trust and any other owner, as the Trustee deems proper, any property in which the trust owns an undivided interest.

(d) **Lease.** To lease trust property for terms within or extending beyond the term of the trust, for any purpose.

(e) **Real Estate.** To operate, maintain, repair, rehabilitate, alter, erect, improve, or remove any improvements on real estate; to subdivide real estate; to grant easements, give consents, and enter into contracts relating to real estate or its use; and to release or dedicate any interest in real estate.

(f) **Borrow.** To borrow money for any purpose; to encumber or hypothecate trust property by mortgage, deed of trust, or otherwise; and to maintain, prepay, renew, or extend any indebtedness upon such terms as the Trustee deems appropriate.

(g) **Loans.** To lend money to any person or entity, including, but not limited to, a beneficiary hereunder, upon such terms and with such security as the Trustee deems advisable.

(h) **Securities.** To engage in all actions necessary to the effective administration of securities including, but not limited to, the authority to: vote securities in person or by proxy; engage in a voting trust or voting agreement; exercise any options, rights, or privileges pertaining to any trust property; and consent to or participate in mergers, consolidations, sales of assets, recapitalizations, reorganizations, dissolutions, or other alterations of corporate structure affecting securities held by the Trustee.

(i) **Business Powers.** To enter into, carry on, and expand or acquire additional interests in (through the investment or loan of trust funds) any business activity, in sole proprietorship, general or limited partnership, joint venture, corporate or other form (and to convert from one form to another), including, but not limited to, any business interest which may be contributed to the trust, to employ agents and confer upon them the authority to manage and operate such business activity without liability for the acts of any such agents or for any loss, liability or indebtedness of such business, if the agents are selected and retained with reasonable care; and to sell, liquidate, or otherwise terminate any business interest, including, but not limited to, the fulfillment of any agreement for the disposition of any such business interest.

(j) **Litigation.** To commence or defend at the expense of the trust such litigation with respect to the trust estate as the Trustee deems advisable.

(k) **Claims.** To collect, pay, contest, compromise, settle, renew, or abandon any claims or demands of or against the trust estate, on whatever terms the Trustee deems advisable.

(l) **Additional Property.** To receive from any source additional property which is acceptable to the Trustee, and add it to the trust estate.

(m) **Agents.** To employ attorneys, auditors, brokers, investment advisors, depositaries, and agents with or without discretionary powers, to employ a trust company or bank with trust powers as agent for the purpose of performing any delegable duties of the administration, and to pay all expenses and fees so incurred.

(n) **Nominee.** To hold securities and other property in bearer form or in the name of a Trustee or nominee with or without disclosure of any fiduciary relationship.

(o) **Miscellaneous Powers.** Generally, to do and perform any and all acts, things, or deeds which an individual could do with respect to property and which, in the judgment of the Trustee, may be necessary or proper for the investment, management, protection and promotion of the property of the trust estate.

(p) **Tax Elections.** Unless otherwise expressly directed hereunder, to exercise any tax option, allocation or election permitted by law as the Trustee determines in the Trustee's sole discretion.

(q) **Division and Distribution.** To make all allocations, distributions, or divisions contemplated by this instrument; to allocate, distribute and divide different kinds or disproportionate shares of property or undivided interests in property among the beneficiaries or trusts, in cash or in kind, or both, without regard to the income tax basis of specific property allocated to any beneficiary or trust, even though shares may as a result be composed differently, and to determine the value of any property so allocated, divided or distributed.

(r) **Reliance.** To rely upon any notice, certificate, affidavit, or other document or evidence believed by the Trustee to be genuine and accurate, in making any payment or distribution. The Trustee shall incur no liability for a disbursement or distribution made in good faith and without actual notice or knowledge of a changed condition or status affecting any person's interest in the trust or any other matter.

Court Supervision. The Trustee shall not be required to qualify before or be appointed by any court; nor shall the Trustee be required to obtain the order or approval of any court in the exercise of any power or discretion.

Periodic Accounting. The Trustee shall make reports at least annually to those beneficiaries who may receive current distributions, such reports to reflect the property held in trust, the receipts, disbursements, and distributions made during the accounting period, and such other information as may be necessary to convey the condition of and changes to the trust estate.

Beneficiary Under Disability. Where a beneficiary is under the disability of minority or, in the Trustee's opinion, any other legal, physical or mental disability, a parent, custodian or guardian who, entirely in the Trustee's discretion, is acceptable to the Trustee may, in carrying out the provisions of this Trust Agreement, act and receive notice in the beneficiary's place, and sign any instrument for the beneficiary.

Spendthrift Trusts. All trusts created under this Trust Agreement are spendthrift trusts. No beneficiary may anticipate, by assignment or otherwise, a beneficial interest in the principal or income of the trusts created hereunder; nor may any beneficiary sell, transfer, encumber, or in any way charge an interest in trust income or principal prior to actually receiving it. Neither the income nor the principal of any trust established hereunder shall be subject to any execution, garnishment, attachment, bankruptcy, claims for alimony or support, other legal proceeding of any character, legal sequestration, levy or sale, or in any other event or manner be applicable or subject, voluntarily or involuntarily, to the payment of a beneficiary's debts. The Trustee shall make distributions to or for each beneficiary according to the terms hereof, notwithstanding any purported sale, assignment, hypothecation, transfer, attachment, or judicial process.

Limitation on Distributions.

(a) **Support Obligation.** Any other provision of this Trust Agreement notwithstanding, no distribution shall be made which discharges, in whole or in part, the Trustee's legal obligations, from time to time existing, to support, educate or otherwise provide for any of the trust beneficiaries. When determining these legal obligations, the existence of the trust estate and funds made available by it shall not be taken into consideration.

(b) **Distribution to Trustee/Beneficiary.** Notwithstanding anything to the contrary in this Trust Agreement, no Trustee shall have the authority to make discretionary distributions to that person as beneficiary, except to the extent the distributions are for the beneficiary's health, maintenance, support or education. If the Trustee is otherwise in this Trust Agreement authorized to make a distribution beyond that standard, the distributions shall be so limited.

Rule Against Perpetuities. Every trust created hereunder (or through the exercise of a power of appointment granted in this Trust Agreement) must vest not later than twenty-one (21) years after my death and descendants living at the time the trust created hereunder first becomes irrevocable. If a trust is not vested within that period, it will terminate as of the maximum vesting date. In the event of termination, the Trustee shall distribute each trust to its income beneficiaries determined at the time of distribution in the proportions to which they are entitled to receive income.

Out-of-State Properties. If the Trustee must act in a jurisdiction in which a person or entity serving as Trustee is unable or unwilling to act, the other or others serving as Trustee may act in that jurisdiction. If no Trustee is able or willing to act, the Trustee may appoint an ancillary trustee for that jurisdiction and may confer upon the ancillary trustee such rights, powers, discretions and duties, exercisable without court order, to act with respect to such matters as the Trustee deems proper. The ancillary trustee shall be responsible to the Trustee for any property it administers. The Trustee may pay the ancillary trustee reasonable compensation for services and may absolve the ancillary trustee from any requirement to furnish bond or other security.

ARTICLE VIII

AMENDMENT AND REVOCATION OF TRUST

I may amend, revoke or modify this Trust Agreement in whole or in part by an instrument signed and acknowledged by me and delivered to the Trustee. Amendment or modification of the Trust Agreement shall be effective immediately upon delivery of the instrument to the Trustee, except that changes affecting the Trustee's duties, liabilities, or compensation shall not be effective without the Trustee's written consent. On my death, this Trust Agreement may no longer be amended or modified, and the trust created hereunder shall become irrevocable.

ARTICLE IX

MISCELLANEOUS PROVISIONS

Applicable Law. The validity, construction, and administration of each trust created hereunder shall be governed by the laws of the State of _____.

Adoption. For purposes of this Trust Agreement, a person shall be regarded as having been legally adopted by another only if the adoption is by court proceedings, the finality of which is not being contested by the adopting person.

Survival. Any person must survive by thirty (30) days for a gift made in this Trust Agreement which directly or indirectly requires such person's survival of another to be effective.

Education. "Education" shall include preparatory, collegiate, postgraduate, professional and vocational education; specialized formal or informal training in music, the stage, handicrafts, the arts or sports or athletic endeavors, whether by private instruction or otherwise; and any other activity, including foreign or domestic travel, which tends to develop the talents and potential of the beneficiary, regardless of age. Education shall also include all tuition, board, lodging fees, books and equipment, travel expenses and other expenses incidental thereto.

Executor. "Executor" shall include personal representative, executrix, administrator and administratrix.

Health. "Health" shall include medical, dental, hospital and nursing care expenses, and other expenses of invalidism, and distributions for the "health" of a beneficiary may, in the discretion of the Trustee include any part or all of the costs of purchasing or maintaining hospital or medical insurance and disability income insurance coverage for such beneficiary and/or any person in whom such beneficiary has an insurable interest.

Binding Agreement. This agreement shall extend to and be binding upon the heirs, executors, administrators, successors and assigns of the parties.

Use of Words. As used in this instrument, the masculine, feminine, and neuter gender, and the singular or plural of any word includes the others unless the context indicates otherwise.

Unenforceable Provision. If any provision of this Trust Agreement is unenforceable, the remaining provisions shall be given effect, unless to do so would produce an unreasonable result.

Titles, Headings, and Captions. All titles, headings, and captions used in this Trust Agreement have been included for convenience only and should not be construed in interpreting this instrument.

IN WITNESS WHEREOF, I as Grantor and Trustee have hereunto set my hand, on the day and year first above written in multiple originals.

_____   _____
Witness   Grantor

_____   _____
Witness   Trustee

STATE OF _____ §
                                                      §
COUNTY OF _____ §

    BEFORE ME, the undersigned authority, on this day personally appeared _____, Grantor and Trustee, known to me to be the person whose name is subscribed to the foregoing instrument and acknowledged to me that he/she executed the same for the purposes and consideration therein expressed.

    GIVEN UNDER MY HAND AND SEAL OF OFFICE this ____ day of _____, _____.

                        _____
                        Notary Public
                        My Commission Expires:

This page intentionally left blank.

_____ LIVING TRUST

THIS AGREEMENT OF TRUST is entered into at _____, State of _____, this _____ day of _____, _____, by and between _____, as Grantor and Trustee. This Trust, as from time to time amended, shall be known as the "_____ LIVING TRUST dated _____, _____."

ARTICLE I

My Children. My Children are: _____

_____.

ARTICLE II

FUNDING

Initial Funding. I hereby transfer to Trustee the sum of Ten Dollars ($10.00).

Additional Funding. From time to time the trust may be funded with additional property by me or by any other person in any manner. All property transferred, assigned, conveyed or delivered to the Trustee shall be held, administered and distributed by the Trustee in accordance with the terms of this Trust Agreement.

ARTICLE III

ADMINISTRATION OF TRUST DURING MY LIFETIME

Distributions of Income. While I am living, the Trustee shall distribute the trust's net income as directed in writing by me from time to time. In default of such direction, the Trustee shall pay to or expend on behalf of me all of the trust's net income from the Trust quarterly or more frequently.

Distributions of Principal. The Trustee shall pay to or expend for my benefit such part or all of the principal of the trust as I may request, from time to time. In default of such direction, the Trustee shall pay to or expend for my benefit so much of the principal of the trust as the Trustee, determines to be necessary or advisable for my health, maintenance and support.

Use of Residential Property. If any real property used by me for residential purposes (whether on a full-time or part-time basis, including recreational property) becomes part of the trust estate, I shall have the right to use and occupy such property without rental or other accounting to the trust estate.

Distributions to My Children. The Trustee shall pay to or expend for the benefit of my minor Children so much of the principal of the trust as the Trustee, in his/her sole discretion, determines to be necessary for the education, health, maintenance and support of my Children. The Trustee shall make such discretionary distributions only after conferring with me. The trust distributions do not need to be equal.

ARTICLE IV

ADMINISTRATION OF TRUST UPON MY DEATH

Payment of Expenses, Claims and Taxes. Upon my death, the Trustee shall, upon the request of the Executor of my estate, pay such part or all of the expenses of the last illness, funeral, and burial, legally enforceable claims against me or my estate and estate administration expenses. The Trustee may also pay any estate, inheritance, or succession taxes, state, federal and foreign, or any other taxes together with interest and penalties thereon that are payable by reason of my death.

ARTICLE V

DISTRIBUTION OF TRUST TO MY CHILDREN

Tangible Personal Property. The Trustee shall distribute my tangible personal property in accordance with any written, signed and dated memorandum prepared by me. Any tangible personal property which is not disposed of by memorandum shall be distributed in equal shares to my surviving Children.

Specific Bequest. The Trustee shall distribute the following property to the named individuals:

_____ to _____

_____ to _____

If any of the individuals named does not survive me, the gift to that person will lapse and the property will pass as provided below.

Division of Trust Estate for My Children. The Trustee shall divide the remaining trust estate, including any additions to the Trust by reason of my death, into separate equal shares as follows: one share for each Child of mine who is then living, and one share for the then living descendants, collectively, of each deceased Child of mine with one or more descendants then living. The Trustee shall administer a share for each Child in a separate trust, and a share for the Descendants of each deceased Child, pursuant to the provisions of Article VI, following.

ARTICLE VI

TRUSTS FOR CHILDREN AND DESCENDANTS

Separate Trust for Child. Each trust for the benefit of a Child shall be administered and distributed upon the following terms:

(a) **Distributions to Child.** The Trustee shall distribute to the Child all of the trust's net income quarterly or more frequently and so much of the principal of the trust as the Trustee deems necessary to provide for the Child's health, maintenance, education and support.

When the Child attains age _____, the Trustee shall distribute to the Child _____ of the value of the then remaining trust estate.

When the Child attains age _____, the Trustee shall distribute to the Child the remaining trust estate.

(b) **Termination of Trust.** If not earlier terminated by distribution of the entire trust estate under the foregoing provisions, the trust shall terminate upon the death of the Child. The Trustee shall distribute the remaining trust estate to the Child's then living descendants, pursuant to the limitation described in subsection (c) hereof. If there are no descendants of the Child then living, the Trustee shall distribute the remaining trust estate to my then living descendants, per stirpes.

(c) **Distribution to Descendants of a Deceased Child.** Property which is to be distributed under this subsection to the descendants of a deceased Child shall be distributed, per stirpes, to those descendants living at the event causing the distribution hereunder.

Contingent Distribution. If my spouse, my Children and their descendants and all of my descendants are deceased, the trust estate then remaining shall be distributed, to the following individuals in the amounts specified:

_____ to_____

_____ to_____

ARTICLE VII

THE TRUSTEE

Successor Trustees. During my lifetime, if I cannot serve as Trustee, I will appoint a successor Trustee. If I do not appoint a successor trustee, or after my death, the successor trustee shall be _____. If

_____ is not able to serve, the successor trustee(s) shall be _____.
If the successor trustee fails or ceases to serve, _____
shall be successor trustee. If all successor trustees fail or cease to serve, a majority in number of the income beneficiaries of the trust at that time shall appoint a successor trustee. Any appointment under this section shall be by a signed, acknowledged instrument delivered to the successor trustee.

Removal of Trustee. During my life, I may remove a trustee at any time for any reason. After my death or if I am incapacitated and unable to remove the trustee, _____ _____ may remove the trustee. If _____is not alive or is unable to exercise this power, _____ shall have the power to remove a trustee.

Resignation of Trustee. A Trustee may resign as to any one or more of the trusts created hereunder by giving written notice to all co-trustees then serving, if any, the current income beneficiaries, the successor trustee if identified in this Trust Agreement, and to those persons, if any, authorized in this Trust Agreement to appoint the successor trustee. Notice shall be delivered at least thirty (30) days prior to the date of resignation.

Trustee's Fees. The Trustee shall be entitled to reasonable fees commensurate with the Trustee's duties and responsibilities, taking into account the value and nature of the trust estate and the time and work involved. The Trustee shall be reimbursed for reasonable costs and expenses incurred in connection with fiduciary duties.

Bond. The Trustee shall not be required to furnish bond or other security.

Liability of Trustee. A Trustee shall only be liable for willful misconduct or gross negligence, and shall not be liable for breach of fiduciary duty by virtue of mistake or error in judgment.

Incapacity of Individual Trustee. This Section shall apply in the event a Trustee becomes unable to discharge the duties of Trustee by reason of accident, physical or mental illness or deterioration, or other cause, and does not resign. Upon certification by two medical doctors that each has examined the Trustee and has concluded that the Trustee is unable to discharge such duties, the Trustee shall cease to serve, as if the Trustee had resigned, effective the date of the certification.

ARTICLE VIII

TRUST ADMINISTRATION

Trustee Powers: Investment and Management of Trust Estate. Subject to any limitation stated elsewhere in this instrument, the Trustee shall have, with respect to each trust established hereunder, all of the powers granted to trustees by common law and by applicable statutes as amended from time to time. In addition, the trustee shall have the following powers:

(a) **Retain Property.** To retain any property received from any source, regardless of lack of diversification, risk, or nonproductivity.

(b) **Invest.** To invest the trust estate in any kind of property, without being limited by any law dealing with the character, risk, productivity, diversification, wasting nature of, or otherwise concerning, investments by trustees.

(c) **Sell.** By public offering or private negotiation, to sell, exchange, assign, transfer, or otherwise dispose of all or any real or personal trust property and give options for these purposes, for such price and on such terms, with such covenants of warranty and such security for deferred payment as the Trustee deems proper. To partition between the trust and any other owner, as the Trustee deems proper, any property in which the trust owns an undivided interest.

(d) **Lease.** To lease trust property for terms within or extending beyond the term of the trust, for any purpose.

(e) **Real Estate.** To operate, maintain, repair, rehabilitate, alter, erect, improve, or remove any improvements on real estate; to subdivide real estate; to grant easements, give consents, and enter into contracts relating to real estate or its use; and to release or dedicate any interest in real estate.

(f) **Borrow.** To borrow money for any purpose; to encumber or hypothecate trust property by mortgage, deed of trust, or otherwise; and to maintain, prepay, renew, or extend any indebtedness upon such terms as the Trustee deems appropriate.

(g) **Loans.** To lend money to any person or entity, including, but not limited to, a beneficiary hereunder, upon such terms and with such security as the Trustee deems advisable.

(h) **Securities.** To engage in all actions necessary to the effective administration of securities including, but not limited to, the authority to: vote securities in person or by proxy; engage in a voting trust or voting agreement; exercise any options, rights, or privileges pertaining to any trust property; and consent to or participate in mergers,

consolidations, sales of assets, recapitalizations, reorganizations, dissolutions, or other alterations of corporate structure affecting securities held by the Trustee.

(i) **Business Powers.** To enter into, carry on, and expand or acquire additional interests in (through the investment or loan of trust funds) any business activity, in sole proprietorship, general or limited partnership, joint venture, corporate or other form (and to convert from one form to another), including, but not limited to, any business interest which may be contributed to the trust, to employ agents and confer upon them the authority to manage and operate such business activity without liability for the acts of any such agents or for any loss, liability or indebtedness of such business, if the agents are selected and retained with reasonable care; and to sell, liquidate, or otherwise terminate any business interest, including, but not limited to, the fulfillment of any agreement for the disposition of any such business interest.

(j) **Litigation.** To commence or defend at the expense of the trust such litigation with respect to the trust estate as the Trustee deems advisable.

(k) **Claims.** To collect, pay, contest, compromise, settle, renew, or abandon any claims or demands of or against the trust estate, on whatever terms the Trustee deems advisable.

(l) **Additional Property.** To receive from any source additional property which is acceptable to the Trustee, and add it to the trust estate.

(m) **Agents.** To employ attorneys, auditors, brokers, investment advisors, depositaries, and agents with or without discretionary powers, to employ a trust company or bank with trust powers as agent for the purpose of performing any delegable duties of the administration, and to pay all expenses and fees so incurred.

(n) **Nominee.** To hold securities and other property in bearer form or in the name of a Trustee or nominee with or without disclosure of any fiduciary relationship.

(o) **Miscellaneous Powers.** Generally, to do and perform any and all acts, things, or deeds which an individual could do with respect to property and which, in the judgment of the Trustee, may be necessary or proper for the investment, management, protection and promotion of the property of the trust estate.

(p) **Tax Elections.** Unless otherwise expressly directed hereunder, to exercise any tax option, allocation or election permitted by law as the Trustee determines in the Trustee's sole discretion.

(q) **Division and Distribution.** To make all allocations, distributions, or divisions contemplated by this instrument; to allocate, distribute and divide different kinds or disproportionate shares of property or undivided interests in property among the beneficiaries or trusts, in cash or in kind, or both, without regard to the income tax basis of specific property allocated to any beneficiary or trust, even though shares may as a result be composed differently, and to determine the value of any property so allocated, divided or distributed.

(r) **Reliance.** To rely upon any notice, certificate, affidavit, or other document or evidence believed by the Trustee to be genuine and accurate, in making any payment or distribution. The Trustee shall incur no liability for a disbursement or distribution made in good faith and without actual notice or knowledge of a changed condition or status affecting any person's interest in the trust or any other matter.

Court Supervision. The Trustee shall not be required to qualify before or be appointed by any court; nor shall the Trustee be required to obtain the order or approval of any court in the exercise of any power or discretion.

Periodic Accounting. The Trustee shall make reports at least annually to those beneficiaries who may receive current distributions, such reports to reflect the property held in trust, the receipts, disbursements, and distributions made during the accounting period, and such other information as may be necessary to convey the condition of and changes to the trust estate.

Beneficiary Under Disability. Where a beneficiary is under the disability of minority or, in the Trustee's opinion, any other legal, physical or mental disability, a parent, custodian or guardian who, entirely in the Trustee's discretion, is acceptable to the Trustee may, in carrying out the provisions of this Trust Agreement, act and receive notice in the beneficiary's place, and sign any instrument for the beneficiary.

Spendthrift Trusts. All trusts created under this Trust Agreement are spendthrift trusts. No beneficiary may anticipate, by assignment or otherwise, a beneficial interest in the principal or income of the trusts created hereunder; nor may any beneficiary sell, transfer, encumber, or in any way charge an interest in trust income or principal prior to actually receiving it. Neither the income nor the principal of any trust established hereunder shall be subject to any execution, garnishment, attachment, bankruptcy, claims for alimony or support, other legal proceeding of any character, legal sequestration, levy or sale, or in any other event or manner be applicable or subject, voluntarily or involuntarily, to the payment of a beneficiary's debts. The Trustee shall make distributions to or for each beneficiary according to the terms hereof, notwithstanding any purported sale, assignment, hypothecation, transfer, attachment, or judicial process.

Limitation on Distributions.

(a) **Support Obligation.** Any other provision of this Trust Agreement notwithstanding, no distribution shall be made which discharges, in whole or in part, the Trustee's legal obligations, from time to time existing, to support, educate or otherwise provide for any of the trust beneficiaries. When determining these legal obligations, the existence of the trust estate and funds made available by it shall not be taken into consideration.

(b) **Distribution to Trustee/Beneficiary.** Notwithstanding anything to the contrary in this Trust Agreement, no Trustee shall have the authority to make discretionary distributions to that person as beneficiary, except to the extent the distributions are for the beneficiary's health, maintenance, support or education. If the Trustee is otherwise in this Trust Agreement authorized to make a distribution beyond that standard, the distributions shall be so limited.

Rule Against Perpetuities. Every trust created hereunder (or through the exercise of a power of appointment granted in this Trust Agreement) must vest not later than twenty-one (21) years after my death and descendants living at the time the trust created hereunder first becomes irrevocable. If a trust is not vested within that period, it will terminate as of the maximum vesting date. In the event of termination, the Trustee shall distribute each trust to its income beneficiaries determined at the time of distribution in the proportions to which they are entitled to receive income.

Out-of-State Properties. If the Trustee must act in a jurisdiction in which a person or entity serving as Trustee is unable or unwilling to act, the other or others serving as Trustee may act in that jurisdiction. If no Trustee is able or willing to act, the Trustee may appoint an ancillary trustee for that jurisdiction and may confer upon the ancillary trustee such rights, powers, discretions and duties, exercisable without court order, to act with respect to such matters as the Trustee deems proper. The ancillary trustee shall be responsible to the Trustee for any property it administers. The Trustee may pay the ancillary trustee reasonable compensation for services and may absolve the ancillary trustee from any requirement to furnish bond or other security.

ARTICLE IX

AMENDMENT AND REVOCATION OF TRUST

I may amend, revoke or modify this Trust Agreement in whole or in part by an instrument signed and acknowledged by me and delivered to the Trustee. Amendment or modification of the Trust Agreement shall be effective immediately upon delivery of the instrument to the Trustee, except that changes affecting the Trustee's duties, liabilities, or compensation shall not be effective without the Trustee's written consent. On my death, this Trust Agreement may no longer be amended or modified, and the trust created hereunder shall become irrevocable.

ARTICLE X

MISCELLANEOUS PROVISIONS

Applicable Law. The validity, construction, and administration of each trust created hereunder shall be governed by the laws of the State of _____.

Adoption. For purposes of this Trust Agreement, a person shall be regarded as having been legally adopted by another only if the adoption is by court proceedings, the finality of which is not being contested by the adopting person.

Survival. Any person must survive by thirty (30) days for a gift made in this Trust Agreement which directly or indirectly requires such person's survival of another to

be effective.

Education. "Education" shall include preparatory, collegiate, postgraduate, professional and vocational education; specialized formal or informal training in music, the stage, handicrafts, the arts or sports or athletic endeavors, whether by private instruction or otherwise; and any other activity, including foreign or domestic travel, which tends to develop the talents and potential of the beneficiary, regardless of age. Education shall also include all tuition, board, lodging fees, books and equipment, travel expenses and other expenses incidental thereto.

Executor. "Executor" shall include personal representative, executrix, administrator and administratrix.

Health. "Health" shall include medical, dental, hospital, and nursing care expenses, and other expenses of invalidism, and distributions for the "health" of a beneficiary may, in the discretion of the Trustee include any part or all of the costs of purchasing or maintaining hospital or medical insurance and disability income insurance coverage for such beneficiary and/or any person in whom such beneficiary has an insurable interest.

Binding Agreement. This agreement shall extend to and be binding upon the heirs, executors, administrators, successors and assigns of the parties.

Use of Words. As used in this instrument, the masculine, feminine, and neuter gender, and the singular or plural of any word includes the others unless the context indicates otherwise.

Unenforceable Provision. If any provision of this Trust Agreement is unenforceable, the remaining provisions shall be given effect, unless to do so would produce an unreasonable result.

Titles, Headings, and Captions. All titles, headings, and captions used in this Trust Agreement have been included for convenience only and should not be construed in interpreting this instrument.

IN WITNESS WHEREOF, I as Grantor and Trustee have hereunto set my hand, on the day and year first above written in multiple originals.

_____

Witness

_____

Grantor

_____

Witness

_____

Trustee

STATE OF _____ §
                                                                                    §
COUNTY OF _____ §

BEFORE ME, the undersigned authority, on this day personally appeared _____, Grantor and Trustee, known to me to be the person whose name is subscribed to the foregoing instrument and acknowledged to me that he/she executed the same for the purposes and consideration therein expressed.

GIVEN UNDER MY HAND AND SEAL OF OFFICE this ____ day of _____, _____.

_____

Notary Public
My Commission Expires:

MEMORANDUM OF DISPOSITION
OF TANGIBLE PERSONAL PROPERTY

Pursuant to the terms of my Living Trust dated _____ , _____ , I have requested the distribution of certain items of my tangible property in accordance with a writing or memorandum, and this memorandum is made for such purpose. If the named beneficiary of a particular item does not survive me by more than thirty days, such item shall be disposed of as though it had not been listed herein.

Description Of Item of
Tangible Personal Property

Name of Beneficiary
and Address

Dated:_____

_____
Witness

_____
Signature of property owner

_____
Witness

_____
Witness

INSTRUCTIONS FOR USE OF PERSONAL PROPERTY MEMORANDUM

1. For such a memorandum to be effective, your trust must expressly refer to disposition of your personal property by a memorandum or written list.

2. The memorandum should not include items already specifically disposed of by you in your Will or Trust.

3. This memorandum is designed for disposing of such items as jewelry, furniture, antiques, artwork, china, silverware, sports equipment, coin and stamp collections, and similar items of household goods and personal effects. This memorandum is not intended to apply to the disposition of money, of promissory notes or other evidence of indebtedness, of real estate, of securities, or of any property used in a trade or business.

4. The memorandum should be dated and signed by you.

5. You should clearly describe each item so that it can be easily identified and will not be confused with another similar item.

6. Each designated beneficiary should be identified by his or her proper name and relationship to you. The address of the beneficiary should be added if he or she does not live in the same household as you.

7. You should consider providing for an alternative beneficiary if the first designated beneficiary does not survive you.

8. You may change the recipients or property designated in the memorandum from time to time or revise or revoke the entire memorandum. Changes should be made only by a new memorandum patterned after this form and the old memorandum should be destroyed. Changes should never be made by striking through an item or by other alterations made on the memorandum after it has been executed; this might create a question as to the validity of the entire memorandum since it might not be possible at a later time to determine whether you or someone else made such changes.

9. If it is desired that a named beneficiary should receive the property only if he or she survives both you and some other person (such as your spouse), that desire should be expressed after the beneficiary's name.

AMENDMENT
TO
THE _____ LIVING TRUST

Dated _____, _____

    This Amendment to THE _____ LIVING TRUST, dated _____, _____ (the "Trust"), by _____ _____, as Grantor and as Trustee. Pursuant to the power of amendment reserved by me in Article _____ of the Trust, Grantor hereby amends the Trust as follows:

ITEM 1.

    Grantor hereby deletes the following paragraph of the Trust in its entirety, and substitutes in its place the following:

Deleted paragraph:

Replacement paragraph:

ITEM 2.

Grantor hereby adds the following paragraph to the Trust:

IN WITNESS WHEREOF, _____ has hereunder caused his/her name to be subscribed as Grantor and as Trustee of this Amendment to THE _____ LIVING TRUST, dated _____, _____, at the City of _____, County of _____, State of _____, on this _____ day of _____, _____.

_____   _____
Witness   Grantor

_____   _____
Witness   Trustee

THE STATE OF _____ §

§

COUNTY OF _____ §

    BEFORE ME, the undersigned authority, a Notary Public in and for said County and State, on this day personally appeared _____, known to me to be the person whose name is subscribed to the annexed or foregoing instrument, and acknowledged to me that he/she executed the same for the purposes and consideration therein expressed and in the capacities therein stated.

    GIVEN UNDER MY HAND AND SEAL OF OFFICE, this the _____ day of _____, _____.

_____
Notary Public
My commission expires:

REVOCATION OF

THE _____LIVING TRUST

On _____, _____, I, _____,
as trustee and grantor, executed a certain trust agreement, wherein I reserved the right at any time
or times to amend or revoke the trust agreement in whole or in part by an instrument in writing
delivered to the trustee.

Pursuant to the right reserved to me under the trust agreement, I hereby revoke the trust
agreement in its entirety and direct that the trust property held thereunder be conveyed by the
trustee to me.

IN WITNESS WHEREOF, I have signed this revocation this _____ day of
_____, _____.

_____   _____
Witness   Grantor

_____
Witness

STATE OF _____ §
                                   §
COUNTY OF _____ §

I, _____, Notary Public, hereby certify that
_____, personally known to me to be the same per-
son whose name is signed to the foregoing instrument, appeared before me this day in person and
acknowledged that he/she signed the instrument as his/her free and voluntary act, for the uses
and purposes therein set forth.

Given under my hand and official seal this _____ day of _____, _____.

_____
Notary Public
My commission expires:

This page intentionally left blank.

ASSIGNMENT OF PERSONAL PROPERTY

The undersigned does hereby transfer and assign, without consideration and solely in order to change formal title, all of his/her right, title and interest in and to the following property to _____, Trustee of the _____LIVING TRUST, dated _____, _____, and any amendments thereto:

All personal property now or hereafter located in the principal and any other residences of the undersigned.

Dated this _____ day of _____, _____.

_____
(Name)

STATE OF _____ §
§
COUNTY OF _____ §

Subscribed and acknowledged before me this _____ day of _____, _____, by _____ , known to me to be the person whose name is subscribed to the foregoing instrument and acknowledged to me that he/she executed the same for the purposes and consideration therein expressed.

GIVEN UNDER MY HAND AND SEAL OF OFFICE this _____ day of _____, _____.

_____
Notary Public
My Commission Expires:

This page intentionally left blank.

Personal Property Assignment

Date: _____

    The undersigned, _____,
as assignor(s), in consideration of the sum of one dollar, receipt of which is acknowledged, and
other good and valuable consideration, hereby assigns, transfers, and delivers to _____
_____ as assignee, the following goods:

Assignor(s):   Assignee:

_____   _____

_____

_____

This page intentionally left blank.

Personal Property Assignment

Date: _____

    The undersigned, _____,
as assignor, in consideration of the sum of one dollar, receipt of which is acknowledged, and other
good and valuable consideration, hereby assigns, transfers, and delivers to _____
_____ as assignees, the following goods:

_____ shall

own the above-listed goods:

    ❑   as husband and wife, in an estate by the entireties.

    ❑   as joint tenants with full rights of survivorship.

    ❑   as husband and wife, as joint tenants with full rights of survivorship.

Assignor: Assignees:

_____   _____

_____

_____

_____

This page intentionally left blank.

Form **SS-4**
(Rev. April 2000)
Department of the Treasury
Internal Revenue Service

Application for Employer Identification Number

(For use by employers, corporations, partnerships, trusts, estates, churches, government agencies, certain individuals, and others. See instructions.)

▶ **Keep a copy for your records.**

EIN

OMB No. 1545-0003

Please type or print clearly.

1	Name of applicant (legal name) (see instructions)

2 Trade name of business (if different from name on line 1)	3 Executor, trustee, "care of" name

4a Mailing address (street address) (room, apt., or suite no.)	5a Business address (if different from address on lines 4a and 4b)
4b City, state, and ZIP code	5b City, state, and ZIP code

6	County and state where principal business is located

7	Name of principal officer, general partner, grantor, owner, or trustor—SSN or ITIN may be required (see instructions) ▶

8a Type of entity (Check only one box.) (see instructions)

Caution: *If applicant is a limited liability company, see the instructions for line 8a.*

☐ Sole proprietor (SSN) _____
☐ Partnership   ☐ Personal service corp.
☐ REMIC   ☐ National Guard
☐ State/local government ☐ Farmers' cooperative
☐ Church or church-controlled organization
☐ Other nonprofit organization (specify) ▶ _____
☐ Other (specify) ▶

☐ Estate (SSN of decedent) _____
☐ Plan administrator (SSN) _____
☐ Other corporation (specify) ▶ _____
☐ Trust
☐ Federal government/military
(enter GEN if applicable) _____

8b If a corporation, name the state or foreign country (if applicable) where incorporated

State	Foreign country

9 Reason for applying (Check only one box.) (see instructions)
☐ Started new business (specify type) ▶ _____
☐ Hired employees (Check the box and see line 12)
☐ Created a pension plan (specify type) ▶

☐ Banking purpose (specify purpose) ▶ _____
☐ Changed type of organization (specify new type) ▶ _____
☐ Purchased going business
☐ Created a trust (specify type) ▶ _____
☐ Other (specify) ▶

10 Date business started or acquired (month, day, year) (see instructions)	11 Closing month of accounting year (see instructions)

12 First date wages or annuities were paid or will be paid (month, day, year). **Note:** *If applicant is a withholding agent, enter date income will first be paid to nonresident alien. (month, day, year)* . . . . ▶

13 Highest number of employees expected in the next 12 months. **Note:** *If the applicant does not expect to have any employees during the period, enter 0. (see instructions)* . . . . ▶

	Nonagricultural	Agricultural	Household

14 Principal activity (see instructions) ▶

15 Is the principal business activity manufacturing? . . . . ☐ Yes ☐ No
If "Yes," principal product and raw material used ▶

16 To whom are most of the products or services sold? Please check one box.   ☐ Business (wholesale)
☐ Public (retail)   ☐ Other (specify) ▶   ☐ N/A

17a Has the applicant ever applied for an employer identification number for this or any other business? . . . . ☐ Yes ☐ No
Note: *If "Yes," please complete lines 17b and 17c.*

17b If you checked "Yes" on line 17a, give applicant's legal name and trade name shown on prior application, if different from line 1 or 2 above.
Legal name ▶   Trade name ▶

17c Approximate date when and city and state where the application was filed. Enter previous employer identification number if known.

Approximate date when filed (mo., day, year)	City and state where filed	Previous EIN

Under penalties of perjury, I declare that I have examined this application, and to the best of my knowledge and belief, it is true, correct, and complete.

Business telephone number (include area code)
( )

Fax telephone number (include area code)
( )

Name and title (Please type or print clearly.) ▶

Signature ▶   Date ▶

Note: *Do not write below this line. For official use only.*

Please leave blank ▶	Geo.	Ind.	Class	Size	Reason for applying

For Privacy Act and Paperwork Reduction Act Notice, see page 4.   Cat. No. 16055N   Form **SS-4** (Rev. 4-2000)

General Instructions

Section references are to the Internal Revenue Code unless otherwise noted.

Purpose of Form

Use Form SS-4 to apply for an employer identification number (EIN). An EIN is a nine-digit number (for example, 12-3456789) assigned to sole proprietors, corporations, partnerships, estates, trusts, and other entities for tax filing and reporting purposes. The information you provide on this form will establish your business tax account.

Caution: *An EIN is for use in connection with your business activities only. Do **not** use your EIN in place of your social security number (SSN).*

Who Must File

You must file this form if you have not been assigned an EIN before and:

● You pay wages to one or more employees including household employees.

● You are required to have an EIN to use on any return, statement, or other document, even if you are not an employer.

● You are a withholding agent required to withhold taxes on income, other than wages, paid to a nonresident alien (individual, corporation, partnership, etc.). A withholding agent may be an agent, broker, fiduciary, manager, tenant, or spouse, and is required to file **Form 1042,** Annual Withholding Tax Return for U.S. Source Income of Foreign Persons.

● You file **Schedule C,** Profit or Loss From Business, **Schedule C-EZ,** Net Profit From Business, or **Schedule F,** Profit or Loss From Farming, of **Form 1040,** U.S. Individual Income Tax Return, **and** have a Keogh plan or are required to file excise, employment, or alcohol, tobacco, or firearms returns.

The following must use EINs even if they do not have any employees:

● State and local agencies who serve as tax reporting agents for public assistance recipients, under Rev. Proc. 80-4, 1980-1 C.B. 581, should obtain a separate EIN for this reporting. See **Household employer** on page 3.

● Trusts, except the following:

1. Certain grantor-owned trusts. (See the **Instructions for Form 1041,** U.S. Income Tax Return for Estates and Trusts.)

2. Individual retirement arrangement (IRA) trusts, unless the trust has to file **Form 990-T,** Exempt Organization Business Income Tax Return. (See the **Instructions for Form 990-T.)**

● Estates

● Partnerships

● REMICs (real estate mortgage investment conduits) (See the **Instructions for Form 1066,** U.S. Real Estate Mortgage Investment Conduit (REMIC) Income Tax Return.)

● Corporations

● Nonprofit organizations (churches, clubs, etc.)

● Farmers' cooperatives

● Plan administrators (A plan administrator is the person or group of persons specified as the administrator by the instrument under which the plan is operated.)

When To Apply for a New EIN

New Business. If you become the new owner of an existing business, **do not** use the EIN of the former owner. **If you already have an EIN, use that number.** If you do not have an EIN, apply for one on this form. If you become the "owner" of a corporation by acquiring its stock, use the corporation's EIN.

Changes in Organization or Ownership. If you already have an EIN, you may need to get a new one if either the organization or ownership of your business changes. If you incorporate a sole proprietorship or form a partnership, you must get a new EIN. However, **do not** apply for a new EIN if:

● You change only the name of your business,

● You elected on **Form 8832,** Entity Classification Election, to change the way the entity is taxed, or

● A partnership terminates because at least 50% of the total interests in partnership capital and profits were sold or exchanged within a 12-month period. (See Regulations section 301.6109-1(d)(2)(iii).) The EIN for the terminated partnership should continue to be used.

Note: *If you are electing to be an "S corporation," be sure you file **Form 2553,** Election by a Small Business Corporation.*

File Only One Form SS-4. File only one Form SS-4, regardless of the number of businesses operated or trade names under which a business operates. However, each corporation in an affiliated group must file a separate application.

EIN Applied for, But Not Received. If you do not have an EIN by the time a return is due, write "Applied for" and the date you applied in the space shown for the number. **Do not** show your social security number (SSN) as an EIN on returns.

If you do not have an EIN by the time a tax deposit is due, send your payment to the Internal Revenue Service Center for your filing area. (See **Where To Apply** below.) Make your check or money order payable to "United States Treasury" and show your name (as shown on Form SS-4), address, type of tax, period covered, and date you applied for an EIN. Send an explanation with the deposit.

For more information about EINs, see **Pub. 583,** Starting a Business and Keeping Records, and **Pub. 1635,** Understanding Your EIN.

How To Apply

You can apply for an EIN either by mail or by telephone. You can get an EIN immediately by calling the Tele-TIN number for the service center for your state, or you can send the completed Form SS-4 directly to the service center to receive your EIN by mail.

Application by Tele-TIN. Under the Tele-TIN program, you can receive your EIN by telephone and use it immediately to file a return or make a payment. To receive an EIN by telephone, complete Form SS-4, then call the Tele-TIN number listed for your state under **Where To Apply.** The person making the call must be authorized to sign the form. (See **Signature** on page 4.)

An IRS representative will use the information from the Form SS-4 to establish your account and assign you an EIN. Write the number you are given on the upper right corner of the form and sign and date it.

*Mail or fax (facsimile) the signed Form SS-4 **within 24 hours** to the Tele-TIN Unit at the service center address for your state.* The IRS representative will give you the fax number. The fax numbers are also listed in Pub. 1635.

Taxpayer representatives can receive their client's EIN by telephone if they first send a fax of a completed **Form 2848,** Power of Attorney and Declaration of Representative, or **Form 8821,** Tax Information Authorization, to the Tele-TIN unit. The Form 2848 or Form 8821 will be used solely to release the EIN to the representative authorized on the form.

Application by Mail. Complete Form SS-4 at least 4 to 5 weeks before you will need an EIN. Sign and date the application and mail it to the service center address for your state. You will receive your EIN in the mail in approximately 4 weeks.

Where To Apply

The Tele-TIN numbers listed below will involve a long-distance charge to callers outside of the local calling area and can be used only to apply for an EIN. **The numbers may change without notice.** Call 1-800-829-1040 to verify a number or to ask about the status of an application by mail.

If your principal business, office or agency, or legal residence in the case of an individual, is located in: ▼	Call the Tele-TIN number shown or file with the Internal Revenue Service Center at: ▼
Florida, Georgia, South Carolina	Attn: Entity Control Atlanta, GA 39901 770-455-2360
New Jersey, New York (New York City and counties of Nassau, Rockland, Suffolk, and Westchester)	Attn: Entity Control Holtsville, NY 00501 516-447-4955
New York (all other counties), Connecticut, Maine, Massachusetts, New Hampshire, Rhode Island, Vermont	Attn: Entity Control Andover, MA 05501 978-474-9717
Illinois, Iowa, Minnesota, Missouri, Wisconsin	Attn: Entity Control Stop 6800 2306 E. Bannister Rd. Kansas City, MO 64999 816-926-5999
Delaware, District of Columbia, Maryland, Pennsylvania, Virginia	Attn: Entity Control Philadelphia, PA 19255 215-516-6999
Indiana, Kentucky, Michigan, Ohio, West Virginia	Attn: Entity Control Cincinnati, OH 45999 859-292-5467

Kansas, New Mexico, Oklahoma, Texas	Attn: Entity Control Austin, TX 73301 512-460-7843
Alaska, Arizona, California (counties of Alpine, Amador, Butte, Calaveras, Colusa, Contra Costa, Del Norte, El Dorado, Glenn, Humboldt, Lake, Lassen, Marin, Mendocino, Modoc, Napa, Nevada, Placer, Plumas, Sacramento, San Joaquin, Shasta, Sierra, Siskiyou, Solano, Sonoma, Sutter, Tehama, Trinity, Yolo, and Yuba), Colorado, Idaho, Montana, Nebraska, Nevada, North Dakota, Oregon, South Dakota, Utah, Washington, Wyoming	Attn: Entity Control Mail Stop 6271 P.O. Box 9941 Ogden, UT 84201 801-620-7645
California (all other counties), Hawaii	Attn: Entity Control Fresno, CA 93888 559-452-4010
Alabama, Arkansas, Louisiana, Mississippi, North Carolina, Tennessee	Attn: Entity Control Memphis, TN 37501 901-546-3920
If you have no legal residence, principal place of business, or principal office or agency in any state	Attn: Entity Control Philadelphia, PA 19255 215-516-6999

Specific Instructions

The instructions that follow are for those items that are not self-explanatory. Enter N/A (nonapplicable) on the lines that do not apply.

Line 1. Enter the legal name of the entity applying for the EIN exactly as it appears on the social security card, charter, or other applicable legal document.

Individuals. Enter your first name, middle initial, and last name. If you are a sole proprietor, enter your individual name, not your business name. Enter your business name on line 2. Do not use abbreviations or nicknames on line 1.

Trusts. Enter the name of the trust.

Estate of a decedent. Enter the name of the estate.

Partnerships. Enter the legal name of the partnership as it appears in the partnership agreement. **Do not** list the names of the partners on line 1. See the specific instructions for line 7.

Corporations. Enter the corporate name as it appears in the corporation charter or other legal document creating it.

Plan administrators. Enter the name of the plan administrator. A plan administrator who already has an EIN should use that number.

Line 2. Enter the trade name of the business if different from the legal name. The trade name is the "doing business as" name.

Note: *Use the full legal name on line 1 on all tax returns filed for the entity. However, if you enter a trade name on line 2 and choose to use the trade name instead of the legal name, enter the trade name on all returns you file. To prevent processing delays and errors, **always** use either the legal name only or the trade name only on all tax returns.*

Line 3. Trusts enter the name of the trustee. Estates enter the name of the executor, administrator, or other fiduciary. If the entity applying has a designated person to receive tax information, enter that person's name as the "care of" person. Print or type the first name, middle initial, and last name.

Line 7. Enter the first name, middle initial, last name, and SSN of a principal officer if the business is a corporation; of a general partner if a partnership; of the owner of a single member entity that is disregarded as an entity separate from its owner; or of a grantor, owner, or trustor if a trust. If the person in question is an alien individual with a previously assigned individual taxpayer identification number (ITIN), enter the ITIN in the space provided, instead of an SSN. You are not required to enter an SSN or ITIN if the reason you are applying for an EIN is to make an entity classification election (see Regulations section 301.7701-1 through 301.7701-3), and you are a nonresident alien with no effectively connected income from sources within the United States.

Line 8a. Check the box that best describes the type of entity applying for the EIN. If you are an alien individual with an ITIN previously assigned to you, enter the ITIN in place of a requested SSN.

Caution: *This is not an election for a tax classification of an entity. See "Limited liability company (LLC)" below.*

If not specifically mentioned, check the "Other" box, enter the type of entity and the type of return that will be filed (for example, common trust fund, Form 1065). Do not enter N/A. If you are an alien individual applying for an EIN, **see the Line 7** instructions above.

Sole proprietor. Check this box if you file Schedule C, C-EZ, or F (Form 1040) and have a qualified plan, or are required to file excise, employment, or alcohol, tobacco, or firearms returns, or are a payer of gambling winnings. Enter your SSN (or ITIN) in the space provided. If you are a nonresident alien with are a nonresident alien with no effectively connected income from sources within the United States, you do not need to enter an SSN or ITIN.

REMIC. Check this box if the entity has elected to be treated as a real estate mortgage investment conduit (REMIC). See the Instructions for Form 1066 for more information.

Other nonprofit organization. Check this box if the nonprofit organization is other than a church or church-controlled organization and specify the type of nonprofit organization (for example, an educational organization).

If the organization also seeks tax-exempt status, you must file either **Package 1023,** Application for Recognition of Exemption, or **Package 1024,** Application for Recognition of Exemption Under Section 501(a). Get **Pub. 557,** Tax Exempt Status for Your Organization, for more information.

Group exemption number (GEN). If the organization is covered by a group exemption letter, enter the four-digit GEN. (Do not confuse the GEN with the nine-digit EIN.) If you do not know the GEN, contact the parent organization. Get Pub. 557 for more information about group exemption numbers.

Withholding agent. If you are a withholding agent required to file Form 1042, check the "Other" box and enter "Withholding agent."

Personal service corporation. Check this box if the entity is a personal service corporation. An entity is a personal service corporation for a tax year only if:

● The principal activity of the entity during the testing period (prior tax year) for the tax year is the performance of personal services substantially by employee-owners, and

● The employee-owners own at least 10% of the fair market value of the outstanding stock in the entity on the last day of the testing period.

Personal services include performance of services in such fields as health, law, accounting, or consulting. For more information about personal service corporations, see the **Instructions for Forms 1120 and 1120-A,** and **Pub. 542,** Corporations.

Limited liability company (LLC). See the definition of limited liability company in the **Instructions for Form 1065,** U.S. Partnership Return of Income. An LLC with two or more members can be a partnership or an association taxable as a corporation. An LLC with a single owner can be an association taxable as a corporation or an entity disregarded as an entity separate from its owner. See Form 8832 for more details.

Note: *A domestic LLC with at least two members that does not file Form 8832 is classified as a partnership for Federal income tax purposes.*

● If the entity is classified as a partnership for Federal income tax purposes, check the "partnership" box.

● If the entity is classified as a corporation for Federal income tax purposes, check the "Other corporation" box and write "limited liability co." in the space provided.

● If the entity is disregarded as an entity separate from its owner, check the "Other" box and write in "disregarded entity" in the space provided.

Plan administrator. If the plan administrator is an individual, enter the plan administrator's SSN in the space provided.

Other corporation. This box is for any corporation other than a personal service corporation. If you check this box, enter the type of corporation (such as insurance company) in the space provided.

Household employer. If you are an individual, check the "Other" box and enter "Household employer" and your SSN. If you are a state or local agency serving as a tax reporting agent for public assistance recipients who become household employers, check the "Other" box and enter "Household employer agent." If you are a trust that qualifies as a household employer, you do not need a separate EIN for reporting tax information relating to household employees; use the EIN of the trust.

QSub. For a qualified subchapter S subsidiary (QSub) check the "Other" box and specify "QSub."

Line 9. Check only **one** box. Do not enter N/A.

Started new business. Check this box if you are starting a new business that requires an EIN. If you check this box, enter the type of business being started. **Do not** apply if you already have an EIN and are only adding another place of business.

Hired employees. Check this box if the existing business is requesting an EIN because it has hired or is hiring employees and is therefore required to file employment tax returns. **Do not** apply if you already have an EIN and are only hiring employees. For information on the applicable employment taxes for family members, see **Circular E,** Employer's Tax Guide (Publication 15).

Created a pension plan. Check this box if you have created a pension plan and need an EIN for reporting purposes. Also, enter the type of plan.

Note: *Check this box if you are applying for a trust EIN when a new pension plan is established.*

Banking purpose. Check this box if you are requesting an EIN for banking purposes only, and enter the banking purpose (for example, a bowling league for depositing dues or an investment club for dividend and interest reporting).

Changed type of organization. Check this box if the business is changing its type of organization, for example, if the business was a sole proprietorship and has been incorporated or has become a partnership. If you check this box, specify in the space provided the type of change made, for example, "from sole proprietorship to partnership."

Purchased going business. Check this box if you purchased an existing business. **Do not** use the former owner's EIN. **Do not** apply for a new EIN if you already have one. Use your own EIN.

Created a trust. Check this box if you created a trust, and enter the type of trust created. For example, indicate if the trust is a nonexempt charitable trust or a split-interest trust.

Note: *Do **not** check this box if you are applying for a trust EIN when a new pension plan is established. Check "Created a pension plan."*

Exception. Do **not** file this form for certain grantor-type trusts. The trustee does not need an EIN for the trust if the trustee furnishes the name and TIN of the grantor/owner and the address of the trust to all payors. See the Instructions for Form 1041 for more information.

Other (specify). Check this box if you are requesting an EIN for any other reason, and enter the reason.

Line 10. If you are starting a new business, enter the starting date of the business. If the business you acquired is already operating, enter the date you acquired the business. Trusts should enter the date the trust was legally created. Estates should enter the date of death of the decedent whose name appears on line 1 or the date when the estate was legally funded.

Line 11. Enter the last month of your accounting year or tax year. An accounting or tax year is usually 12 consecutive months, either a calendar year or a fiscal year (including a period of 52 or 53 weeks). A calendar year is 12 consecutive months ending on December 31. A fiscal year is either 12 consecutive months ending on the last day of any month other than December or a 52-53 week year. For more information on accounting periods, see **Pub. 538,** Accounting Periods and Methods.

Individuals. Your tax year generally will be a calendar year.

Partnerships. Partnerships generally must adopt one of the following tax years:
• The tax year of the majority of its partners,
• The tax year common to all of its principal partners,
• The tax year that results in the least aggregate deferral of income, or
• In certain cases, some other tax year.
See the Instructions for Form 1065 for more information.

REMIC. REMICs must have a calendar year as their tax year.

Personal service corporations. A personal service corporation generally must adopt a calendar year unless:
• It can establish a business purpose for having a different tax year, or
• It elects under section 444 to have a tax year other than a calendar year.

Trusts. Generally, a trust must adopt a calendar year except for the following:
• Tax-exempt trusts,
• Charitable trusts, and
• Grantor-owned trusts.

Line 12. If the business has or will have employees, enter the date on which the business began or will begin to pay wages. If the business does not plan to have employees, enter N/A.

Withholding agent. Enter the date you began or will begin to pay income to a nonresident alien. This also applies to individuals who are required to file Form 1042 to report alimony paid to a nonresident alien.

Line 13. For a definition of agricultural labor (farmwork), see **Circular A,** Agricultural Employer's Tax Guide (Publication 51).

Line 14. Generally, enter the exact type of business being operated (for example, advertising agency, farm, food or beverage establishment, labor union, real estate agency, steam laundry, rental of coin-operated vending machine, or investment club). Also state if the business will involve the sale or distribution of alcoholic beverages.

Governmental. Enter the type of organization (state, county, school district, municipality, etc.).

Nonprofit organization (other than governmental). Enter whether organized for religious, educational, or humane purposes, and the principal activity (for example, religious organization—hospital, charitable).

Mining and quarrying. Specify the process and the principal product (for example, mining bituminous coal, contract drilling for oil, or quarrying dimension stone).

Contract construction. Specify whether general contracting or special trade contracting. Also, show the type of work normally performed (for example, general contractor for residential buildings or electrical subcontractor).

Food or beverage establishments. Specify the type of establishment and state whether you employ workers who receive tips (for example, lounge—yes).

Trade. Specify the type of sales and the principal line of goods sold (for example, wholesale dairy products, manufacturer's representative for mining machinery, or retail hardware).

Manufacturing. Specify the type of establishment operated (for example, sawmill or vegetable cannery).

Signature. The application must be signed by (a) the individual, if the applicant is an individual, (b) the president, vice president, or other principal officer, if the applicant is a corporation, (c) a responsible and duly authorized member or officer having knowledge of its affairs, if the applicant is a partnership or other unincorporated organization, or (d) the fiduciary, if the applicant is a trust or an estate.

How To Get Forms and Publications

Phone. You can order forms, instructions, and publications by phone 24 hours a day, 7 days a week. Just call 1-800-TAX-FORM (1-800-829-3676). You should receive your order or notification of its status within 10 workdays.

Personal computer. With your personal computer and modem, you can get the forms and information you need using IRS's Internet Web Site at **www.irs.gov** or File Transfer Protocol at **ftp.irs.gov.**

CD-ROM. For small businesses, return preparers, or others who may frequently need tax forms or publications, a CD-ROM containing over 2,000 tax products (including many prior year forms) can be purchased from the National Technical Information Service (NTIS).

To order **Pub. 1796,** Federal Tax Products on CD-ROM, call **1-877-CDFORMS** (1-877-233-6767) toll free or connect to **www.irs.gov/cdorders**

Privacy Act and Paperwork Reduction Act Notice. We ask for the information on this form to carry out the Internal Revenue laws of the United States. We need it to comply with section 6109 and the regulations thereunder which generally require the inclusion of an employer identification number (EIN) on certain returns, statements, or other documents filed with the Internal Revenue Service. Information on this form may be used to determine which Federal tax returns you are required to file and to provide you with related forms and publications. We disclose this form to the Social Security Administration for their use in determining compliance with applicable laws. We will be unable to issue an EIN to you unless you provide all of the requested information which applies to your entity.

You are not required to provide the information requested on a form that is subject to the Paperwork Reduction Act unless the form displays a valid OMB control number. Books or records relating to a form or its instructions must be retained as long as their contents may become material in the administration of any Internal Revenue law. Generally, tax returns/return information are confidential, as required by section 6103.

The time needed to complete and file this form will vary depending on individual circumstances. The estimated average time is:

Recordkeeping	7 min.
Learning about the law or the form	22 min.
Preparing the form	46 min.
Copying, assembling, and sending the form to the IRS	20 min.

If you have comments concerning the accuracy of these time estimates or suggestions for making this form simpler, we would be happy to hear from you. You can write to the Tax Forms Committee, Western Area Distribution Center, Rancho Cordova, CA 95743-0001. **Do not** send the form to this address. Instead, see **Where To Apply** on page 2.

Form **1040**

Department of the Treasury—Internal Revenue Service
U.S. Individual Income Tax Return 2001

(99) IRS Use Only—Do not write or staple in this space.

For the year Jan. 1–Dec. 31, 2001, or other tax year beginning _____, 2001, ending _____, 20___

OMB No. 1545-0074

Label

(See instructions on page 19.)

Use the IRS label. Otherwise, please print or type.

L A B E L H E R E	Your first name and initial	Last name	Your social security number
	If a joint return, spouse's first name and initial	Last name	Spouse's social security number
	Home address (number and street). If you have a P.O. box, see page 19.	Apt. no.	
	City, town or post office, state, and ZIP code. If you have a foreign address, see page 19.		

▲ **Important!** ▲

You **must** enter your SSN(s) above.

Presidential Election Campaign
(See page 19.)

Note. Checking "Yes" will not change your tax or reduce your refund.

Do you, or your spouse if filing a joint return, want $3 to go to this fund? . . . . ▶

You: ☐ Yes ☐ No   Spouse: ☐ Yes ☐ No

Filing Status

Check only one box.

1 ☐ Single
2 ☐ Married filing joint return (even if only one had income)
3 ☐ Married filing separate return. Enter spouse's social security no. above and full name here. ▶ _____
4 ☐ Head of household (with qualifying person). (See page 19.) If the qualifying person is a child but not your dependent, enter this child's name here. ▶ _____
5 ☐ Qualifying widow(er) with dependent child (year spouse died ▶ ___). (See page 19.)

Exemptions

6a ☐ **Yourself.** If your parent (or someone else) can claim you as a dependent on his or her tax return, **do not** check box 6a . . . .

b ☐ **Spouse** . . . .

If more than six dependents, see page 20.

c Dependents:

(1) First name Last name	(2) Dependent's social security number	(3) Dependent's relationship to you	(4)✔ if qualifying child for child tax credit (see page 20)
			☐
			☐
			☐
			☐
			☐
			☐

No. of boxes checked on 6a and 6b ___

No. of your children on 6c who:
• lived with you ___
• did not live with you due to divorce or separation (see page 20) ___

Dependents on 6c not entered above ___

Add numbers entered on lines above ▶ ☐

d Total number of exemptions claimed . . . .

Income

Attach Forms W-2 and W-2G here. Also attach Form(s) 1099-R if tax was withheld.

If you did not get a W-2, see page 21.

Enclose, but do not attach, any payment. Also, please use **Form 1040-V.**

7	Wages, salaries, tips, etc. Attach Form(s) W-2	**7**
8a	**Taxable** interest. Attach Schedule B if required	**8a**
b	**Tax-exempt** interest. Do not include on line 8a . . . **8b**	
9	Ordinary dividends. Attach Schedule B if required	**9**
10	Taxable refunds, credits, or offsets of state and local income taxes (see page 22) . .	**10**
11	Alimony received	**11**
12	Business income or (loss). Attach Schedule C or C-EZ	**12**
13	Capital gain or (loss). Attach Schedule D if required. If not required, check here ▶ ☐	**13**
14	Other gains or (losses). Attach Form 4797	**14**
15a	Total IRA distributions **15a** ___	b Taxable amount (see page 23)	**15b**
16a	Total pensions and annuities **16a** ___	b Taxable amount (see page 23)	**16b**
17	Rental real estate, royalties, partnerships, S corporations, trusts, etc. Attach Schedule E	**17**
18	Farm income or (loss). Attach Schedule F	**18**
19	Unemployment compensation	**19**
20a	Social security benefits **20a** ___	b Taxable amount (see page 25)	**20b**
21	Other income. List type and amount (see page 27) _____	**21**
22	Add the amounts in the far right column for lines 7 through 21. This is your **total income ▶**	**22**

Adjusted Gross Income

23	IRA deduction (see page 27)	**23**
24	Student loan interest deduction (see page 28)	**24**
25	Archer MSA deduction. Attach Form 8853	**25**
26	Moving expenses. Attach Form 3903	**26**
27	One-half of self-employment tax. Attach Schedule SE . .	**27**
28	Self-employed health insurance deduction (see page 30) .	**28**
29	Self-employed SEP, SIMPLE, and qualified plans . .	**29**
30	Penalty on early withdrawal of savings	**30**
31a	Alimony paid b Recipient's SSN ▶ _____	**31a**
32	Add lines 23 through 31a	**32**
33	Subtract line 32 from line 22. This is your **adjusted gross income** . . . . . ▶	**33**

For Disclosure, Privacy Act, and Paperwork Reduction Act Notice, see page 72.   Cat. No. 11320B   Form **1040** (2001)

Tax and Credits	34	Amount from line 33 (adjusted gross income)	34	

Standard Deduction for-
- People who checked any box on line 35a or 35b **or** who can be claimed as a dependent, see page 31.
- All others:

Single, $4,550

Head of household, $6,650

Married filing jointly or Qualifying widow(er), $7,600

Married filing separately, $3,800

35a	Check if: ☐ **You** were 65 or older, ☐ Blind; ☐ **Spouse** was 65 or older, ☐ Blind. Add the number of boxes checked above and enter the total here . . . . ▶ 35a ☐
b	If you are married filing separately and your spouse itemizes deductions, or you were a dual-status alien, see page 31 and check here . . . . . ▶ 35b ☐
36	**Itemized deductions** (from Schedule A) **or** your **standard deduction** (see left margin) . ⸱⸱ 36
37	Subtract line 36 from line 34 37
38	If line 34 is $99,725 or less, multiply $2,900 by the total number of exemptions claimed on line 6d. If line 34 is over $99,725, see the worksheet on page 32 . . . . ⸱⸱ 38
39	**Taxable income.** Subtract line 38 from line 37. If line 38 is more than line 37, enter -0- 39
40	**Tax** (see page 33). Check if any tax is from **a** ☐ Form(s) 8814 **b** ☐ Form 4972 . . . 40
41	**Alternative minimum tax** (see page 34). Attach Form 6251 41
42	Add lines 40 and 41 . . . . ▶ 42
43	Foreign tax credit. Attach Form 1116 if required . . . . ⸱⸱ 43
44	Credit for child and dependent care expenses. Attach Form 2441 44
45	Credit for the elderly or the disabled. Attach Schedule R . . 45
46	Education credits. Attach Form 8863 . . . . . . ⸱⸱ 46
47	Rate reduction credit. See the worksheet on page 36 . . ⸱⸱ 47
48	Child tax credit (see page 37) . . . . ⸱⸱ 48
49	Adoption credit. Attach Form 8839 . . . . . . ⸱⸱ 49
50	Other credits from: **a** ☐ Form 3800 **b** ☐ Form 8396 **c** ☐ Form 8801 **d** ☐ Form (specify)_____ 50
51	Add lines 43 through 50. These are your **total credits** 51
52	Subtract line 51 from line 42. If line 51 is more than line 42, enter -0-. . . . . . ▶ 52

Other Taxes	53	Self-employment tax. Attach Schedule SE 53	
	54	Social security and Medicare tax on tip income not reported to employer. Attach Form 4137 . ⸱ 54	
	55	Tax on qualified plans, including IRAs, and other tax-favored accounts. Attach Form 5329 if required ⸱⸱ 55	
	56	Advance earned income credit payments from Form(s) W-2 56	
	57	Household employment taxes. Attach Schedule H 57	
	58	Add lines 52 through 57. This is your **total tax** . . . . ▶ 58	

Payments	59	Federal income tax withheld from Forms W-2 and 1099 . ⸱⸱ 59	

If you have a qualifying child, attach Schedule EIC.

60	2001 estimated tax payments and amount applied from 2000 return ⸱⸱ 60
61a	**Earned income credit (EIC)** . . . . ⸱⸱ 61a
b	Nontaxable earned income . ⸱⸱	61b	
62	Excess social security and RRTA tax withheld (see page 51) 62
63	Additional child tax credit. Attach Form 8812 63
64	Amount paid with request for extension to file (see page 51) 64
65	Other payments. Check if from **a** ☐ Form 2439 **b** ☐ Form 4136 65
66	Add lines 59, 60, 61a, and 62 through 65. These are your **total payments** . . . . . ▶ 66

Refund	67	If line 66 is more than line 58, subtract line 58 from line 66. This is the amount you **overpaid**	67

Direct deposit? See page 51 and fill in 68b, 68c, and 68d.

68a	Amount of line 67 you want **refunded to you** . . . . ▶ 68a
▶ b	Routing number |_____| ▶ **c** Type: ☐ Checking ☐ Savings
▶ d	Account number |_____|
69	Amount of line 67 you want **applied to your 2002 estimated tax** ▶	69	

Amount You Owe	70	**Amount you owe.** Subtract line 66 from line 58. For details on how to pay, see page 52 ▶	70
	71	Estimated tax penalty. Also include on line 70 . . . . ⸱⸱	71	

Third Party Designee

Do you want to allow another person to discuss this return with the IRS (see page 53)? ☐ **Yes.** Complete the following. ☐ **No**

Designee's name ▶　　　　　Phone no. ▶ (　　)　　　　Personal identification number (PIN) ▶ |____|

Sign Here

Joint return? See page 19.

Keep a copy for your records.

Under penalties of perjury, I declare that I have examined this return and accompanying schedules and statements, and to the best of my knowledge and belief, they are true, correct, and complete. Declaration of preparer (other than taxpayer) is based on all information of which preparer has any knowledge.

Your signature	Date	Your occupation	Daytime phone number ( )
Spouse's signature. If a joint return, **both** must sign.	Date	Spouse's occupation	

Paid Preparer's Use Only

Preparer's signature ▶	Date	Check if self-employed ☐	Preparer's SSN or PTIN
Firm's name (or yours if self-employed), address, and ZIP code ▶		EIN	
		Phone no. ( )	

Form **1040** (2001)

Form **1041**

Department of the Treasury—Internal Revenue Service

U.S. Income Tax Return for Estates and Trusts

2001

OMB No. 1545-0092

For calendar year 2001 or fiscal year beginning _____, 2001, and ending _____, 20____

A Type of entity:

- [ ] Decedent's estate
- [ ] Simple trust
- [ ] Complex trust
- [ ] Grantor type trust
- [ ] Bankruptcy estate–Ch. 7
- [ ] Bankruptcy estate–Ch. 11
- [ ] Pooled income fund

B Number of Schedules K-1 attached (see instructions) ▶

Name of estate or trust (If a grantor type trust, see page 10 of the instructions.)

Name and title of fiduciary

Number, street, and room or suite no. (If a P.O. box, see page 10 of the instructions.)

City or town, state, and ZIP code

C Employer identification number

D Date entity created

E Nonexempt charitable and split-interest trusts, check applicable boxes (see page 11 of the instructions):

- [ ] Described in section 4947(a)(1)
- [ ] Not a private foundation
- [ ] Described in section 4947(a)(2)

F Check applicable boxes:

- [ ] Initial return
- [ ] Final return
- [ ] Amended return
- [ ] Change in fiduciary's name
- [ ] Change in fiduciary's address

G Pooled mortgage account (see page 12 of the instructions):

- [ ] Bought
- [ ] Sold Date:

Income

1	Interest income	1
2	Ordinary dividends	2
3	Business income or (loss) (attach Schedule C or C-EZ (Form 1040))	3
4	Capital gain or (loss) (attach Schedule D (Form 1041))	4
5	Rents, royalties, partnerships, other estates and trusts, etc. (attach Schedule E (Form 1040))	5
6	Farm income or (loss) (attach Schedule F (Form 1040))	6
7	Ordinary gain or (loss) (attach Form 4797)	7
8	Other income. List type and amount _____	8
9	**Total income.** Combine lines 1 through 8 . . . . ▶	9

Deductions

10	Interest. Check if Form 4952 is attached ▶ [ ]	10
11	Taxes	11
12	Fiduciary fees	12
13	Charitable deduction (from Schedule A, line 7)	13
14	Attorney, accountant, and return preparer fees	14
15a	Other deductions **not** subject to the 2% floor (attach schedule)	15a
b	Allowable miscellaneous itemized deductions subject to the 2% floor	15b
16	**Total.** Add lines 10 through 15b	16
17	Adjusted total income or (loss). Subtract line 16 from line 9. Enter here and on Schedule B, line 1 ▶	17
18	Income distribution deduction (from Schedule B, line 15) (attach Schedules K-1 (Form 1041))	18
19	Estate tax deduction (including certain generation-skipping taxes) (attach computation) . .	19
20	Exemption . . . . ▶	20
21	**Total deductions.** Add lines 18 through 20	21

Tax and Payments

22	Taxable income. Subtract line 21 from line 17. If a loss, see page 17 of the instructions	22
23	**Total tax** (from Schedule G, line 7)	23
24	**Payments: a** 2001 estimated tax payments and amount applied from 2000 return . . .	24a
b	Estimated tax payments allocated to beneficiaries (from Form 1041-T)	24b
c	Subtract line 24b from line 24a	24c
d	Tax paid with extension of time to file: [ ] Form 2758 [ ] Form 8736 [ ] Form 8800	24d
e	Federal income tax withheld. If any is from Form(s) 1099, check ▶ [ ]	24e
	Other payments: **f** Form 2439 _____ ; **g** Form 4136 _____ ; Total ▶	24h
25	**Total payments.** Add lines 24c through 24e, and 24h . . . . ▶	25
26	Estimated tax penalty (see page 17 of the instructions)	26
27	**Tax due.** If line 25 is smaller than the total of lines 23 and 26, enter amount owed . . .	27
28	**Overpayment.** If line 25 is larger than the total of lines 23 and 26, enter amount overpaid	28
29	Amount of line 28 to be: **a** Credited to 2002 estimated tax ▶ ; **b** Refunded ▶	29

Sign Here ▶

Under penalties of perjury, I declare that I have examined this return, including accompanying schedules and statements, and to the best of my knowledge and belief, it is true, correct, and complete. Declaration of preparer (other than taxpayer) is based on all information of which preparer has any knowledge.

| Signature of fiduciary or officer representing fiduciary | Date | ▶ EIN of fiduciary if a financial institution | May the IRS discuss this return with the preparer shown below (see page 7)? [ ] Yes [ ] No |

Paid Preparer's Use Only

Preparer's signature ▶		Date	Check if self-employed [ ]	Preparer's SSN or PTIN
Firm's name (or yours if self-employed), address, and ZIP code ▶			EIN	
			Phone no. ( )	

For Paperwork Reduction Act Notice, see the separate instructions.

Cat. No. 11370H

Form **1041** (2001)

Schedule A	Charitable Deduction. Do not complete for a simple trust or a pooled income fund.		
1	Amounts paid or permanently set aside for charitable purposes from gross income (see page 18)	1	
2	Tax-exempt income allocable to charitable contributions (see page 18 of the instructions) . .	2	
3	Subtract line 2 from line 1	3	
4	Capital gains for the tax year allocated to corpus and paid or permanently set aside for charitable purposes	4	
5	Add lines 3 and 4	5	
6	Section 1202 exclusion allocable to capital gains paid or permanently set aside for charitable purposes (see page 18 of the instructions)	6	
7	**Charitable deduction.** Subtract line 6 from line 5. Enter here and on page 1, line 13	7	

Schedule B	Income Distribution Deduction		
1	Adjusted total income (see page 18 of the instructions)	1	
2	Adjusted tax-exempt interest	2	
3	Total net gain from Schedule D (Form 1041), line 16, column (1) (see page 19 of the instructions)	3	
4	Enter amount from Schedule A, line 4 (reduced by any allocable section 1202 exclusion). . .	4	
5	Capital gains for the tax year included on Schedule A, line 1 (see page 19 of the instructions)	5	
6	Enter any gain from page 1, line 4, as a negative number. If page 1, line 4, is a loss, enter the loss as a positive number	6	
7	**Distributable net income (DNI).** Combine lines 1 through 6. If zero or less, enter -0-	7	
8	If a complex trust, enter accounting income for the tax year as determined under the governing instrument and applicable local law **8**		
9	Income required to be distributed currently	9	
10	Other amounts paid, credited, or otherwise required to be distributed	10	
11	Total distributions. Add lines 9 and 10. If greater than line 8, see page 19 of the instructions	11	
12	Enter the amount of tax-exempt income included on line 11	12	
13	Tentative income distribution deduction. Subtract line 12 from line 11	13	
14	Tentative income distribution deduction. Subtract line 2 from line 7. If zero or less, enter -0-	14	
15	**Income distribution deduction.** Enter the smaller of line 13 or line 14 here and on page 1, line 18	15	

Schedule G	Tax Computation (see page 20 of the instructions)		
1	**Tax: a** ☐ Tax rate schedule or ☐ Schedule D (Form 1041) . .	1a	
	b Tax on lump-sum distributions (attach Form 4972).	1b	
	c Alternative minimum tax (from Schedule I, line 39).	1c	
	d **Total.** Add lines 1a through 1c . . . . ▶	1d	
2a	Foreign tax credit (attach Form 1116)	2a	
b	Other nonbusiness credits (attach schedule)	2b	
c	General business credit. Enter here and check which forms are attached: ☐ Form 3800 ☐ Forms (specify) ▶ _____	2c	
d	Credit for prior year minimum tax (attach Form 8801)	2d	
3	**Total credits.** Add lines 2a through 2d . . . . ▶	3	
4	Subtract line 3 from line 1d. If zero or less, enter -0-	4	
5	Recapture taxes. Check if from: ☐ Form 4255 ☐ Form 8611	5	
6	Household employment taxes. Attach Schedule H (Form 1040)	6	
7	**Total tax.** Add lines 4 through 6. Enter here and on page 1, line 23 . . . . . ▶	7	

Other Information		Yes	No
1	Did the estate or trust receive tax-exempt income? If "Yes," attach a computation of the allocation of expenses Enter the amount of tax-exempt interest income and exempt-interest dividends ▶ $ _____		
2	Did the estate or trust receive all or any part of the earnings (salary, wages, and other compensation) of any individual by reason of a contract assignment or similar arrangement?		
3	At any time during calendar year 2001, did the estate or trust have an interest in or a signature or other authority over a bank, securities, or other financial account in a foreign country? . . . . See page 21 of the instructions for exceptions and filing requirements for Form TD F 90-22.1. If "Yes," enter the name of the foreign country ▶ _____		
4	During the tax year, did the estate or trust receive a distribution from, or was it the grantor of, or transferor to, a foreign trust? If "Yes," the estate or trust may have to file Form 3520. See page 21 of the instructions . .		
5	Did the estate or trust receive, or pay, any qualified residence interest on seller-provided financing? If "Yes," see page 21 for required attachment		
6	If this is an estate or a complex trust making the section 663(b) election, check here (see page 21) . ..▶ ☐		
7	To make a section 643(e)(3) election, attach Schedule D (Form 1041), and check here (see page 21). ..▶ ☐		
8	If the decedent's estate has been open for more than 2 years, attach an explanation for the delay in closing the estate, and check here ▶ ☐		
9	Are any present or future trust beneficiaries skip persons? See page 21 of the instructions		

Schedule I   Alternative Minimum Tax (see pages 21 through 27 of the instructions)

Part I- Estate's or Trust's Share of Alternative Minimum Taxable Income

1	Adjusted total income or (loss) (from page 1, line 17)	1	
2	Net operating loss deduction. Enter as a positive amount	2	
3	Add lines 1 and 2	3	

4 **Adjustments and tax preference items:**

a	Interest	4a	
b	Taxes	4b	
c	Miscellaneous itemized deductions (from page 1, line 15b)	4c	
d	Refund of taxes	4d ( )	
e	Depreciation of property placed in service after 1986	4e	
f	Circulation and research and experimental expenditures	4f	
g	Mining exploration and development costs	4g	
h	Long-term contracts entered into after February 28, 1986	4h	
i	Amortization of pollution control facilities	4i	
j	Installment sales of certain property	4j	
k	Adjusted gain or loss (including incentive stock options).	4k	
l	Certain loss limitations	4l	
m	Tax shelter farm activities	4m	
n	Passive activities	4n	
o	Beneficiaries of other trusts or decedent's estates	4o	
p	Tax-exempt interest from specified private activity bonds	4p	
q	Depletion	4q	
r	Accelerated depreciation of real property placed in service before 1987	4r	
s	Accelerated depreciation of leased personal property placed in service before 1987	4s	
t	Intangible drilling costs	4t	
u	Other adjustments	4u	

5	Combine lines 4a through 4u	5	
6	Add lines 3 and 5	6	
7	Alternative tax net operating loss deduction (see page 25 of the instructions for limitations) .	7	
8	Adjusted alternative minimum taxable income. Subtract line 7 from line 6.	8	

Note: *Complete Part II below before going to line 9.*

9	Income distribution deduction from line 27 below	9	
10	Estate tax deduction (from page 1, line 19)	10	
11	Add lines 9 and 10	11	
12	Estate's or trust's share of alternative minimum taxable income. Subtract line 11 from line 8 .	12	

If line 12 is:

- $22,500 or less, stop here and enter -0- on Schedule G, line 1c. The estate or trust is not liable for the alternative minimum tax.
- Over $22,500, but less than $165,000, go to line 28.
- $165,000 or more, enter the amount from line 12 on line 34 and go to line 35.

Part II- Income Distribution Deduction on a Minimum Tax Basis

13	Adjusted alternative minimum taxable income (see page 25 of the instructions)	13	
14	Adjusted tax-exempt interest (other than amounts included on line 4p)	14	
15	Total net gain from Schedule D (Form 1041), line 16, column (1). If a loss, enter -0-	15	
16	Capital gains for the tax year allocated to corpus and paid or permanently set aside for charitable purposes (from Schedule A, line 4)	16	
17	Capital gains paid or permanently set aside for charitable purposes from gross income (see page 26 of the instructions)	17	
18	Capital gains computed on a minimum tax basis included on line 8	18 ( )	
19	Capital losses computed on a minimum tax basis included on line 8. Enter as a positive amount	19	
20	Distributable net alternative minimum taxable income (DNAMTI). Combine lines 13 through 19. If zero or less, enter -0-	20	
21	Income required to be distributed currently (from Schedule B, line 9)	21	
22	Other amounts paid, credited, or otherwise required to be distributed (from Schedule B, line 10)	22	
23	Total distributions. Add lines 21 and 22	23	
24	Tax-exempt income included on line 23 (other than amounts included on line 4p)	24	
25	Tentative income distribution deduction on a minimum tax basis. Subtract line 24 from line 23	25	
26	Tentative income distribution deduction on a minimum tax basis. Subtract line 14 from line 20. If zero or less, enter -0-	26	
27	**Income distribution deduction on a minimum tax basis.** Enter the smaller of line 25 or line 26. Enter here and on line 9	27	

Part III- Alternative Minimum Tax

28	Exemption amount			28	$22,500	00
29	Enter the amount from line 12	29				
30	Phase-out of exemption amount	30	$75,000	00		
31	Subtract line 30 from line 29. If zero or less, enter -0-	31				
32	Multiply line 31 by 25% (.25)			32		
33	Subtract line 32 from line 28. If zero or less, enter -0-			33		
34	Subtract line 33 from line 29			34		
35	Go to Part IV of Schedule I to figure line 35 if the estate or trust has a gain on lines 15c and 16 of column (2) of Schedule D (Form 1041) (as refigured for the AMT, if necessary). **All others:** If line 34 is-					
	• $175,000 or less, multiply line 34 by 26% (.26).					
	• Over $175,000, multiply line 34 by 28% (.28) and subtract $3,500 from the result			35		
36	Alternative minimum foreign tax credit (see page 26 of instructions)			36		
37	Tentative minimum tax. Subtract line 36 from line 35			37		
38	Enter the tax from Schedule G, line 1a (minus any foreign tax credit from Schedule G, line 2a)			38		
39	**Alternative minimum tax.** Subtract line 38 from line 37. If zero or less, enter -0-. Enter here and on Schedule G, line 1c			39		

Part IV- Line 35 Computation Using Maximum Capital Gains Rates

Caution: *If the estate or trust **did not** complete Part V of Schedule D (Form 1041), see page 27 of the instructions before completing this part.*

40	Enter the amount from line 34		40		
41	Enter the amount from Schedule D (Form 1041), line 21, or line 9 of the Schedule D Tax Worksheet, whichever applies (as refigured for AMT, if necessary)	41			
42	Enter the amount from Schedule D (Form 1041), line 15b, column (2) (as refigured for AMT, if necessary)	42			
43	Add lines 41 and 42. If zero or less, enter -0-	43			
44	Enter the amount from Schedule D (Form 1041), line 21, or line 4 of the Schedule D Tax Worksheet, whichever applies (as refigured for AMT, if necessary)	44			
45	Enter the **smaller** of line 43 or line 44		45		
46	Subtract line 45 from line 40. If zero or less, enter -0-		46		
47	If line 46 is $175,000 or less, multiply line 46 by 26% (.26). Otherwise, multiply line 46 by 28% (.28) and subtract $3,500 from the result ▶		47		
48	Enter the amount from Schedule D (Form 1041), line 26, or line 16 of the Schedule D Tax Worksheet (as figured for the regular tax)		48		
49	Enter the **smallest** of line 40, line 41, or line 48		49		
50	Enter the estate's or trust's allocable portion of qualified 5-year gain, if any, from Schedule D (Form 1041) line 27 (as refigured for the AMT, if necessary)	50			
51	Enter the smaller of line 49 or line 50		51		
52	Multiply line 51 by 8% (.08) ▶		52		
53	Subtract line 51 from line 49		53		
54	Multiply line 53 by 10% (.10) ▶		54		
55	Enter the **smaller** of line 40 or line 41		55		
56	Enter the amount from line 49		56		
57	Subtract line 56 from line 55. If zero or less, enter -0-		57		
58	Multiply line 57 by 20% (.20) ▶		58		
59	Enter the amount from line 40		59		
60	Add lines 46, 49, and 57		60		
61	Subtract line 60 from line 59		61		
62	Multiply line 61 by 25% (.25) ▶		62		
63	Add lines 47, 52, 54, 58, and 62		63		
64	If line 40 is $175,000 or less, multiply line 40 by 26% (.26). Otherwise, multiply line 40 by 28% (.28) and subtract $3,500 from the result		64		
65	Enter the **smaller** of line 63 or line 64 here and on line 35 ▶		65		

SCHEDULE D (Form 1041) Department of the Treasury Internal Revenue Service	**Capital Gains and Losses** ▶ Attach to Form 1041 (or Form 5227). See the separate instructions for Form 1041 (or Form 5227).	OMB No. 1545-0092 20**01**

Name of estate or trust | Employer identification number

Note: *Form 5227 filers need to complete **only** Parts I and II.*

Part I — Short-Term Capital Gains and Losses—Assets Held One Year or Less

(a) Description of property (Example, 100 shares 7% preferred of "Z" Co.)	(b) Date acquired (mo., day, yr.)	(c) Date sold (mo., day, yr.)	(d) Sales price	(e) Cost or other basis (see page 29)	(f) Gain or (Loss) (col. (d) less col. (e))	
1						

2 Short-term capital gain or (loss) from Forms 4684, 6252, 6781, and 8824 . .	**2**	
3 Net short-term gain or (loss) from partnerships, S corporations, and other estates or trusts	**3**	
4 Short-term capital loss carryover. Enter the amount, if any, from line 9 of the 2000 Capital Loss Carryover Worksheet	**4** ( )
5 **Net short-term gain or (loss).** Combine lines 1 through 4 in column (f). Enter here and on line 14 below . . . . ▶	**5**	

Part II — Long-Term Capital Gains and Losses—Assets Held More Than One Year

(a) Description of property (Example, 100 shares 7% preferred of "Z" Co.)	(b) Date acquired (mo., day, yr.)	(c) Date sold (mo., day, yr.)	(d) Sales price	(e) Cost or other basis (see page 29)	(f) Gain or (Loss) (col. (d) less col. (e))	(g) 28% Rate Gain or (Loss) *(see instr. below)
6						

7 Long-term capital gain or (loss) from Forms 2439, 4684, 6252, 6781, and 8824 . .	**7**	
8 Net long-term gain or (loss) from partnerships, S corporations, and other estates or trusts .	**8**	
9 Capital gain distributions	**9**	
10 Gain from Form 4797, Part I	**10**	
11 Long-term capital loss carryover. Enter in both columns (f) and (g) the amount, if any, from line 14, of the 2000 Capital Loss Carryover Worksheet	**11** ( )( )
12 Combine lines 6 through 11 in column (g)	**12**	
13 **Net long-term gain or (loss).** Combine lines 6 through 11 in column (f). Enter here and on line 15 below . . . . ▶	**13**	

***28% rate gain or loss** includes **all** "collectibles gains and losses" (as defined on page 30 of the instructions) and up to 50% of the eligible gain on qualified small business stock (see page 28 of the instructions).

Part III — Summary of Parts I and II

		(1) Beneficiaries' (see page 30)	(2) Estate's or trust's	(3) Total
14	**Net short-term gain or (loss)** (from line 5 above)	**14**		
15	**Net long-term gain or (loss):**			
a	28% rate gain or (loss) (from line 12 above)	**15a**		
b	Unrecaptured section 1250 gain (see line 17 of the worksheet on page 31)	**15b**		
c	Total for year (from line 13 above)	**15c**		
16	**Total net gain or (loss).** Combine lines 14 and 15c . ▶	**16**		

Note: *If line 16, column (3), is a net gain, enter the gain on Form 1041, line 4. If lines 15c and 16, column (2), are net gains, go to Part V, and **do not** complete Part IV. If line 16, column (3), is a net loss, complete Part IV and the **Capital Loss Carryover Worksheet**, as necessary.*

For Paperwork Reduction Act Notice, see the Instructions for Form 1041.   Cat. No. 11376V   Schedule D (Form 1041) 2001

Part IV   Capital Loss Limitation

17   Enter here and enter as a (loss) on Form 1041, line 4, the **smaller** of:

   a   The loss on line 16, column (3) **or**

   b $3,000 .   .   .   .   **17** (   )

If the loss on line 16, column (3), is more than $3,000, **or** if Form 1041, page 1, line 22, is a loss, complete the **Capital Loss Carryover Worksheet** on page 32 of the instructions to determine your capital loss carryover.

Part V   **Tax Computation Using Maximum Capital Gains Rates** (Complete this part **only** if both lines 15c and 16 in column (2) are gains, and Form 1041, line 22 is more than zero.)

   Note: If line 15a, column (2) or line 15b, column (2) is more than zero, complete the worksheet on page 34 of the instructions to figure the amount to enter on lines 20, 27, and 38 below and skip all other lines below. Otherwise, go to line 18.

18   Enter taxable income from Form 1041, line 22   .   .   .   .   **18**

19   Enter the **smaller** of line 15c or 16 in column (2)   **19**

20   If the estate or trust is filing Form 4952, enter the amount from line 4e; otherwise, enter -0- ▶   **20**

21   Subtract line 20 from line 19. If zero or less, enter -0- **21**

22   Subtract line 21 from line 18. If zero or less, enter -0- **22**

23   Figure the tax on the amount on line 22. Use the 2001 Tax Rate Schedule on page 20 of the instructions **23**

24   Enter the **smaller** of the amount on line 18 or $1,800   .   .   .   .   .   **24**

If line 24 is greater than line 22, go to line 25. Otherwise, skip lines 25 through 31 and go to line 32.

25   Enter the amount from line 22   .   .   .   .   **25**

26   Subtract line 25 from line 24. If zero or less, enter -0- and go to line 32   **26**

27   Enter the estate's or trust's allocable portion of qualified 5-year gain, if any, from line 7c of the worksheet on page 33   .   .   .   .   **27**

28   Enter the **smaller** of line 26 or line 27   .   .   .   .   **28**

29   Multiply line 28 by 8% (.08) **29**

30   Subtract line 28 from line 26   .   .   .   .   **30**

31   Multiply line 30 by 10% (.10) **31**

If the amounts on lines 21 and 26 are the same, skip lines 32 through 35 and go to line 36.

32   Enter the **smaller** of line 18 or line 21   .   .   .   .   **32**

33   Enter the amount, if any, from line 26   .   .   .   .   **33**

34   Subtract line 33 from line 32   .   .   .   .   **34**

35   Multiply line 34 by 20% (.20) **35**

36   Add lines 23, 29, 31, and 35   .   .   .   .   **36**

37   Figure the tax on the amount on line 18. Use the 2001 Tax Rate Schedule on page 20 of the instructions **37**

38   **Tax on all taxable income (including capital gains).** Enter the **smaller** of line 36 or line 37 here and on line 1a of Schedule G, Form 1041   .   .   .   .   **38**

SCHEDULE K-1 (Form 1041)

Beneficiary's Share of Income, Deductions, Credits, etc.

Department of the Treasury
Internal Revenue Service

for the calendar year 2001, or fiscal year

beginning .... , 2001, ending .... , 20 ....
► Complete a separate Schedule K-1 for each beneficiary.

OMB No. 1545-0092

2001

Name of trust or decedent's estate

☐ Amended K-1
☐ Final K-1

Beneficiary's identifying number ►	Estate's or trust's EIN ►
Beneficiary's name, address, and ZIP code	Fiduciary's name, address, and ZIP code

(a) Allocable share item		(b) Amount	(c) Calendar year 2001 Form 1040 filers enter the amounts in column (b) on:
1	Interest	**1**	Schedule B, Part I, line 1
2	Ordinary dividends	**2**	Schedule B, Part II, line 5
3	Net short-term capital gain	**3**	Schedule D, line 5
4	Net long-term capital gain: **a** Total for year	**4a**	Schedule D, line 12, column (f)
b	28% rate gain	**4b**	Schedule D, line 12, column (g)
c	Qualified 5-year gain	**4c**	Line 4 of the worksheet for Schedule D, line 29
d	Unrecaptured section 1250 gain	**4d**	Line 11 of the worksheet for Schedule D, line 19
5a	Annuities, royalties, and other nonpassive income before directly apportioned deductions	**5a**	Schedule E, Part III, column (f)
b	Depreciation	**5b**	Include on the applicable line of the appropriate tax form
c	Depletion	**5c**	
d	Amortization	**5d**	
6a	Trade or business, rental real estate, and other rental income before directly apportioned deductions (see instructions)	**6a**	Schedule E, Part III
b	Depreciation	**6b**	Include on the applicable line of the appropriate tax form
c	Depletion	**6c**	
d	Amortization	**6d**	
7	Income for minimum tax purposes	**7**	
8	Income for regular tax purposes (add lines 1, 2, 3, 4a, 5a, and 6a)	**8**	
9	Adjustment for minimum tax purposes (subtract line 8 from line 7)	**9**	Form 6251, line 12
10	Estate tax deduction (including certain generation-skipping transfer taxes)	**10**	Schedule A, line 27
11	Foreign taxes	**11**	Form 1040, line 43 or Schedule A, line 8
12	Adjustments and tax preference items (itemize):		
a	Accelerated depreciation	**12a**	Include on the applicable line of Form 6251
b	Depletion	**12b**	
c	Amortization	**12c**	
d	Exclusion items	**12d**	2002 Form 8801
13	Deductions in the final year of trust or decedent's estate:		
a	Excess deductions on termination (see instructions)	**13a**	Schedule A, line 22
b	Short-term capital loss carryover	**13b** ( )	Schedule D, line 5
c	Long-term capital loss carryover	**13c** ( )	Schedule D, line 12, columns (f) and (g)
d	Net operating loss (NOL) carryover for regular tax purposes	**13d** ( )	Form 1040, line 21
e	NOL carryover for minimum tax purposes	**13e**	See the instructions for Form 6251, line 20
f	....	**13f**	Include on the applicable line of the appropriate tax form
g	....	**13g**	
14	Other (itemize):		
a	Payments of estimated taxes credited to you	**14a**	Form 1040, line 60
b	Tax-exempt interest	**14b**	Form 1040, line 8b
c	....	**14c**	Include on the applicable line of the appropriate tax form
d	....	**14d**	
e	....	**14e**	
f	....	**14f**	
g	....	**14g**	
h		**14h**	

For Paperwork Reduction Act Notice, see the Instructions for Form 1041.   Cat. No. 11380D   **Schedule K-1 (Form 1041) 2001**

Instructions for Beneficiary Filing Form 1040

Note: *The fiduciary's instructions for completing Schedule K-1 are in the Instructions for Form 1041.*

General Instructions

Purpose of Form

The fiduciary of a trust or decedent's estate uses Schedule K-1 to report your share of the trust's or estate's income, credits, deductions, etc. **Keep it for your records. Do not file it with your tax return.** A copy has been filed with the IRS.

Inconsistent Treatment of Items

Generally, you must report items shown on your Schedule K-1 (and any attached schedules) the same way that the estate or trust treated the items on its return.

If the treatment on your original or amended return is inconsistent with the estate's or trust's treatment, or if the estate or trust was required to but has not filed a return, you must file **Form 8082,** Notice of Inconsistent Treatment or Administrative Adjustment Request (AAR), with your original or amended return to identify and explain any inconsistency (or to note that an estate or trust return has not been filed).

If you are required to file Form 8082 but fail to do so, you may be subject to the accuracy-related penalty. This penalty is in addition to any tax that results from making your amount or treatment of the item consistent with that shown on the estate's or trust's return. Any deficiency that results from making the amounts consistent may be assessed immediately.

Errors

If you believe the fiduciary has made an error on your Schedule K-1, notify the fiduciary and ask for an amended or a corrected Schedule K-1. **Do not** change any items on your copy. Be sure that the fiduciary sends a copy of the amended Schedule K-1 to the IRS. **If you are unable to reach an agreement with the fiduciary regarding the inconsistency, you must file Form 8082.**

Tax Shelters

If you receive a copy of **Form 8271,** Investor Reporting of Tax Shelter Registration Number, see the Instructions for Form 8271 to determine your reporting requirements.

Beneficiaries of Generation-Skipping Trusts

If you received **Form 706-GS(D-1),** Notification of Distribution From a Generation-Skipping Trust, and paid a generation-skipping transfer (GST) tax on **Form 706-GS(D),** Generation-Skipping Transfer Tax Return for Distributions, you can deduct the GST tax paid on income distributions on Schedule A (Form 1040), line 8. To figure the deduction, see the Instructions for Form 706-GS(D).

Specific Instructions

Lines 3 and 4

If there is an attachment to this Schedule K-1 reporting a disposition of a passive activity, see the Instructions for **Form 8582,** Passive Activity Loss Limitations, for information on the treatment of dispositions of interests in a passive activity.

Lines 6b through 6d

The deductions on lines 6b through 6d may be subject to the passive loss limitations of Internal Revenue Code section 469, which generally limits deductions from passive activities to the income from those activities. The rules for applying these limitations to beneficiaries have not yet been issued. For more details, see **Pub. 925,** Passive Activity and At-Risk Rules.

Line 12d

If you pay alternative minimum tax in 2001, the amount on line 12d will help you figure any minimum tax credit for 2002. See the 2002 **Form 8801,** Credit for Prior Year Minimum Tax- Individuals, Estates, and Trusts, for more information.

Line 14a

To figure any underpayment and penalty on **Form 2210,** Underpayment of Estimated Tax by Individuals, Estates, and Trusts, treat the amount entered on line 14a as an estimated tax payment made on January 15, 2002.

Lines 14c through 14h

The amount of gross farming and fishing income is included on line 6a. This income is also separately stated on line 14 to help you determine if you are subject to a penalty for underpayment of estimated tax. Report the amount of gross farming and fishing income on Schedule E (Form 1040), line 41.

Form **706**		**United States Estate (and Generation-Skipping Transfer) Tax Return**			OMB No. 1545-0015

(Rev. November 2001)

Estate of a citizen or resident of the United States (see separate instructions).
To be filed for decedents dying after December 31, 2000, and before January 1, 2002.
For Paperwork Reduction Act Notice, see page 25 of the separate instructions.

Department of the Treasury
Internal Revenue Service

Part 1.—Decedent and Executor

1a Decedent's first name and middle initial (and maiden name, if any)   **1b** Decedent's last name   **2** Decedent's Social Security No.

3a Legal residence (domicile) at time of death (county, state, and ZIP code, or foreign country)   **3b** Year domicile established   **4** Date of birth   **5** Date of death

6a Name of executor (see page 4 of the instructions)   **6b** Executor's address (number and street including apartment or suite no. or rural route; city, town, or post office; state; and ZIP code)

6c Executor's social security number (see page 4 of the instructions)

7a Name and location of court where will was probated or estate administered   **7b** Case number

8 If decedent died testate, check here ▶ ☐ and attach a certified copy of the will.   **9** If Form 4768 is attached, check here ▶ ☐

10 If Schedule R-1 is attached, check here ▶ ☐

Part 2.—Tax Computation

1	Total gross estate less exclusion (from Part 5, Recapitulation, page 3, item 12)	**1**
2	Total allowable deductions (from Part 5, Recapitulation, page 3, item 23)	**2**
3	Taxable estate (subtract line 2 from line 1)	**3**
4	Adjusted taxable gifts (total taxable gifts (within the meaning of section 2503) made by the decedent after December 31, 1976, other than gifts that are includible in decedent's gross estate (section 2001(b)))	**4**
5	Add lines 3 and 4	**5**
6	Tentative tax on the amount on line 5 from Table A on page 12 of the instructions	**6**
7a	If line 5 exceeds $10,000,000, enter the lesser of line 5 or $17,184,000. If line 5 is $10,000,000 or less, skip lines 7a and 7b and enter -0- on line 7c **7a**	
b	Subtract $10,000,000 from line 7a **7b**	
c	Enter 5% (.05) of line 7b	**7c**
8	Total tentative tax (add lines 6 and 7c)	**8**
9	Total gift tax payable with respect to gifts made by the decedent after December 31, 1976. Include gift taxes by the decedent's spouse for such spouse's share of split gifts (section 2513) only if the decedent was the donor of these gifts and they are includible in the decedent's gross estate (see instructions)	**9**
10	Gross estate tax (subtract line 9 from line 8)	**10**
11	Maximum unified credit (applicable credit amount) against estate tax . **11**	
12	Adjustment to unified credit (applicable credit amount). (This adjustment may not exceed $6,000. See page 4 of the instructions.) **12**	
13	Allowable unified credit (applicable credit amount) (subtract line 12 from line 11)	**13**
14	Subtract line 13 from line 10 (but do not enter less than zero)	**14**
15	Credit for state death taxes. Do not enter more than line 14. Figure the credit by using the amount on line 3 less $60,000. See Table B in the instructions and **attach credit evidence** (see instructions) ..	**15**
16	Subtract line 15 from line 14	**16**
17	Credit for Federal gift taxes on pre-1977 gifts (section 2012) (attach computation) **17**	
18	Credit for foreign death taxes (from Schedule(s) P). (Attach Form(s) 706-CE.) **18**	
19	Credit for tax on prior transfers (from Schedule Q) **19**	
20	Total (add lines 17, 18, and 19)	**20**
21	Net estate tax (subtract line 20 from line 16)	**21**
22	Generation-skipping transfer taxes (from Schedule R, Part 2, line 10)	**22**
23	Total transfer taxes (add lines 21 and 22)	**23**
24	Prior payments. Explain in an attached statement **24**	
25	United States Treasury bonds redeemed in payment of estate tax . **25**	
26	Total (add lines 24 and 25)	**26**
27	Balance due (or overpayment) (subtract line 26 from line 23)	**27**

Under penalties of perjury, I declare that I have examined this return, including accompanying schedules and statements, and to the best of my knowledge and belief, it is true, correct, and complete. Declaration of preparer other than the executor is based on all information of which preparer has any knowledge.

Signature(s) of executor(s)   Date

Signature of preparer other than executor   Address (and ZIP code)   Date

Cat. No. 20548R

Estate of:

Part 3- Elections by the Executor

Please check the "Yes" or "No" box for each question. (See instructions beginning on page 5.) | Yes | No

1	Do you elect alternate valuation?		1		
2	Do you elect special use valuation? If "Yes," you must complete and attach Schedule A-1.		2		
3	Do you elect to pay the taxes in installments as described in section 6166? If "Yes," you must attach the additional information described on page 8 of the instructions.		3		
4	Do you elect to postpone the part of the taxes attributable to a reversionary or remainder interest as described in section 6163?		4		

Part 4- General Information (Note: *Please attach the necessary supplemental documents.* **You must attach the death certificate.**)
(See instructions on page 9.)

Authorization to receive confidential tax information under Regs. sec. 601.504(b)(2)(i); to act as the estate's representative before the IRS; and to make written or oral presentations on behalf of the estate if return prepared by an attorney, accountant, or enrolled agent for the executor:

Name of representative (print or type)	State	Address (number, street, and room or suite no., city, state, and ZIP code)

I declare that I am the ☐ attorney/ ☐ certified public accountant/ ☐ enrolled agent (you must check the applicable box) for the executor and prepared this return for the executor. I am not under suspension or disbarment from practice before the Internal Revenue Service and am qualified to practice in the state shown above.

Signature	CAF number	Date	Telephone number

1 Death certificate number and issuing authority (attach a copy of the death certificate to this return).

2 Decedent's business or occupation. If retired, check here ▶ ☐ and state decedent's former business or occupation.

3 Marital status of the decedent at time of death:

☐ Married

☐ Widow or widower- Name, SSN, and date of death of deceased spouse ▶ --

☐ Single
☐ Legally separated
☐ Divorced- Date divorce decree became final ▶

4a Surviving spouse's name	**4b** Social security number	**4c** Amount received (see page 9 of the instructions)

5 Individuals (other than the surviving spouse), trusts, or other estates who receive benefits from the estate (do not include charitable beneficiaries shown in Schedule O) (see instructions). For Privacy Act Notice (applicable to individual beneficiaries only), see the Instructions for Form 1040.

Name of individual, trust, or estate receiving $5,000 or more	Identifying number	Relationship to decedent	Amount (see instructions)

All unascertainable beneficiaries and those who receive less than $5,000 ▶

Total

Please check the "Yes" or "No" box for each question. | Yes | No

		Yes	No
6	Does the gross estate contain any section 2044 property (qualified terminable interest property (QTIP) from a prior gift or estate) (see page 9 of the instructions)?		

(continued on next page)

Part 4- General Information *(continued)*

Please check the "Yes" or "No" box for each question.	Yes	No
7a Have Federal gift tax returns ever been filed? . . . . " If "Yes," please attach copies of the returns, if available, and furnish the following information:		
7b Period(s) covered **7c** Internal Revenue office(s) where filed		
If you answer "Yes" to any of questions 8- 16, you must attach additional information as described in the instructions.		
8a Was there any insurance on the decedent's life that is not included on the return as part of the gross estate? . . . . . "		
b Did the decedent own any insurance on the life of another that is not included in the gross estate? . . . . "		
9 Did the decedent at the time of death own any property as a joint tenant with right of survivorship in which **(a)** one or more of the other joint tenants was someone other than the decedent's spouse, and **(b)** less than the full value of the property is included on the return as part of the gross estate? If "Yes," you must complete and attach Schedule E . . . . "		
10 Did the decedent, at the time of death, own any interest in a partnership or unincorporated business or any stock in an inactive or closely held corporation?		
11 Did the decedent make any transfer described in section 2035, 2036, 2037, or 2038 (see the instructions for Schedule G beginning on page 11 of the separate instructions)? If "Yes," you must complete and attach Schedule G . . . . "		
12 Were there in existence at the time of the decedent's death:		
a Any trusts created by the decedent during his or her lifetime? . . . . "		
b Any trusts not created by the decedent under which the decedent possessed any power, beneficial interest, or trusteeship?		
13 Did the decedent ever possess, exercise, or release any general power of appointment? If "Yes," you must complete and attach Schedule H		
14 Was the marital deduction computed under the transitional rule of Public Law 97-34, section 403(e)(3) (Economic Recovery Tax Act of 1981)? If "Yes," attach a separate computation of the marital deduction, enter the amount on item 20 of the Recapitulation, and note on item 20 "computation attached."		
15 Was the decedent, immediately before death, receiving an annuity described in the "General" paragraph of the instructions for Schedule I? If "Yes," you must complete and attach Schedule I . . . . "		
16 Was the decedent ever the beneficiary of a trust for which a deduction was claimed by the estate of a pre-deceased spouse under section 2056(b)(7) and which is not reported on this return? If "Yes," attach an explanation. . . . . "		

Part 5- Recapitulation

Item number	Gross estate		Alternate value	Value at date of death
1	Schedule A- Real Estate	**1**		
2	Schedule B- Stocks and Bonds	**2**		
3	Schedule C- Mortgages, Notes, and Cash	**3**		
4	Schedule D- Insurance on the Decedent's Life (attach Form(s) 712) . . .	**4**		
5	Schedule E- Jointly Owned Property (attach Form(s) 712 for life insurance) . .	**5**		
6	Schedule F- Other Miscellaneous Property (attach Form(s) 712 for life insurance)	**6**		
7	Schedule G- Transfers During Decedent's Life (att. Form(s) 712 for life insurance)	**7**		
8	Schedule H- Powers of Appointment	**8**		
9	Schedule I- Annuities	**9**		
10	Total gross estate (add items 1 through 9)	**10**		
11	Schedule U- Qualified Conservation Easement Exclusion	**11**		
12	Total gross estate less exclusion (subtract item 11 from item 10). Enter here and on line 1 of Part 2- Tax Computation	**12**		

Item number	Deductions		Amount	
13	Schedule J- Funeral Expenses and Expenses Incurred in Administering Property Subject to Claims	**13**		
14	Schedule K- Debts of the Decedent	**14**		
15	Schedule K- Mortgages and Liens	**15**		
16	Total of items 13 through 15	**16**		
17	Allowable amount of deductions from item 16 (see the instructions for item 17 of the Recapitulation) . .	**17**		
18	Schedule L- Net Losses During Administration	**18**		
19	Schedule L- Expenses Incurred in Administering Property Not Subject to Claims	**19**		
20	Schedule M- Bequests, etc., to Surviving Spouse	**20**		
21	Schedule O- Charitable, Public, and Similar Gifts and Bequests	**21**		
22	Schedule T- Qualified Family-Owned Business Interest Deduction	**22**		
23	Total allowable deductions (add items 17 through 22). Enter here and on line 2 of the Tax Computation	**23**		

Estate of:

SCHEDULE A- Real Estate

- *For jointly owned property that must be disclosed on Schedule E, see the instructions on the reverse side of Schedule E.*
- *Real estate that is part of a sole proprietorship should be shown on Schedule F.*
- *Real estate that is included in the gross estate under section 2035, 2036, 2037, or 2038 should be shown on Schedule G.*
- *Real estate that is included in the gross estate under section 2041 should be shown on Schedule H.*
- *If you elect section 2032A valuation, you must complete Schedule A and Schedule A-1.*

Item number	Description	Alternate valuation date	Alternate value	Value at date of death
1				

Total from continuation schedules or additional sheets attached to this schedule			
TOTAL. (Also enter on Part 5, Recapitulation, page 3, at item 1.)			

(If more space is needed, attach the continuation schedule from the end of this package or additional sheets of the same size.)

(See the instructions on the reverse side.)

form 18

Form 709

Department of the Treasury
Internal Revenue Service

United States Gift (and Generation-Skipping Transfer) Tax Return

(Section 6019 of the Internal Revenue Code) (For gifts made during calendar year 2001)

► **See separate instructions.**

OMB No. 1545-0020

2001

Part 1—General Information

1 Donor's first name and middle initial	2 Donor's last name	3 Donor's social security number

4 Address (number, street, and apartment number)	5 Legal residence (domicile) (county and state)

6 City, state, and ZIP code	7 Citizenship

		Yes	No
8	If the donor died during the year, check here ► ☐ and enter date of death		
9	If you received an extension of time to file this Form 709, check here ► ☐ and attach the Form 4868, 2688, 2350, or extension letter		
10	Enter the total number of separate donees listed on Schedule A—count each person only once. ►		
11a	Have you (the donor) previously filed a Form 709 (or 709-A) for any other year? If the answer is "No," do not complete line 11b		
11b	If the answer to line 11a is "Yes," has your address changed since you last filed Form 709 (or 709-A)?		
12	Gifts by husband or wife to third parties.—Do you consent to have the gifts (including generation-skipping transfers) made by you and by your spouse to third parties during the calendar year considered as made one-half by each of you? (See instructions.) (If the answer is "Yes," the following information must be furnished and your spouse must sign the consent shown below. **If the answer is "No," skip lines 13–18 and go to Schedule A.**)		
13	Name of consenting spouse **14** SSN		
15	Were you married to one another during the entire calendar year? (see instructions)		
16	If the answer to 15 is "No," check whether ☐ married ☐ divorced or ☐ widowed, and give date (see instructions) ►		
17	Will a gift tax return for this calendar year be filed by your spouse?		
18	**Consent of Spouse—**I consent to have the gifts (and generation-skipping transfers) made by me and by my spouse to third parties during the calendar year considered as made one-half by each of us. We are both aware of the joint and several liability for tax created by the execution of this consent.		

Consenting spouse's signature ►   Date ►

Part 2—Tax Computation

1	Enter the amount from Schedule A, Part 3, line 15	1	
2	Enter the amount from Schedule B, line 3	2	
3	Total taxable gifts (add lines 1 and 2)	3	
4	Tax computed on amount on line 3 (see Table for Computing Tax in separate instructions)	4	
5	Tax computed on amount on line 2 (see Table for Computing Tax in separate instructions)	5	
6	Balance (subtract line 5 from line 4)	6	
7	Maximum unified credit (nonresident aliens, see instructions)	7	220,550 00
8	Enter the unified credit against tax allowable for all prior periods (from Sch. B, line 1, col. C)	8	
9	Balance (subtract line 8 from line 7)	9	
10	Enter 20% (.20) of the amount allowed as a specific exemption for gifts made after September 8, 1976, and before January 1, 1977 (see instructions)	10	
11	Balance (subtract line 10 from line 9)	11	
12	Unified credit (enter the smaller of line 6 or line 11)	12	
13	Credit for foreign gift taxes (see instructions)	13	
14	Total credits (add lines 12 and 13)	14	
15	Balance (subtract line 14 from line 6) (do not enter less than zero)	15	
16	Generation-skipping transfer taxes (from Schedule C, Part 3, col. H, Total)	16	
17	Total tax (add lines 15 and 16)	17	
18	Gift and generation-skipping transfer taxes prepaid with extension of time to file	18	
19	If line 18 is less than line 17, enter **balance due** (see instructions)	19	
20	If line 18 is greater than line 17, enter **amount to be refunded**	20	

Attach check or money order here.

Sign Here

Under penalties of perjury, I declare that I have examined this return, including any accompanying schedules and statements, and to the best of my knowledge and belief, it is true, correct, and complete. Declaration of preparer (other than donor) is based on all information of which preparer has any knowledge.

► _____   Date _____
     Signature of donor

Paid Preparer's Use Only

Preparer's signature ►	Date	Check if self-employed ► ☐
Firm's name (or yours if self-employed), address, and ZIP code ►		Phone no. ► ( )

For Disclosure, Privacy Act, and Paperwork Reduction Act Notice, see page 12 of the separate instructions for this form.   Cat. No. 16783M   Form **709** (2001)

SCHEDULE A   Computation of Taxable Gifts (Including Transfers in Trust)

A   Does the value of any item listed on Schedule A reflect any valuation discount? If the answer is "Yes," see instructions . Yes ☐ No ☐

B   ☐ ◄ Check here if you elect under section 529(c)(2)(B) to treat any transfers made this year to a qualified state tuition program as made ratably over a 5-year period beginning this year. See instructions. Attach explanation.

Part 1- Gifts Subject Only to Gift Tax. *Gifts less political organization, medical, and educational exclusions—see instructions*

A Item number	B • Donee's name and address • Relationship to donor (if any) • Description of gift • If the gift was made by means of a trust, enter trust's EIN and attach a description or copy of the trust instrument (see instructions) • If the gift was of securities, give CUSIP number	C Donor's adjusted basis of gift	D Date of gift	E Value at date of gift
1				

Total of Part 1 (add amounts from Part 1, column E) . . . . ▶

Part 2- Gifts That are Direct Skips and are Subject to Both Gift Tax and Generation-Skipping Transfer Tax. You must list the gifts in chronological order. *Gifts less political organization, medical, and educational exclusions—see instructions. (Also list here direct skips that are subject only to the GST tax at this time as the result of the termination of an "estate tax inclusion period." See instructions.)*

A Item number	B • Donee's name and address • Relationship to donor (if any) • Description of gift • If the gift was made by means of a trust, enter trust's EIN and attach a description or copy of the trust instrument (see instructions) • If the gift was of securities, give CUSIP number	C Donor's adjusted basis of gift	D Date of gift	E Value at date of gift
1				

Total of Part 2 (add amounts from Part 2, column E) . . . . ▶

Part 3- Taxable Gift Reconciliation

1	Total value of gifts of donor (add totals from column E of Parts 1 and 2)	**1**	
2	One-half of items _____ attributable to spouse (see instructions)	**2**	
3	Balance (subtract line 2 from line 1)	**3**	
4	Gifts of spouse to be included (from Schedule A, Part 3, line 2 of spouse's return- see instructions) . .	**4**	

If any of the gifts included on this line are also subject to the generation-skipping transfer tax, check here ▶ ☐ and enter those gifts also on Schedule C, Part 1.

5	Total gifts (add lines 3 and 4)	**5**	
6	Total annual exclusions for gifts listed on Schedule A (including line 4, above) (see instructions)	**6**	
7	Total included amount of gifts (subtract line 6 from line 5)	**7**	

Deductions (see instructions)

8	Gifts of interests to spouse for which a marital deduction will be claimed, based on items _____ of Schedule A	**8**		
9	Exclusions attributable to gifts on line 8	**9**		
10	Marital deduction- subtract line 9 from line 8	**10**		
11	Charitable deduction, based on items _____ less exclusions . .	**11**		
12	Total deductions- add lines 10 and 11		**12**	
13	Subtract line 12 from line 7		**13**	
14	Generation-skipping transfer taxes payable with this Form 709 (from Schedule C, Part 3, col. H, Total) . .		**14**	
15	Taxable gifts (add lines 13 and 14). Enter here and on line 1 of the Tax Computation on page 1 . . .		**15**	

(If more space is needed, attach additional sheets of same size.)   Form **709** (2001)

SCHEDULE A	Computation of Taxable Gifts *(continued)*

16 Terminable Interest (QTIP) Marital Deduction. (See instructions for line 8 of Schedule A.)

If a trust (or other property) meets the requirements of qualified terminable interest property under section 2523(f), and

   a. The trust (or other property) is listed on Schedule A, and

   b. The value of the trust (or other property) is entered in whole or in part as a deduction on line 8, Part 3 of Schedule A,

then the donor shall be deemed to have made an election to have such trust (or other property) treated as qualified terminable interest property under section 2523(f).

If less than the entire value of the trust (or other property) that the donor has included in Part 1 of Schedule A is entered as a deduction on line 8, the donor shall be considered to have made an election only as to a fraction of the trust (or other property). The numerator of this fraction is equal to the amount of the trust (or other property) deducted on line 10 of Part 3, Schedule A. The denominator is equal to the total value of the trust (or other property) listed in Part 1 of Schedule A.

If you make the QTIP election (see instructions for line 8 of Schedule A), the terminable interest property involved will be included in your spouse's gross estate upon his or her death (section 2044). If your spouse disposes (by gift or otherwise) of all or part of the qualifying life income interest, he or she will be considered to have made a transfer of the entire property that is subject to the gift tax (see Transfer of Certain Life Estates on page 4 of the instructions).

17 Election Out of QTIP Treatment of Annuities

☐ ◄ Check here if you elect under section 2523(f)(6) **NOT** to treat as qualified terminable interest property any joint and survivor annuities that are reported on Schedule A and would otherwise be treated as qualified terminable interest property under section 2523(f). (See instructions.) Enter the item numbers (from Schedule A) for the annuities for which you are making this election ►

SCHEDULE B	Gifts From Prior Periods

If you answered "Yes" on line 11a of page 1, Part 1, see the instructions for completing Schedule B. If you answered "No," skip to the Tax Computation on page 1 (or Schedule C, if applicable).

A Calendar year or calendar quarter (see instructions)	B Internal Revenue office where prior return was filed	C Amount of unified credit against gift tax for periods after December 31, 1976	D Amount of specific exemption for prior periods ending before January 1, 1977	E Amount of taxable gifts

1	Totals for prior periods (without adjustment for reduced specific exemption)	**1**			
2	Amount, if any, by which total specific exemption, line 1, column D, is more than $30,000		**2**		
3	Total amount of taxable gifts for prior periods (add amount, column E, line 1, and amount, if any, on line 2). (Enter here and on line 2 of the Tax Computation on page 1.)		**3**		

(If more space is needed, attach additional sheets of same size.)

Form **709** (2001)

SCHEDULE C	Computation of Generation-Skipping Transfer Tax

Note: *Inter vivos direct skips that are completely excluded by the GST exemption must still be fully reported (including value and exemptions claimed) on Schedule C.*

Part 1- Generation-Skipping Transfers

A Item No. (from Schedule A, Part 2, col. A)	B Value (from Schedule A, Part 2, col. E)	C Split Gifts (enter ½ of col. B) (see instructions)	D Subtract col. C from col. B	E Nontaxable portion of transfer	F Net Transfer (subtract col. E from col. D)
1					
2					
3					
4					
5					
6					

	Split gifts from spouse's Form 709 (enter item number)	Value included from spouse's Form 709	Nontaxable portion of transfer	Net transfer (subtract col. E from col. D)
If you elected gift splitting and your spouse was required to file a separate Form 709 (see the instructions for "Split Gifts"), you must enter all of the gifts shown on Schedule A, Part 2, of your spouse's Form 709 here.	S-			
	S-			
In column C, enter the item number of each gift in the order it appears in column A of your spouse's Schedule A, Part 2. We have	S-			
preprinted the prefix "S-" to distinguish your spouse's item numbers from your own when you complete column A of Schedule C, Part 3.	S-			
	S-			
	S-			
In column D, for each gift, enter the amount reported in column C, Schedule C, Part 1, of your spouse's Form 709.	S-			
	S-			

Part 2- GST Exemption Reconciliation (Section 2631) and Section 2652(a)(3) Election

Check box ▶ ☐ if you are making a section 2652(a)(3) (special QTIP) election (see instructions)

Enter the item numbers (from Schedule A) of the gifts for which you are making this election ▶ . . . .

1	Maximum allowable exemption (see instructions)	1	
2	Total exemption used for periods before filing this return	2	
3	Exemption available for this return (subtract line 2 from line 1)	3	
4	Exemption claimed on this return (from Part 3, col. C total, below)	4	
5	Exemption allocated to transfers not shown on Part 3, below. **You must attach a Notice of Allocation.** (See instructions.)	5	
6	Add lines 4 and 5	6	
7	Exemption available for future transfers (subtract line 6 from line 3)	7	

Part 3- Tax Computation

A Item No. (from Schedule C, Part 1)	B Net transfer (from Schedule C, Part 1, col. F)	C GST Exemption Allocated	D Divide col. C by col. B	E Inclusion Ratio (subtract col. D from 1.000)	F Maximum Estate Tax Rate	G Applicable Rate (multiply col. E by col. F)	H Generation-Skipping Transfer Tax (multiply col. B by col. G)
1					55% (.55)		
2					55% (.55)		
3					55% (.55)		
4					55% (.55)		
5					55% (.55)		
6					55% (.55)		
					55% (.55)		
					55% (.55)		
					55% (.55)		
					55% (.55)		

| Total exemption claimed. Enter here and on line 4, Part 2, above. May not exceed line 3, Part 2, above . . . . . | **Total generation-skipping transfer tax.** Enter here, on line 14 of Schedule A, Part 3, and on line 16 of the Tax Computation on page 1 . . . . | |

(If more space is needed, attach additional sheets of same size.)   ✸   Form **709** (2001)

INDEX

SPHINX® PUBLISHING'S NATIONAL TITLES
Valid in All 50 States

LEGAL SURVIVAL IN BUSINESS

The Complete Book of Corporate Forms	$24.95
How to Form a Limited Liability Company	$22.95
Incorporate in Delaware from Any State	$24.95
Incorporate in Nevada from Any State	$24.95
How to Form a Nonprofit Corporation (2E)	$24.95
How to Form Your Own Corporation (3E)	$24.95
How to Form Your Own Partnership (2E)	$24.95
How to Register Your Own Copyright (4E)	$24.95
How to Register Your Own Trademark (3E)	$21.95
Most Valuable Business Legal Forms You'll Ever Need (3E)	$21.95
The Small Business Owner's Guide to Bankruptcy	$21.95

LEGAL SURVIVAL IN COURT

Crime Victim's Guide to Justice (2E)	$21.95
Grandparents' Rights (3E)	$24.95
Help Your Lawyer Win Your Case (2E)	$14.95
Jurors' Rights (2E)	$12.95
Legal Research Made Easy (3E)	$21.95
Winning Your Personal Injury Claim (2E)	$24.95
Your Rights When You Owe Too Much	$16.95

LEGAL SURVIVAL IN REAL ESTATE

Essential Guide to Real Estate Contracts	$18.95
Essential Guide to Real Estate Leases	$18.95
How to Buy a Condominium or Townhome (2E)	$19.95

LEGAL SURVIVAL IN PERSONAL AFFAIRS

Cómo Hacer su Propio Testamento	$16.95
Cómo Solicitar su Propio Divorcio	$24.95
Cómo Restablecer su propio Crédito y Renegociar sus Deudas	$21.95
Guía de Inmigración a Estados Unidos (3E)	$24.95
Guía de Justicia para Víctimas del Crimen	$21.95
The 529 College Savings Plan	$16.95
How to File Your Own Bankruptcy (5E)	$21.95
How to File Your Own Divorce (4E)	$24.95
How to Make Your Own Simple Will (3E)	$18.95
How to Write Your Own Living Will (2E)	$16.95
How to Write Your Own Premarital Agreement (3E)	$24.95
Living Trusts and Other Ways to Avoid Probate (3E)	$24.95
Manual de Beneficios para el Seguro Social	$18.95
Mastering the MBE	$16.95
Most Valuable Personal Legal Forms You'll Ever Need	$24.95
Neighbor v. Neighbor (2E)	$16.95
The Nanny and Domestic Help Legal Kit	$22.95
The Power of Attorney Handbook (4E)	$19.95
Repair Your Own Credit and Deal with Debt	$18.95
The Social Security Benefits Handbook (3E)	$18.95
Social Security Q&A	$12.95
Sexual Harassment:Your Guide to Legal Action	$18.95
Teen Rights	$22.95
Unmarried Parents' Rights	$19.95
U.S. Immigration Step by Step	$21.95
U.S.A. Immigration Guide (4E)	$24.95
The Visitation Handbook	$18.95
Win Your Unemployment Compensation Claim (2E)	$21.95
Your Right to Child Custody, Visitation and Support (2E)	$24.95

Legal Survival Guides are directly available from Sourcebooks, Inc., or from your local bookstores.
Prices are subject to change without notice.

For credit card orders call 1–800–432–7444, write P.O. Box 4410, Naperville, IL 60567-4410
or fax 630-961-2168

Find more legal information at: **www.SphinxLegal.com**

SPHINX® PUBLISHING ORDER FORM

Qty	ISBN	Title	Retail	Ext.
		SPHINX PUBLISHING NATIONAL TITLES		
___	1-57248-148-X	Cómo Hacer su Propio Testamento	$16.95	___
___	1-57248-147-1	Cómo Solicitar su Propio Divorcio	$24.95	___
___	1-57248-226-5	Cómo Restablecer su propio Crédito y Renegociar sus Deudas	$21.95	___
___	1-57248-238-9	The 529 College Savings Plan	$16.95	___
___	1-57248-166-8	The Complete Book of Corporate Forms	$24.95	___
___	1-57248-163-3	Crime Victim's Guide to Justice (2E)	$21.95	___
___	1-57248-159-5	Essential Guide to Real Estate Contracts	$18.95	___
___	1-57248-160-9	Essential Guide to Real Estate Leases	$18.95	___
___	1-57248-139-0	Grandparents' Rights (3E)	$24.95	___
___	1-57248-188-9	Guía de Inmigración a Estados Unidos (3E)	$24.95	___
___	1-57248-187-0	Guía de Justicia para Víctimas del Crimen	$21.95	___
___	1-57248-103-X	Help Your Lawyer Win Your Case (2E)	$14.95	___
___	1-57248-164-1	How to Buy a Condominium or Townhome (2E)	$19.95	___
___	1-57248-191-9	How to File Your Own Bankruptcy (5E)	$21.95	___
___	1-57248-132-3	How to File Your Own Divorce (4E)	$24.95	___
___	1-57248-083-1	How to Form a Limited Liability Company	$22.95	___
___	1-57248-231-1	How to Form a Nonprofit Corporation (2E)	$24.95	___
___	1-57248-133-1	How to Form Your Own Corporation (3E)	$24.95	___
___	1-57248-224-9	How to Form Your Own Partnership (2E)	$24.95	___
___	1-57248-232-X	How to Make Your Own Simple Will (3E)	$18.95	___
___	1-57248-200-1	How to Register Your Own Copyright (4E)	$24.95	___
___	1-57248-104-8	How to Register Your Own Trademark (3E)	$21.95	___
___	1-57248-118-8	How to Write Your Own Living Will (2E)	$16.95	___
___	1-57248-156-0	How to Write Your Own Premarital Agreement (3E)	$24.95	___
___	1-57248-230-3	Incorporate in Delaware from Any State	$24.95	___
___	1-57248-158-7	Incorporate in Nevada from Any State	$24.95	___
___	1-57071-333-2	Jurors' Rights (2E)	$12.95	___
___	1-57248-223-0	Legal Research Made Easy (3E)	$21.95	___
___	1-57248-165-X	Living Trusts and Other Ways to Avoid Probate (3E)	$24.95	___
___	1-57248-186-2	Manual de Beneficios para el Seguro Social	$18.95	___
___	1-57248-220-6	Mastering the MBE	$16.95	___
___	1-57248-167-6	Most Valuable Bus. Legal Forms You'll Ever Need (3E)	$21.95	___
___	1-57248-130-7	Most Valuable Personal Legal Forms You'll Ever Need	$24.95	___
___	1-57248-098-X	The Nanny and Domestic Help Legal Kit	$22.95	___
___	1-57248-089-0	Neighbor v. Neighbor (2E)	$16.95	___
___	1-57248-169-2	The Power of Attorney Handbook (4E)	$19.95	___
___	1-57248-149-8	Repair Your Own Credit and Deal with Debt	$18.95	___
___	1-57248-217-6	Sexual Harassment: Your Guide to Legal Action	$18.95	___
___	1-57248-219-2	The Small Business Owner's Guide to Bankruptcy	$21.95	___
___	1-57248-168-4	The Social Security Benefits Handbook (3E)	$18.95	___
___	1-57248-216-8	Social Security Q&A	$12.95	___
___	1-57248-221-4	Teen Rights	$22.95	___
___	1-57071-399-5	Unmarried Parents' Rights	$19.95	___
___	1-57248-161-7	U.S.A. Immigration Guide (4E)	$24.95	___
___	1-57248-192-7	The Visitation Handbook	$18.95	___
___	1-57248-225-7	Win Your Unemployment Compensation Claim (2E)	$21.95	___
___	1-57248-138-2	Winning Your Personal Injury Claim (2E)	$24.95	___
___	1-57248-162-5	Your Right to Child Custody, Visitation and Support (2E)	$24.95	___
___	1-57248-157-9	Your Rights When You Owe Too Much	$16.95	___
		CALIFORNIA TITLES		
___	1-57248-150-1	CA Power of Attorney Handbook (2E)	$18.95	___
___	1-57248-151-X	How to File for Divorce in CA (3E)	$26.95	___
___	1-57071-356-1	How to Make a CA Will	$16.95	___
___	1-57248-145-5	How to Probate and Settle an Estate in California	$26.95	___
___	1-57248-146-3	How to Start a Business in CA	$18.95	___
___	1-57248-194-3	How to Win in Small Claims Court in CA (2E)	$18.95	___
___	1-57248-196-X	The Landlord's Legal Guide in CA	$24.95	___
		FLORIDA TITLES		
___	1-57071-363-4	Florida Power of Attorney Handbook (2E)	$16.95	___
___	1-57248-176-5	How to File for Divorce in FL (7E)	$26.95	___
___	1-57248-177-3	How to Form a Corporation in FL (5E)	$24.95	___

SPHINX® PUBLISHING ORDER FORM

Qty	ISBN	Title	Retail	Ext.
_____	1-57248-203-6	How to Form a Limited Liability Co. in FL (2E)	$24.95	_____
_____	1-57071-401-0	How to Form a Partnership in FL	$22.95	_____
	Form Continued on Following Page		**SUBTOTAL**	
_____	1-57248-113-7	How to Make a FL Will (6E)	$16.95	_____
_____	1-57248-088-2	How to Modify Your FL Divorce Judgment (4E)	$24.95	_____
_____	1-57248-144-7	How to Probate and Settle an Estate in FL (4E)	$26.95	_____
_____	1-57248-081-5	How to Start a Business in FL (5E)	$16.95	_____
_____	1-57248-204-4	How to Win in Small Claims Court in FL (7E)	$18.95	_____
_____	1-57248-202-8	Land Trusts in Florida (6E)	$29.95	_____
_____	1-57248-123-4	Landlords' Rights and Duties in FL (8E)	$21.95	_____
		GEORGIA TITLES		
_____	1-57248-137-4	How to File for Divorce in GA (4E)	$21.95	_____
_____	1-57248-180-3	How to Make a GA Will (4E)	$21.95	_____
_____	1-57248-140-4	How to Start a Business in Georgia (2E)	$16.95	_____
		ILLINOIS TITLES		
_____	1-57248-206-0	How to File for Divorce in IL (3E)	$24.95	_____
_____	1-57248-170-6	How to Make an IL Will (3E)	$16.95	_____
_____	1-57248-247-8	How to Start a Business in IL (3E)	$21.95	_____
_____	1-57248-078-5	Landlords' Rights & Duties in IL	$21.95	_____
		MASSACHUSETTS TITLES		
_____	1-57248-128-5	How to File for Divorce in MA (3E)	$24.95	_____
_____	1-57248-115-3	How to Form a Corporation in MA	$24.95	_____
_____	1-57248-108-0	How to Make a MA Will (2E)	$16.95	_____
_____	1-57248-106-4	How to Start a Business in MA (2E)	$18.95	_____
_____	1-57248-209-5	The Landlord's Legal Guide in MA	$24.95	_____
		MICHIGAN TITLES		
_____	1-57248-215-X	How to File for Divorce in MI (3E)	$24.95	_____
_____	1-57248-182-X	How to Make a MI Will (3E)	$16.95	_____
_____	1-57248-183-8	How to Start a Business in MI (3E)	$18.95	_____
		MINNESOTA TITLES		
_____	1-57248-142-0	How to File for Divorce in MN	$21.95	_____
_____	1-57248-179-X	How to Form a Corporation in MN	$24.95	_____
_____	1-57248-178-1	How to Make a MN Will (2E)	$16.95	_____
		NEW YORK TITLES		
_____	1-57248-193-5	Child Custody, Visitation and Support in NY	$26.95	_____
_____	1-57248-141-2	How to File for Divorce in NY (2E)	$26.95	_____
_____	1-57248-105-6	How to Form a Corporation in NY	$24.95	_____

Qty	ISBN	Title	Retail	Ext.
_____	1-57248-095-5	How to Make a NY Will (2E)	$16.95	_____
_____	1-57248-199-4	How to Start a Business in NY (2E)	$18.95	_____
_____	1-57248-198-6	How to Win in Small Claims Court in NY (2E)	$18.95	_____
_____	1-57248-197-8	Landlords' Legal Guide in NY	$24.95	_____
_____	1-57071-188-7	New York Power of Attorney Handbook	$19.95	_____
_____	1-57248-122-6	Tenants' Rights in NY	$21.95	_____
		NORTH CAROLINA TITLES		
_____	1-57248-185-4	How to File for Divorce in NC (3E)	$22.95	_____
_____	1-57248-129-3	How to Make a NC Will (3E)	$16.95	_____
_____	1-57248-184-6	How to Start a Business in NC (3E)	$18.95	_____
_____	1-57248-091-2	Landlords' Rights & Duties in NC	$21.95	_____
		OHIO TITLES		
_____	1-57248-190-0	How to File for Divorce in OH (2E)	$24.95	_____
_____	1-57248-174-9	How to Form a Corporation in OH	$24.95	_____
_____	1-57248-173-0	How to Make an OH Will	$16.95	_____
		PENNSYLVANIA TITLES		
_____	1-57248-242-7	Child Custody, Visitation and Support in Pennsylvania	$26.95	_____
_____	1-57248-211-7	How to File for Divorce in PA (3E)	$26.95	_____
_____	1-57248-094-7	How to Make a PA Will (2E)	$16.95	_____
_____	1-57248-112-9	How to Start a Business in PA (2E)	$18.95	_____
_____	1-57071-179-8	Landlords' Rights and Duties in PA	$19.95	_____
		TEXAS TITLES		
_____	1-57248-171-4	Child Custody, Visitation, and Support in TX	$22.95	_____
_____	1-57248-172-2	How to File for Divorce in TX (3E)	$24.95	_____
_____	1-57248-114-5	How to Form a Corporation in TX (2E)	$24.95	_____
_____	1-57071-417-7	How to Make a TX Will (2E)	$16.95	_____
_____	1-57248-214-1	How to Probate and Settle an Estate in TX (3E)	$26.95	_____
_____	1-57248-228-1	How to Start a Business in TX (3E)	$18.95	_____
_____	1-57248-111-0	How to Win in Small Claims Court in TX (2E)	$16.95	_____
_____	1-57248-110-2	Landlords' Rights and Duties in TX (2E)	$21.95	_____

SUBTOTAL THIS PAGE _____

SUBTOTAL PREVIOUS PAGE _____

Shipping — $5.00 for 1st book, $1.00 each additional _____

Illinois residents add 6.75% sales tax _____

Connecticut residents add 6.00% sales tax _____

TOTAL _____

To order, call Sourcebooks at 1-800-432-7444 or FAX (630) 961-2168 (Bookstores, libraries, wholesalers—please call for discount)
Prices are subject to change without notice.
Find more legal information at: www.SphinxLegal.com